NO PERMANENT SCARS

No Permanent Scars

Michael Hemery

Silenced Press

First Edition.

ISBN-13: 978-0-9792410-6-2
ISBN-10: 0-9792410-6-5

Library of Congress Control Number: †

Cover graphic design by Bill Reed
Author photo by Drew Hood

More information available at:
www.silencedpress.com

The author would like to thank the editors who first took a chance with these essays:

Drunken Boat: "Reconstruction"
Fearless Confessions: A Writer's Guide to Memoir: "After the Dash"
Los Angeles Review: "Like it Mattered"
Lumina: "Stripes" and "Un/doings"
New Plains Review: "About Us"
Passages North: "With Honors"
Portland Review: "Bad Blood"
Post Road Magazine: "Paul's Boots"
Redivider: "Bites"
Slice: "Ah, Nuts, I'm in Love"
sub-Terrain: "The End"
The Tusculum Review: "Not Only"

Table of Contents

Bumps

Fractures

Abrasions

Ruptures

To Pa, I tried not to use too many adjectives.

Disclaimer

This is how I remember it. Surely when someone else pieces it all together, a date, an age, the way the sun reflected off the lake, the narrative slightly shifts. But the nonfiction essays contained within these pages represent my interpretation and point of view. Many names and a few specifics throughout *No Permanent Scars* have been intentionally changed to protect individuals, but the personal truths remain the same.

Bumps

Not Only

The only reason I'm asking; only a minute of your time; only a warning; only a slight fever; a cold; a rash from shorts rubbing my thighs; the only shorts we could afford; only fifty cents; polyester; pink; only raised my skin when I mowed the lawn. I was fat. Somehow the sweat made friction.

Only a flesh wound; a spider bite; a bee sting; only a steak knife could remove the barb; only babies cry; only stubbed; bumped; bruised; only a sliver, but it still hurt; only a pinch; only a pin prick; only a pint.

The blood drained from my father's arm each month at the clinic, repayment for what Mom borrowed when I was born. In my first few moments, I nearly killed her. The doctor left a piece of placenta inside. He forgot. Or didn't search long enough. Just a scrap of tissue caused the hemorrhaging to begin. Dad squeezed a rubber ball, blood siphoning from his vein to the plastic sack dangling on the metal pole. He said he had a responsibility. Someone else might need it. After he finished, the nurse removed the needle. She plugged the hole in his arm with a cotton bandage, sent him into the waiting room to recover. Dad slipped me his butter cookies, even though the nurse said they were only for him.

Only way we're getting out of here alive; only if the conditions are right; only a fender bender; only a scratch; only bleeding a little; only live once; only minor injuries, not sure how anyone survived.

My only hesitation; only opportunity you'll have; only time; only money; only three shopping days left; the only gifts I asked for.

A pair of handcuffs and a leather briefcase to store my allowance. I'd count my money every day—quarters, dimes, nickels, and pennies. Stacked in neat piles on my dresser. I liked change better than cash—the weight felt more significant. I hated separation, needing, not having. I planned to lock the money in the briefcase. Handcuff it to my wrist. Cart the loot off to school. Mom said the other kids would laugh. I said I'd pay them not to. That Christmas, they were the only gifts I didn't receive. The following summer I bought a small suitcase at a neighbor's garage sale. Seventy-five cents. I filled it with change, rolled in paper wrappers. Duct-taped the case to my wrist. I carried my change to the playground where the neighborhood boys played basketball. The kid whose family bred Doberman Pinschers laughed when I approached. I clicked open latches of the suitcase. Handed him a quarter. He stopped giggling to examine the money. He whipped the piece of silver at my forehead. The other boys joined in, launching loose pebbles and gravel at my skull. I used the suitcase to deflect chunks of asphalt. The change broke free from the paper wrappers, rattling as I moved. I ran home to cry on the front step. I tried to pull off the tape, but it hurt too much. Mom sat next to me. She yanked off the tape in one snap motion. The hairs on my wrist burned.

If only they understood.

Use only cold water; only in the case of an emergency; only break the glass if; only going away for a few; don't worry, it's only the wind; the house shifting; thunder; only permitted in the kitchen; only for special occasions; your only downfall; only under fire because; there's smoke only if there's.

The house next to my grandmother's burned to the studs. Their youngest kid lit a match when his parents were gone. After the fire department left, my folks made me walk through the gutted rooms. Mom said this is what a spark can do. The smell made me dizzy. I shuffled my feet through a pile of black powder that could have been a couch. A kitchen table. Their black lab consumed by flames. The ash left charcoal stains on my shoes.

Insurance will only pay; if only he could take back; only once; only a second.

Running on only an eighth of a tank; only a few minutes left; only things you can count on are taxes and; only breathing because; only hurts when I move; only child.

Julie said I was the exception because every only child she's ever met is spoiled. Selfish. Maladjusted. Emotionally unfit. Rotten. Especially her ex-husband, the cheating bastard.

Only only children.

I told her my wife and I only wanted one. She said just wait. She said we'd want more. She said my child would be lonely. I said I never was lonely. I finger painted with Mom on the patio and pretended I was a disc jockey, playing 45' records for an imaginary audience in my room. Julie said only children are re-clusive. She said I'd want more for my child. She said I'd want my kid to fit in. I asked what would happen if I didn't. She said I was doing something wrong. The only advice she had.

Only mentioned it because; only wish you could have seen; only going to say this once; only chance I'll have.

Blisters

Michael Hemery

With Honors

I

Growing up, I assumed all five-year olds were offered the same academic advice my father gave me each time we discussed school: always do your best, never take the easy way out, follow your passions, and most importantly don't contract the mumps.

My dad stored his report cards from elementary and middle school in a green, fireproof World War II ammo box that he acquired at a local army supply depot. Each time he'd retrieve tax papers or other important documents from the metal box, I'd ask him to retell the story of his youth. At eleven, he moved from France to Cleveland, and was placed in public school without any sort of intervention or ESL tutor. He was forced to learn the English language and an odd system of measurements entirely on his own. Despite this disadvantage, he outscored many of his American peers, proudly flaunting his language skills in French class when the teacher turned to him for advice.

I'd ask to see the report cards every time he opened the box, so he'd pull out the folded pieces of paper, scattering them on the bed.

"What do you think?" he'd ask me. "Your old man's not so bad, eh?" He received straight-A's in every class until his sophomore year. Those report cards were missing from this pile. "I expect the same thing from you. If you're going to succeed, you have to keep up your grades, no excuses."

"Tell me again why your other report cards aren't in here," I said, wanting to hear the story again. "The ones from tenth, eleventh, and twelfth grades."

"It was those darn mumps," he said, sorting the progress reports into a neat stack. "Ever since then I got stupid."

"So mumps make you stupid?" I asked.

"Whatever you do," he warned, "don't get the mumps."

21

II

I never attended preschool, any sort of daycare, or camp. Yet I was over prepared for kindergarten due to my parents' insistence on excelling in the arts and academics. Before I ever set foot in a classroom, we read together each day, pulled a variety of educational games out of the closet, and spent the lazy summer afternoons finger-painting on the patio. They frequently reminded me that I'd be the first in my whole family to attend college, so therefore I must push myself. When it came time to attend "real school," I could barely contain my excitement. The day before I entered kindergarten I recorded a song into my parents' portable tape recorder. The chorus went, *School days, school days, I love school days.* My mom still has the tape—proof of my early enthusiasm for education, even though we no longer own a tape player.

III

A check minus. I held the paper in disbelief as Mrs. Hall, my kindergarten teacher, finished passing out papers to the rest of the students. On the top of my paper, in red marker, she wrote, "Color in the lines next time," followed by a thick check minus. This may not have been my finest display of coloring talent—my crayon strokes frequently broke the black boundary of Goofy's outlined body—but this was in no way check-minus work. It wasn't up to the high standards I'd set with the Donald Duck project where I demonstrated a hint of shading, but it wasn't any worse than the average kindergartner. I contested the grade with Mrs. Hall at the end of the school day after I slung my bag onto my back, preparing for the walk home. I thought perhaps the minus was simply a slip of the pen.

She took the paper from my hand and pointed to the stray lines. "This is not the sort of work I expect from you, Michael. You're better than this."

"But Brad's paper was sloppier than mine, and he at least got a check."

"But you're not Brad."

As my eyes welled, I ran from her room and out the front doors of the school. I'd never received a check-minus on anything. Paranoia overcame me. *There is no way a college will let me in with that sort of grade. I bet that check minus will show up on my report card. What if I've caught the mumps? John looked a little sick the other day on the playground. What if I caught the mumps and am now stupid and can't get into college?*

I crumpled up the paper as I walked home, stuffing it in the branches of a dense bush growing beside the brick school building. I figured I would crush my folks by informing them their son wasn't going to continue his education after high school because of this Goofy disaster. I couldn't bring these marks home to my dad; I was too ashamed. He was an incredible artist, sketching fantastic drawings of Daffy Duck and other cartoon characters for my amusement.

On the walk home I wiped my eyes, trying to compose myself and not let on there was anything amiss. I found that my dad had taken a half-day off of work so we could play soccer together in the front yard. I conjured up some mild enthusiasm while kicking the ball around until I eventually confessed my crime to him.

"Well," Dad said, "where's the paper now?"

"In a bush," I said.

He held me while I cried into his shirtsleeve and then took my hand as we returned to the school to retrieve the check-minus from the bush. But we never found it. It must have blown away or been retrieved by the janitor. Or maybe, he said, it was a trick of my imagination and never existed at all.

IV

After high school my father served in the Coast Guard before working as a pressman for a local newspaper. It was an arduous job that subjected employees to caustic chemicals, hazardous fumes, and exhausting manual labor. My dad's friends lost fingers in the blades of the presses, and the huge rolls of paper had been known to fall off the shelves, permanently disabling several employees. The cracks and creases of my dad's hands were dyed with black ink, despite the number of times he scrubbed them with the pink, chalky soap he stored underneath the utility sink in the basement.

But I loved the smell of the ink. It clung to his navy blue work shirts and was infused in his hair. When he returned home from work, the smell of ink wafted into the kitchen, mixing with the chicken or fish sticks Mom was preparing. Biting and sharp like gasoline, there was something fresh about its presence in a stale room. On those long nights when my dad worked double shifts, my mom would send me to bed, insisting he wouldn't be home until well past midnight, and I needed my rest. She'd leave my bedroom door open just a crack, while waiting up for him in the living room, listening quietly to Billie Holiday records. I'd close my eyes, listening to every word of those records, anxiously awaiting the scent of ink to rouse me.

V

After fifteen years on the pressroom floor, the estimating department realized my dad was gifted with numbers so they offered him a white-collar desk job at a "slightly higher pay scale than his current position" (but also much lower than the other white-collar employees because he didn't possess a college degree). The company needed my dad's assistance in saving the company from financial ruin because he understood the practical matters on the floor but could also design, engineer, and manufacture the needed parts for the presses at a much greater discount than an outside contractor. They flew him to California to evaluate a used press the company was interested in purchasing. "It was the most amazing experience," he said. "From here to LA there are mountains and plains and lakes, everything so beautiful from way up there. The world is evened out. At that elevation there is barely any trace of man."

For Christmas, the company gave my dad $500 and a large tin of caramel, cheese, and butter-flavored popcorn. When he asked why he'd received such a generous gift, his boss said it was the standard bonus for all employees. My dad mentioned that he'd never received a bonus when he worked on the pressroom floor. The man laughed and said they never issued bonuses to "those sort of employees." Dad returned the money and that following Monday returned to his job on the press. He kept the popcorn.

VI

"Upon accepting our invitation into the honors program, you have a moral and intellectual responsibility to understand that you are better than everyone else. That can be a great burden when your peers in high school can't understand that you are intellectually superior."

I chewed on my pen cap. Most of my blue pen caps were dented with imprints of my teeth. My mom and my health teacher lectured that the caps housed hundreds of germs that could potentially cause illness. Despite understanding and appreciating this information, I gnawed away at the plastic until it eventually snapped, forcing me to find a new cap.

The classroom was occupied by two dozen seventh-graders who were instructed to listen to a lecture by the junior-high guidance counselor and then fill out a form indicating our interest in being admitted into the honors program for all subject areas. I raised my hand. I didn't wait to be called on. We were supposed to wait. We were supposed to know better.

"Excuse me," I interrupted from the back of the classroom. "Can you say that again?"

The guidance counselor cleared his throat. "I *said* you must understand that you are the best of the best. You are the brightest and most promising students in the seventh grade; each of you have the potential for greatness. The school has been watching you, and you are better than everyone else."

I unclenched my molars from the pen cap, stood up, and gave the blank form to the secretary who sat near the door. "That's what I thought you said."

VII

My grandmother handed me a $100 bill to "buy new shoes and pants" for my first day of school—the private college ten minutes from my home that I'd been eyeing since kindergarten. The only application I sent out. She wanted me to have the gift because I was the first person in my family ever to attend college. She hoped that I'd be a success and learn what she, her husband, my dad, my mom, her parents, her sister, my cousins, their parents, and on and on and on never had the opportunity to learn. I don't remember what I said back to her. I must have thanked her. I know I hugged her. I also know I didn't spend the money on shoes.

VIII

My dad attended college for one day. He said he'd wanted to go to Case Western Reserve University for drawing and design, but when the admissions counselor met with him, she actually laughed when she looked at his grades. He settled for Cleveland State University. On the first day of school, his science professor insisted that all papers be written longhand in a particular, uppercase font or they would not be accepted for credit. When my dad asked the reasoning behind this request, the professor explained that this was the "handwriting of scholars." My dad withdrew from school the following day. When I asked him why he never stuck it out, he said his mom never really pushed him to continue. She didn't care one way or the other what he did. More likely it was because my father has no patience for unexplained bullshit.

IX

The day of orientation, I was corralled into the school's tennis courts with a few hundred college freshmen. We were instructed to hold hands with the two people standing next to us as we entered the cages. A "student leader" then commanded us to duck under outstretched arms, forming a twisted mess of bodies. A senior standing on a ladder, shouting through a megaphone, told us to untangle ourselves while still holding hands to make a circle around the perimeter of the court. I couldn't comprehend what this had to do with preparing me for the five courses I was scheduled to begin the following day, but I understood this was some sort of "getting to know you," team-building activity. I searched out fellow cynics to commiserate with on the absurdity of this request, rolling my eyes at the eighteen-year-old girl with too much eye makeup who gripped my right hand. She asked what was wrong as she loosened herself from the knot she'd formed with the boy next to her. I said, "You know," nodding my head to the senior on the ladder who was now cheering motivational rhymes. She said, "I don't know." I said, "That's too bad." She asked if I owned a car, because she and her friends had fake IDs and wanted to run to the convenience store after the orientation for beer. She said none of them had wheels and just needed someone, anyone, to make the run for them. I said I didn't have a car. She said she'd seen me in the commuters' meeting earlier that day and knew I had a car.

Ten minutes later, as I ducked underneath arms, twisting my body over and under other freshmen, trying to untangle and free myself from my peers, the girl said she wished she'd been holding hands with someone much more fun. She asked how such a "fucking loser" like me was accepted into college.

I sat at the foot of my parents' bed, sniveling that I didn't want to go back to school. I said I'd always envisioned college as a place filled with academics who were self-motivated and focused on their studies. I wanted to return my ticket of admission. I said neither of them went to college, so I saw no reason why I had to go. My mom stroked my hair, telling me it would be all right. She said tomorrow would be better. They told me I had to go back if I ever planned on changing the world. They lied.

X

After returning to the pressroom floor, my dad began exploring other careers because he said the job wasn't "fun" anymore. When the company changed ownership, they fired most of his friends while expecting the remaining employees to work more for less pay. Dad said it used to be one of the best jobs he'd ever had because his coworkers developed a sense of camaraderie working long hours together to produce the paper. During breaks and lunch his buddies would play pranks on each other (slipping mice into their friends' brown lunch bags and encouraging one another to sit on wet paint). After work they'd share a beer on the curb in front of the building. But the company broke their spirits by increasing restrictions on conversations in the pressroom and shortening their lunch breaks. They were now expected to remain virtually silent while working, as to not distract them from increased production.

My dad took a second job—substituting as a night custodian for an elementary school. He hoped to demonstrate his strong work ethic to the principal so he could eventually be considered for fulltime employment. A year later he quit the printing business when he was hired fulltime to work as a second shift janitor. His few remaining friends in the pressroom were jealous.

One evening while emptying the principal's trashcan, my dad overheard the man complaining to his secretary about an error on his computer. My dad was a self-taught computer genius. He'd always remained ahead of the trends—he owned a Commodore 64 and a modem before anyone even heard of the Internet. As he relined the garbage can he offered the principal a brief explanation on how to resolve the error and prevent it from occurring again.

Once computers began to be integrated into the school for teacher use, my dad became the unofficial technology coordinator. Administrators asked him to abandon his mop and vacuum throughout the day to do in-service instruction for teachers. One time my dad was asked by the superintendent to give a lecture on computers in the elementary school's gymnasium. My mom and I had the day off, so we sat in the back and listened to his speech. After receiving a round of applause at the conclusion of his lecture, he didn't wait until the room was empty to begin stacking chairs and sweeping the floor clean.

XI

"Pick up the paper," I said to my student who cleared the tattered notebook paper scraps off his desk onto the carpeted floor.

"No," he said, leaning back in his chair.

"I said pick up the paper, *now*." The room of twenty-nine other students fell silent.

"No," he said. "Do I look like a janitor?"

XII

From the Yale handbook: "To ensure that undergraduate students are exposed to a range of ideas and disciplines during their time at Yale, Yale College requires them to fulfill a variety of distributional requirements, which must be met by certain milestone points. As knowledge of more than one language and familiarity with more than one culture will become increasingly important in the world of the twenty-first century for professionals in every field, the distributional requirements include foreign language study."

XIII

My dad is bilingual.
The janitor is bilingual.
My grandfather is bilingual.
My grandfather was a janitor, too.
That janitor was bilingual, too.
My undergraduate creative writing instructor used to be a janitor.
My undergraduate creative writing instructor is not bilingual.

XIV

"Mr. Hemery," one of my former students said, rushing into my classroom. "I heard that the nonfiction English class I'm signed up for next year is the dumb English class. Is that true?"

The English department at the high school where I teach recently revised the curriculum to be more demanding and engaging for all levels of students. We strove to find challenging selections to motivate different types of learners to read the books and participate in intellectual classroom discussions. We still offered AP English—the course for students who'd been following the honors track for the past three years, but introduced two new courses: Nonfiction and Fiction.

At the curriculum meeting I said, "The whole point is to instill some sense of passion about reading. It's naïve to assume all people are passionate about the same things." After hours of deliberation, we successfully created reading lists for each of the non-AP classes that would hopefully spur engaging real-life conversations, including *Nickel and Dimed,* a book about trying to live on minimum wage, and *Fast Food Nation,* an exposé on big business's exploitation of America.

"Who told you Nonfiction was the 'dumb' class?" I asked the student.

"Well, one of my friends said that she had to take AP; otherwise, she'd be bored because those other classes were for *regular* students."

"We worked really hard to make sure our classes prepare students for both college and work. I don't know who is spreading these rumors, but they're wrong," I said.

The student hesitated and then said, "She heard it from her teacher."

XV

    Bumper sticker:
    My child is an honor student at _____ school.
    Bumper sticker:
    My kid can beat up your honor student.

XVI

    My dad refuses to read fiction. He'll read my wife's poetry, but that's about as close to the "not real" as he'll get. I've tried to explain to him that fiction is a reflection of reality's concerns.

"Then why not deal with reality itself?" he asked. "It's fucked up enough, isn't it? What's the point of reading something that's not real? That just seems like a waste of time. Enough people avoid reality. And fiction is usually too wordy. Just get to the point, already, you know? Besides, I've never liked adjectives."

XVII

"Iago isn't a faggot," Shawn, one of my senior English students, said outside my classroom.

"Mrs. Mitter said there is evidence that Iago *is* gay," said another male student's voice that I couldn't identify.

"He's a pissed off, evil motherfucker, but he ain't gay. Everything he does is calculated and precise and he brought down Othello because of pure revenge for fucking him over as lieutenant. He's a badass motherfucker."

"Well, maybe it's because we read *Othello* in AP English and your teacher doesn't think you can handle that discussion in regular English."

"Maybe it's because you've never seen real evil."

XVIII

My wife and I met my parents for breakfast recently and Dad recounted the intricate details of the sailing books we bought him for Christmas. He does this all the time, but before we presented him with his gifts this year, I made him promise to restrain himself from telling us every minute fact. I'm not really interested in sailing.

He's read all of Bernard Moitessier's works but said he lost some respect for the author in his last book because Moitessier started to become a "mooch," writing the book because he needed the money, rather than for the love of sailing. At breakfast my dad talked about some teacher from Stanford who teaches college courses on his boat, while sailing the coast of Europe. He told about a crew that survived a journey to Antarctica, but the boat sank on their return home in a small bay off the coast of South America when manmade debris crashed into it. He ended the morning by explaining the details of the crew of the *Endurance* who traveled to Antarctica in 1914 and survived. When they returned, they decided to join the military and fight for their country during World War I. They said it was the right thing to do. Nearly every man died in battle. According to Dad, man fucks everything up.

XVIV

One of my students slipped his book bag off his shoulder as he entered my Broadcasting class. He's typically one of the first in the room. "I have a question for you," he said. "In AP English yesterday, our teacher said that we're the only class that is required to make cross references in our research papers because none of the other students can handle it. She said that they can't even get their citations done correctly, let alone understand more sophisticated constructions. Is that true?"

He emphasized the word *true* as if he couldn't even fathom not cross-referencing citations.

"Sophomore year we primarily focus on the concept of research in general," I said. "We stress how to take information from multiple sources, create a thesis and then support it with details. There is another paper junior year that is a little more advanced, but my seniors aren't required to write a research paper like AP. I suppose they expect a little more out of you guys because you will most likely take higher-level English courses in college."

The student nodded his head and said, "Since you don't teach your students how to really write a *true* research paper, do you ever feel like you are short-changing them?"

"Not really," I said. "Most students will only write research papers in school. In some way or another they may work on something similar in their jobs, like compiling data, but unless you're a college professor, an MLA-formatted research paper isn't going to mean a whole heck of a lot after college. I think it's all about getting people to think, rather than the nitty-gritty details. That's why I like teaching English, because we get to talk about real concepts and philosophies. I don't get too hung up on the little stuff."

"But still, I feel bad for you having to teach those kids. Don't you ever feel like you're wasting your time?"

I really like this student quite a bit. He's a good kid with good intentions and will surely run his own company someday. He has a likeable personality and is always prepared for class. Despite my fondness for the boy, I still cleared my throat and answered, "Never."

XX

1. Senior retaking my literature class because he refused to complete any homework first semester and failed the course:
    a. Assisted the industrial arts teacher and a NASA engineer in the design and construction of a robot that placed second in statewide competition.
    b. Overheard me complaining to another teacher that my mobile broadcasting cart had no cable management.
        i. Welded and installed two intricate wire hangers on my cart without my knowledge, and left a note that read, "Merry Christmas, Hemery."

2. Sophomore who received 53% on his research paper because of incorrect formatting on citations and, despite hours of extra help before and after school, lacks the ability to form coherent sentences:

a. Could easily be accepted into any art school in the country because he is an art prodigy.

b. Writes poetry at sixteen that promises to one day be published by the most respected literary magazines.

3. Sophomore in my fifth period class who was suspended for asking his math teacher to "kindly shut the fuck up" and spent last Wednesday in the office due to an infraction of the dress code (holes in his jeans):

a. Believes John Lennon was the greatest gift to society.

b. Can play much of the Beatles library on his guitar (he brought me an audio recording of himself playing to prove it).

4. Sophomore failing my third period class because she's not read one of the ten novels we've covered this year:

a. Can quote hundreds of lines, word for word, from the great movies of the past century.

5. Sophomore failing my third period class because he plagiarized his persuasive essay:

a. Plans on joining the military in two years to "protect" his older brother who's been serving in Iraq.

6. Senior who sleeps in my class each day:

a. Works nights in a factory.

i. Uses money to pay for:

1. Groceries.

2. His own apartment.

b. His mother is addicted to heroin.

c. His father left when he was two.

7. Senior failing my composition class:

    a. Can rebuild the engine of his Toyota Corolla, modifying it for illegal street racing.

8. Sophomore who has piercings in his tongue, ears, nose, and lips; a tattoo of Satan on his bicep; and is receiving 6% in my class:

    a. Asked if I'm willing to "round up" his grade and winked.

    b. Stopped by to say, "Thanks for everything" and "I'm sorry I didn't do anything in your class, but I really did enjoy the shit you talked about. You get it, man" the day he was permanently removed from my class by his assistant principal because of his failing grades and "complete lack of effort."

XXI

Note my dad left on my desk the day before I started my senior year of college:

August 23, 1998

School starts again tomorrow, seems hard to believe summer has passed us by so quickly, it always does. Seemed longer when I was a kid, there was always time to do nothing. I was looking for a quote having to deal with "education," after all that's what tomorrow and the next months will be all about, but I ran across this one, and really that's all I really wanted to say today. I don't spare my words and often times speak out of emotion, not thinking, just feeling, and not saying the right things, and for that I'm sorry, so I hope this quote explains...you and me.

Michael Hemery

"Oh, the comfort, the inexpressible comfort of feeling safe with a person; having neither to weigh thoughts nor to measure words but to pour them all out, just as it is, chaff and grain together, knowing that a faithful hand will take and sift them, keeping what is worth keeping, and then, with the breath of kindness blow the rest away."

-George Eliot

Have a great school year, and be "Good," always,
Love ya with all my heart,
Pops

Stripes

Rap music was dangerous to a twelve-year-old white kid in the suburbs whose only taste of street culture occurred when I attended Cleveland's annual Christmas lighting ceremony downtown and a black man with saggy jeans collected money for parking. The music enchanted me, so with each new tape, I'd pine over the insert, mimicking poses of the men on the cover and reading the lyrics to every song.

I never played rap on the family stereo, because my parents would surely have confiscated the tapes—profanity, drugs, and sex were not approved topics. So I listened to the tapes on my portable Walkman in the tree house or when I mowed the neighbors' lawns, the sound of the mower providing an extra layer of protective clamor between the outside and me.

Listening to Public Enemy and Young MC, I sometimes donned a slight swagger as I trailed behind the mower or made gestures with my free hand (the one not holding onto the lever that kept the blades spinning) like I was scratching an invisible record.

I rapped along with the tapes, even though Mom once witnessed me engaging in this activity and commented that I looked like a fool muttering to myself in the middle of the yard. I figured she just didn't understand my transformation.

One afternoon I looked up from the mower and noticed my neighbor digging a hole to plant a new oak tree, bundled in burlap on the sidewalk. His two boys were playing near the rock pile at the back of his property, pretending to shoot each other with branches that served as makeshift rocket launchers.

When I looked up again a few stripes later, the boys harassed their tan Labrador whose leash, a rope secured to his collar, was knotted to a metal post buried in the ground. One boy whacked the dog on the rump with a stick while the other repeatedly dropped pebbles on his head. They'd wound the rope tightly around the stake, so despite the dog's best efforts, he was unable to escape the boys' torments.

I bobbed my head slightly, singing along with the tape, "My uzi weighs a ton, because I'm public enemy number one." The mower's blades snagged on a particularly dense patch of grass and stalled. I took advantage of the downtime to use both of my hands to scratch imaginary records before yanking on the engine cable twice to revive the mower.

As I turned the mower around at the end of the lawn I observed the neighbor, who'd abandoned his hole, crouching near his son, holding the boy's hand and turning it over repeatedly as if he was studying it.

I finished a row and took a break to wipe the sweat from my face onto the sleeve of my t-shirt. I beat the drumbeats from the song onto the metal handlebar and moved my shoulders back and forth to the beats. The mower sputtered slightly, but regained its stamina after I pushed it forward to complete another line.

On my return row, I paused when I saw the man grab his dog by the collar with his left hand and closed-fisted begin to beat him in the face. The son who'd had his hand examined was no longer in the yard, but the other boy stood near the rock pile, his arms by his sides, stick still in hand, watching his dad.

The dog's legs moved frantically, nails digging into the earth, as he twisted his neck back and forth to free himself from the man's grip. One of his paws scraped the man's arm so the neighbor lifted the dog into the air by its collar, his two front legs now dangling in the air, back paws just barely touching the ground.

The man reeled back and continued to beat the dog, knuckles striking the dog's snout, his eyes, and his head, never the same spot twice in a row.

I know that the dog had screamed. I'd seen his jaws open and close, although I never heard a single cry since my headphones and the mower drowned out any proof.

The animal's front legs, which once flailed erratically, resigned and went limp.

The mower remained motionless, except for its blades, which repeatedly spun over the same patch of grass. I opened my mouth to shout, to scream, but nothing came out.

No longer twisting his neck, the dog now offered zero resistance to the blows.

I know the assault lasted more than a minute and a half, because one song ended and a new one began.

The man dropped the dog to the lawn; his body remained motionless, slumped into a pile of fur and flesh and tail. The man kicked the dog one final time in the stomach with the toe of his boot. It was the kind of kick I'd only seen in movies.

I collapsed, letting go of the handle, the blades stopping immediately.

I buried my face into the grass, inches from the mower, the freshly mowed shavings sticking to the tears. "Stop your fucking crying," the man shouted. I looked up and saw the man grab his son by the shirt and drag him inside the house. "Get the fuck inside and stop fucking crying," he screamed.

It was then that I noticed my headphones had slipped, or been torn, from my head as I buckled to the earth. Yet somewhere beyond the mower, beyond the man's directives, beyond the dog's motionless body, I could still hear the voices from the headphones, but now small and incomprehensible.

Tread Marks

"I'm bored," Jill said, perching her slender body on the wooden frame of the sandbox, not wanting to dirty her white shorts. She wiggled her bare feet in the sand, hugged her bronzed legs close to her body, and rested her chin on her knees. I'd been watching Jill's skin darken all summer, pretending to be coloring in the backyard but secretly gazing at Jill in her bikini. Even though she was nine, four years older than me, I figured I'd marry her some day—she was the only girl I'd ever really known and the whole arrangement seemed convenient. I told her we could have the wedding in my backyard or hers; it didn't matter to me. She just laughed and messed up my hair.

"Seriously, if you boys are going to play cars all day, I'm going home," she continued, referring to Andy, my other neighbor, and me. "I don't want to waste away the rest of the summer."

Although Andy was the same age as Jill, he still ran miniature cars over the tiny dunes with me, pushing hard on the roofs because we both liked the tracks the tires left behind. We could retrace the precise journey of each car, except for the occasional gap where the car would make leaps. The humidity of the Cleveland summers leeched into the sand, making the moist surface perfect for recording history. But at the end of each day, we smoothed out the sand, erasing our presence. "That way we can start fresh tomorrow," Andy would say, working his way from the center of the sandbox to the outside, ensuring his knees didn't dent the freshly raked surface.

"We could play war or make believe we're Care Bears," I suggested to Jill.

"Or we could sit on our skateboards and race down the driveway," Andy said.

41

Jill yawned and stretched her arms, her shirt riding up, exposing her bellybutton. I tried not to stare and pushed down harder on the car.

"We could play pimp and prostitute," said Andy. I stopped rolling the car. "I'll be the pimp, Mike will be the john and you'll be the prostitute." I clapped my hands together, trying to free some of the sand that had stuck to my skin. I said I didn't know how to play "pimp and prostitute," but Andy assured that Jill would teach me.

"I'm usually Brave Heart Lion Care Bear," I said. He was never supposed to be scared of anything.

Jill said pimp and prostitute sounded like more fun than Care Bears, so Andy said we could pretend my enclosed tree house was a cathouse. I said I was allergic to cats, but Andy said I wouldn't be allergic to this type of cat.

Just about the time I was rubbing the sand off the back of my legs to climb the stairs into the make-believe cathouse, my mom called to us from the back door. Andy made a run for the fence gate, but Mom shouted for him to "stop right there."

Jill quietly said, "Oh, shit."

Mom said she'd been listening from the window and if Jill and Andy were going to stay over, they'd better find a better use of their time. Jill asked Mom if she was going to call her mom. Mom shook her head and said no. When Mom went inside to boil us cheese-filled hotdogs with baked beans for lunch, I whispered to Andy, "What's a pimp and a prostitute?"

He said to just forget about it. I apologized to Jill for Mom ruining the game and asked if this would affect our wedding plans. She didn't say anything, but just stared at her toes. Andy said after lunch maybe we'd play Care Bears after all. But as soon as they finished eating, they both went home.

For the remainder of the afternoon, I dragged cars around the make-believe desert. I periodically looked through the fence, but Jill never emerged to sun herself. I constructed a chase scenario with the cars, naming one Pimp, the other Prostitute. They chased each other all afternoon in slow motion, their treads digging lasting imprints in the sand. Finally, I allowed Prostitute to make a clean escape over the side of the sandbox. Pimp crashed into the wall, and I pretended he exploded into flames.

When my dad returned from work that evening I heard him and Mom laughing hysterically. When Mom chortled like that, it was usually at my expense. But unlike the time when I suspended a lawn chair from a tree with a dog chain and nearly castrated myself when the chain slipped between my legs, leaving me dangling nearly upside down, I had no clue what I'd done wrong that afternoon with Jill and Andy. I looked about the abandoned sandbox, studying the marks in the sand. Maybe I should leave them intact to show Andy the next day, but remembered his insistence about starting fresh. I ran my hands over the sand, brushing away the marks, and hurried inside to find out what was so funny.

Keeping Up

When I called my neighbor Kevin one afternoon to play, he scolded me. He said I wasn't allowed to say "play" anymore. He explained when I called him or especially any of the older girls in the neighborhood, I needed to specifically state my intentions. We could go swimming or watch a movie, but not play. He said that word meant something else now. When I asked what, he said I wasn't old enough to know.

My neighborhood overflowed with older girls—sixth graders, two years older than me. I loved their confidence, how they twisted bubble gum around their fingers or bought ice cream sandwiches at the corner store, slamming their change on the counter, walking away without a receipt.

Heeding Kevin's advice, I no longer called Heather, one of the prettiest girls, asking her to play. Instead I suggested we ride bikes. That's what *play* used to mean. I'd ride to Heather's house, then we'd pick up the other girls at their houses, inviting them to join our pack. We'd circle the block for hours. By the end of the morning, we'd gather seven or eight girls, their long blond and brown hair trailing behind as they pedaled their bikes. I always rode somewhere in the middle of that pack—an overweight kid with large, black-framed glasses and striped tube socks pulled up to his calves.

I believe they tolerated my presence because I made them laugh. I changed the lyrics to the popular song, "I Want Your Sex," to "I Want Your Socks." I did impressions of neighbors. I told them humorous stories like how I braided my mom's hair into a knot at the "Dead End Salon," a make-believe business I created one night when my dad worked late. Mom let me tie up her hair, securing it with all sorts of clips. When I finished, I held up a small mirror and shouted, "Voilá!" Mom always clapped. So did the girls when I finished the story. They said,

"Voilá," before poking me in the stomach with their brightly painted fingernails.

I felt safe with the girls—they cared for me like a mother. Once when I fell off my bike while attempting to ride through a ditch, the group stopped to inspect my wounds. Heather pressed on my sliced knee with her bare finger, long enough for the blood to clot. She said I was a goof. That there'd be no permanent scars. Her hand was warm. Soft. She didn't bother to wipe her finger on the grass when she was done to remove the stain. She didn't seem to mind.

By riding in the middle of the girls, I gleaned bits and pieces of various conversations. I learned George Michael was sexy because he moved his hips from side to side. Once I mimicked the movement for the girls. They laughed. I also picked up interesting tips on ways to French-roll pants, apply mascara, find bargains on sandals at the mall, or tell if a boy was a good kisser. I knew some day I'd marry one of the girls, so I paid attention.

As we rode the street, we passed the few boys in the neighborhood throwing baseballs or racing skateboards down driveways. Once Tyler, one of the high-school boys, looked up from his driveway, where he knelt beside his remote control car, to call me a "faggot." His brother John stood next to him and asked if I had a vagina. Missy, a petite girl with a high voice, told me to ignore them. She said they were just jealous because they weren't allowed to ride with them. Sarah, who'd just gotten braces, screamed back, "At least he's not spending his summer with a bunch of guys. That seems a lot gayer to me." Heather said we were done riding for the day. We all returned to her house where I braided their hair while they painted each other's toenails. When I was done with each girl I'd shout "Voilá." They laughed. I bowed and they clapped.

Sometimes Kevin rode with us. I didn't like sharing the girls with another boy, but Kevin taught me a lot of important facts about girls. Besides the "play" tip, he told me never to stare at their boobs, because I'd get hit. He said always to compliment a girl's clothes even if they were ugly. He said girls cared about details like that.

One day he said he was going to ask Missy to go out with him. Kevin rode beside me, asking if I'd talk to her, to see what his chances were of getting a date. I pedaled hard to catch up with her. I was out of breath, so I spoke in pants. She said he was too nice, not bad enough. She said she liked a boy who was dangerous, one who wasn't afraid to get into trouble. She said Kevin wasn't her type. I lagged back to give Kevin the news. He shrugged, saying he was going to go play catch with the guys. He asked if I wanted to join him. I said I'd probably just do a few more laps with the girls.

Toward the end of the summer Heather and Missy rode their bikes up my driveway. My dad was washing the truck while I sat on a lawn chair reading a Batman comic book. Heather said hello to my dad, but he couldn't hear her over the hose's spray. She asked if I wanted to go riding. I told my dad I'd be back in a few hours. The girls mounted their bikes, coasting down the driveway. My dad said to be home before dark. I told him I loved him. He said he loved me, too.

When I caught up with the girls, Missy asked what I said to my dad. I knew she didn't care for sweetness. "I love you" probably wouldn't bode well. I thought up a lie. I said, "My dad said I wasn't allowed to go out tonight, but I told him I was going anyway. He said I'd be in all kinds of trouble, but I don't care. I just left. We don't really get along."

Missy laughed and said, "It looks like we're a bad influence on you." Her pink flip-flops slapped her heels as she pedaled. "You're turning into a real bad ass."

My stomach clenched. I feared my dad heard the lie, the hurtful words. I loved my folks dearly. I glanced over my shoulder to make sure he hadn't heard. But the spray from the hose was still loud. He watched me ride down the street. He waved and smiled. I waved back.

I pedaled to keep up.

That evening we didn't go to anyone's house to watch music videos or play board games. Instead we converged at the playground near the neighborhood elementary school. The girls removed their shoes and took turns pushing each other on the swings. The bottoms of their feet were black, dirty from the asphalt. I watched them stretch out their sun-browned legs, then curl them back. They asked if I wanted to swing. I said no. I was having fun watching.

As the sun began to set, we all sat, circled on the asphalt. I skipped pieces of stone across the parking lot. Missy opened her purse, revealing a pack of cigarettes. She lit one, put it in her mouth, and sucked, the tip glowing red. After a long drag, she opened her mouth, tilting her head back, smoke escaping. It didn't rush out in a hurry, but slowly trickled out before evaporating into the air. She asked if anyone else wanted to try one. Heather said her mom would kill her. The other girls also declined, making up excuses. I didn't make eye contact when she held the pack out to me. Instead I skipped another stone across the parking lot.

I told the girls I'd just seen the movie *Back to the Beach* with my parents. Sarah said she'd wanted to see that all summer, but her mom wouldn't take her. Melissa asked why I didn't invite them along. I said I'd be more than willing to go again. I said I'd buy the popcorn. Heather said she loved beach movies and the song "Wipeout" by the Fat Boys. I told her my dad bought me that record on the way home from the movie. I invited them to stop by to listen whenever they wanted. Missy flicked her cigarette butt into the grass and squeezed my shoulder. She said I was sweet. Her hand reeked of smoke. The smell lingered even after she pulled away.

One of the girls said she bought a new swimsuit last weekend. Another said she had to buy a new bra—her old one was too small. Missy told me to shut my eyes. I asked how come. She said just do it. I squinted just enough to give the illusion they were shut, but was able to see Missy lift her shirt to her chin—her bare stomach, pink bra. She said, "My mom bought me this at the store last week." I'd only seen bras hanging on racks at department stores or brief glimpses in movies, right before my parents sent me from the room.

Missy put her shirt back down, telling me it was okay to look now. Heather said I hadn't shut my eyes in the first place.

Missy arched her back and said, "Guess what else, girls? I got my period the other day."

I didn't understand what that meant. I knew the period as punctuation. It ended things. I never equated it with anything more, especially not a girl's anatomy. My elementary school's maturation talk was brief. The boys and girls were separated into two rooms. Mr. Pilkey stood in front of the boys and said, "Two things will change. You'll grow hair and start to stink." He handed out free sticks of deodorant to each boy in the room. He asked if we had any questions. No one did. Within three minutes we tore onto the playground—chasing each other with the deodorant, coating our hair and shirts with the chalky white paste.

The girls emerged two hours later. They walked slowly towards the playground, single file, in silence. They looked like they'd just been told they were all going to die. We ran up to the girls and asked what took so long. No one answered. Their faces were blank. Brett Cameron said, "You guys getting hair and starting to stink, too?"

Jenny Manther looked up from her shoes and said, "Oh, God, we're going to get hair, too?"

We tried to chase the girls with the deodorant, but they didn't react. None of the girls ran. Instead, they let us smear their shirts and legs. When we grew bored and ran into the field, they huddled in small circles on the playground, whispering.

Now, on that same playground, I was part of that circle, but remained an outsider. I still didn't understand. The girls were all aflutter. They asked questions, wanting to know the details. Sarah said, "Sorry you have to hear all of this, Mike," but they didn't stop. I didn't know what a period was, but figured from the conversation it was a good thing because they congratulated Missy and said she was so lucky. Although, from what I gathered, the details about the blood and the stomach ache didn't seem to support their enthusiasm.

After a bit I said, "I got my period, too."

The girls roared with laughter. I pointed to a scab on my knee and said, "It'd been bleeding something fierce, but I have it under control now." The girls laughed so hard they began to sob. Heather touched the scar on my knee, the same open wound she'd touched before. She said, "Uh-oh, you might be pregnant now." I laughed, too, but wasn't sure why.

Just as the sun set, we mounted our bikes, pedaling down the street. As we passed each girl's house, the pack thinned until just Heather and I rode together. When we reached the end of my driveway we slowed to a stop in the street. I asked Heather what she was doing tomorrow. She said she didn't have any plans. I asked if she wanted to get together. I said, "We could play. The record." I corrected myself before she'd detected the slip. Heather thought for a moment and said that sounded like fun. She leaned over her bike to hug me. Her body was warm, her black shirt retaining the heat from the day. I returned the embrace, promising to call in the morning. I watched her pedal down the street, turning the corner to her house. I stood up on my pedals, pushing down hard so I could make it up the steep incline of our driveway before dark.

Jumbo

It was an honest mistake. I'd only been interning with the nonprofit organization for two weeks when the marketing director asked me to purchase three boxes of paperclips from the office supply store at the end of the block. The career director from my college assured me if I accepted the internship I'd be writing grant reports for the company's annual fund campaign. But instead, I'd only demonstrated my abilities to make double-sided copies and run trivial errands.

"Don't get any of those puny paperclips that easily bend out of shape," my boss said. "I want the industrial strength, jumbo variety." He handed me a scrap of paper with our account number scribbled on it and shouted from his desk as I left his office, "Make sure they're jumbo."

The nonprofit was located eighteen blocks from the center of downtown Cleveland, directly across the street from Cleveland State University. Prior to accepting the internship my junior year of college, I'd never ventured this far east from the heart of the city. As a kid, my folks would drive downtown for Indians baseball games and Christmas lighting festivals on Public Square, but my dad warned me when I turned sixteen and expressed an interest in driving downtown for concerts, "You're safe as long as you stick around the commercial part of downtown, but if you go ten blocks in either direction, you're just asking for trouble."

The company I worked for strayed just east of the business district—the point where black marble edifices with doormen in uniforms turned into chipped brick buildings with rats. Instead of renting space to million-dollar foundations or corporations, our five-floor building, which remained vacant on the third and fourth floors, housed an immigration office, a pizza shop that displayed a "Good Chiken" sign in its front window, and the local branch headquarters for the Black Panthers. The area was a far stretch from the Cleveland suburb where I was raised, with its kickball games and ice cream trucks.

As my new brown loafers clipped along the sidewalk toward the office supply store, I noticed two pigeons trailing after one another several yards away. The one bird briskly strutted along the cement, puffing up his feathers until his entire neck was engorged. As I approached the birds, they began circling one another with more haste, until the pursuer awkwardly mounted the chased and began thrusting his torso into the other bird's behind.

"Do you need anything?" said the female voice.

I'd been so enraptured by the avian humping that I hadn't noticed the stunning dark-skinned woman standing in front of the office supply store window. She wore black, high-heeled shoes with a black silk dress that stopped well above her knees. The top of the dress clung to her chest, while the skirt portion swayed gently as she moved. The office supply store's red neon "OPEN" sign tinted the thick curls of her long brown hair that bounced from her shoulders when she shifted her weight from one foot to the other. Still shaken by the exuberant bird copulation that continued near my feet, I failed to respond to the woman's question. She smiled when she caught my eye and repeated, "Can I get you anything?"

Having only visited office supply chains in the suburbs, I was impressed by the marketing strategy of the locally owned business—curbside service offered by a striking woman with large breasts that stretched open the V-neck of her dress even further, revealing just a hint of her red lace bra.

I shuffled my foot to shoo away the birds and said, "Yes, I actually need three boxes of paperclips. But not the little ones that pop off when they're clipped to a large stack of paper. My boss insisted that I get the jumbo assortment."

When she scrunched up her brow and shook her head at my laborious description of paperclips, I thought she didn't understand the "jumbo" portion of the request so I held out my thumb and index finger to estimate the approximate size of the clips.

"No, honey," she said after I put my hand back down, "you're misinterpreting what I'm asking. Is there *anything* you need?"

It was somewhere between the moment I began to elucidate that I needed large silver clips, but not black binder clips, and when the woman ran her tongue over her bright red lips that I realized she wasn't selling office supplies.

This wasn't the first time a prostitute propositioned me, though I questioned the authenticity of my first encounter. When I was seventeen I had a friend who lived by the freeway near a stretch of cheap motels and gas stations. One evening as I drove home after visiting him, I noticed a woman running toward my car while I waited at a red light. When she began hollering from some distance away, I casually reached down to lock the doors, not wanting to offend her with the loud "thunk" they made when they dropped. Whenever I imagined prostitutes (not that I did often), I pictured sultry redheads, like Julia Roberts in *Pretty Woman*, sexy and smooth. But the woman who approached my car was nothing short of enraged. She screamed, "Let me into that car so I can fuck you! Open the goddamn door, you sonofabitch so I can fuck your brains out!" She pounded on my window with an open hand. I remember driving away when the light turned green, looking at her handprint on my window, thinking, *Wow, she had really big hands.*

Now, I wiped my hands on my pants and said, "Oh, wow, thank you." I could feel my face flushing in embarrassment.

"So, yes?" she asked.

I held my hands out as if to stop her from charging me. "No, I just need the paperclips." She nodded her head. "But it's not you. You're very attractive and I'm sure fine at what you do, but I need to get the paperclips before my boss gets angry. Not that it's a time thing, because it's not. I actually have a girlfriend right now."

I continued to ramble for several more seconds before the woman said, "It's okay, honey, I understand."

"But if I ever need *anything*," I raised the pointer and middle fingers of both hands to make air quotes when I said *anything*, "I'll definitely come back to see you, I promise."

"It's okay, honey," she said. Her smile was gentle. "Good luck with those jumbo clips."

The bell tied to the glass door rang as I entered the store, but none of the three employees behind the desk looked up. Two of the men spoke near the back of the store, while the other woman turned a page of the newspaper sprawled open on the counter. For the next ten minutes I searched the aisles for the paperclips, but could only locate the smaller variety. Not once during my time in the store did one of the employees ask if I needed anything. Since it had been nearly fifteen minutes since my boss sent me on this simple errand, I conceded, approaching the counter to ask the woman where the jumbo paperclips were located. She slowly raised her head from her paper, sighed while glancing at the two men who were still chatting, and replied, "I think they're out of stock."

When I walked back out onto the sidewalk, I checked for the woman in the black dress, but she was gone, leaving behind only the pigeons still chasing each other in circles. I returned to the office and set the three boxes of regular-sized paperclips on my boss's desk.

"This isn't what I asked for," he said.

I shrugged my shoulders and said, "I know."

Hypothetical Child

My wife, Stacie, has lost all naming privileges. I'd already made that mistake with the dog. We were driving home from the city pound, our new German shepherd mix sitting contently on Stacie's lap, when I agreed that she should choose the pup's name. After all, she'd wanted to bring home the dog's brother— a slightly tanner version of our pooch. I insisted on picking a female, because as a child I remembered my dad explaining that girl dogs don't raise their legs to pee and therefore don't kill the shrubs in the backyard. Since I was emphatic about selecting the female, it only seemed fair that Stacie, an equal partner in our relationship, retained naming rights. After twenty minutes of deliberation she announced, "Cherry." I bit my lip. "We'll name her Cherry, because she has this red collar against her black fur. She looks like a little chocolate-covered cherry." She buried her nose in the dog's fur—in Cherry's fur—and began speaking in high-pitched baby talk. "You're our little chocolate-covered cherry, aren't you?"

It would have been a heartless move to question her choice at that juncture. I repressed my silent pleas for a less effeminate name, but held out hope that I could introduce a tougher nickname when Stacie wasn't paying attention. (That plan somehow failed as well; the family now affectionately refers to Cherry as "Smooch McGooch," which is in no way a step in the right direction.) When my male friends inquired about the dog's name, I quietly mumbled "Cherry," which was met with hysterical laughter and jeers about the "fruity" name.

The only sense of justice I felt in the naming debacle occurred after we brought our little cherry cordial to my parents' home, where we lived for two months before purchasing our own home, and Cherry's temperament quickly changed from a sleepy, obedient angel to a holy terror. The second night in the house she proceeded to exhibit the deepest, nastiest growl I'd ever heard rumble forth from a puppy's throat. She chewed through a plastic baby gate, pulled an overstuffed lounge chair from one end of the basement to the other before tearing it into shreds, climbed my parents' basement stairs and ate through the ceiling tile adjacent to the steps, and gnawed their banister into a perfect spear. Suddenly the name "Cherry" didn't quite seem to fit our furry anti-Christ. Although she did develop into a passionate, deeply loving dog, she will kill anything with a tail. It's a tad awkward to be shouting across the backyard, "Cherry! Cherry! Quit shaking that squirrel/ rabbit/ mouse/ chipmunk/ groundhog/ skunk/ cat/ family of opossums and get over here. Dammit Cherry! Stacie, grab a garbage bag and I'll get a shovel; Cherry got another one." A name like Cerberus or Tank would have been more fitting. The guy down the street named his Great Dane Helmet. I secretly wanted to name her Wolverine— after the animal, but more so after the X-Men comic book character that tore his enemies into bloody ribbons with metal claws that protracted from his hands. That seemed a more appropriate name for a dog that loves to shake animals until their backs break.

Due to Stacie's subpar name for our dog, there was no way I was going to give her *carte blanche* in naming our child. The child-naming pursuit is a recent development. When Stacie and I met in college, I explained on our first date that my life goal was to get married and have a child; she swore she'd never marry or even consider the possibility of birthing children. Three years later I convinced her to marry me, while she showed me the benefits of zero parental responsibilities, especially with our hectic professional and personal schedules.

At my previous place of employment, where I was one of two men amongst a stormy sea of women, I casually mentioned one afternoon during lunch that Stacie and I may not have children. Karen, one of the part-time data entry secretaries, informed me I was a "selfish piece of shit."

I didn't quite comprehend how not wanting a child necessarily translated into my being a chunk of feces. In fact, I believed we were making the morally responsible decision by not introducing a child into this world and then proceeding to ignore it in order to tend to other more pressing responsibilities—a scenario played out by many of today's active parents. Karen herself would complain about her kids several times a week.

"Not bringing a child into this world," she explained, "just further confirms that you only care about yourself. Being a parent is all about sacrifices, and you don't seem to want to make any of those sacrifices."

"Exactly," I said. We were in complete agreement. Stress and sacrifice were the two primary reasons Stacie and I were unsure if we wanted a child. We were satisfied with one another's company. We had no immediate desire to muck that up.

And that's how it remained for the first five years of our marriage—we reveled in our solitude, never once broaching the topic of parenting. Life was peaceful and predictable. Smooth sailing. Carefree. Happy times. Easy street.

And then my wife turned thirty.

I'd heard of this elusive biological clock, but assumed Stacie's had never been wound, or maybe she never had hers reset during that whole Y2K fiasco. I imagined Stacie's "timer" more resembled a biological lump of cement that hardened with each passing year. But as her thirtieth birthday approached, Stacie began mentioning the prospect of having a child. She never came right out and said, *I'd like to be a mother.* Instead she took a more passive approach, asking me whether or not I preferred certain names. We'd be reading on our porch swing when she'd say, "What do you think of the name Julian?" Being the respectable male that I am, I ignored her question and continued reading. "Mike," she repeated, "do you like that name or not?"

"Do I like that name? What's the context for a question like that?" I asked. "It depends what I'm naming. Julian seems like a fine name for a cat or a cactus. Is that what you're asking—is Julian a good name for a cactus?"

Exchanges such as these took place often, as I repeatedly disregarded her name inquiries. We were both just beginning our teaching careers and attempting to obtain our master's degrees. Our college loans left us thousands of dollars in debt, so I had no mental capacity to assume one more responsibility—especially the responsibility of parenting. I promptly responded to each proposed name with absolutely no reaction whatsoever. Name after name after name, I'd stare off into nothingness, blocking out the voice that pushed me toward responsibility.

Until she asked, "What about Lily Joy?"

We were eating dinner when she proposed "Lily Joy." I set down my fork, looked up from my plate to Stacie, and asked, "Let's clear something up, are we having a kid or not?"

"I don't know," she said, smiling. "But I'm glad you brought it up. Lately I've been thinking I'd like a little one."

"You realize," I said, "that little one will eventually become a middle school kid who hates us, and then a high school kid who will make horrible choices, wants to stay out all night doing God knows what with his friends, and then sucks every imaginable dime from our bank account only to reject everything we've taught him and become a staunch, right-wing, meat-eating Republican. You've thought of that, haven't you?"

"No," she said, playing with the food on her plate. "But I have thought that someday your folks will be gone, and Thanksgiving will be awfully lonely by ourselves."

I hadn't considered that. My parents, who are admittedly our best friends, live in the house directly behind ours. Stacie and my mom spend the summer afternoons shopping and quilting, while my dad and I sit in front of a computer screen for hours learning new video editing software. Both of Stacie's parents died of cancer when she was in her early twenties, and the rest of her family is dispersed around the country. In our daily bliss, I'd never even considered that some day my parents would be gone. Then the only difference between Thanksgiving and a typical Monday night dinner would be more extravagant meal choices.

"But we can't just have a kid to make sure we're not lonely, can we?" I asked. "That doesn't seem like the right reason. I mean, our kids could move far away from us and not come home for the holidays."

"But they could call," she said.

I moved the food around on my plate.

"Don't you ever want to be part of *it*? Just a little bit? When I first met you, you swore that's all you wanted in life. You said that would make you truly happy."

"It's not going to be named Lily Joy, that's for damn sure," I said.

Stacie smiled.

"Then what do you want to name our kid?"

"Wait, you're not going to trick me into this that easily. Are we having a kid or what?"

"I don't know. I haven't decided yet. And this shouldn't just be my decision. I want you to want a kid, too. So, let me rephrase the question for now: What do you want to name our *hypothetical* child?"

And with that conversation, we agreed to have a hypothetical child. I enjoyed the idea of the little nonentity not crawling around in a hypothetical playpen and not taking walks on hypothetical family outings. Of course, at some point we'd have to meet, sketch out a timeline, take a vote, and if a quorum was met, discuss the next steps in allowing the hypothetical child to manifest itself in the flesh. But, for the time being, we were satisfied with the concept of a hypothetical child. We'd ring out names on car rides or while pushing the cart around the grocery store.

Despite the seemingly lax nature of this "fun" game, it was actually bound to a series of structured rules that all participants were forced to adhere to. First, any names agreed upon must remain confidential. We didn't want to run the risk of family members and friends telling us how ghastly our name choices were or mentioning the rhymes that elementary school kids would make out of the name. Second, all names remained hypothetical. There was never to be any sort of tangible evidence of the naming process. Finally, and most importantly, each party (my wife and me) had unopposed veto rights on any suggested name. It was known throughout the land (our house) as the veto clause. If a name repulsed the other, the name was immediately rejected and was never to be mentioned again. I immediately vetoed "Lily Joy."

For the next year we debated the name of our hypothetical child. Stacie did most of the naming, and I did most of the vetoing. For some time between March and July, when Stacie spent much of her day watering the flowers in the yard, she grew obsessed with garden-themed names. "Lily Joy" was already out. I proceeded to veto Rose, Chrysanthemum, Daisy, Violet, Azalea, and Lavender.

"Why not name our hypothetical child Garden to cover the whole gambit?" I suggested. "Or maybe Thyme or Oregano?" I was smacked.

I did allow one botanical name to slip through: Hyacinth. The Hyacinth concession was a direct result of Stacie's sheer nagging persistence. After mocking the selection, Stacie grew defensive, ignoring the veto rules firmly established at the onset of this process. The situation grew so dire that on Mother's Day I found a hand-made card on the kitchen table with a flower crayoned on the front. Inside it read, "Mommy, don't listen to the bad man. You're my favorite. I love you more than Daddy. Love, your favorite hypothetical child, Hyacinth." Like the day we brought Cherry home from the kennel, Stacie capitalized on my vulnerability to sappiness, so I rescinded my veto. I still had my reservations, especially if the child turned out to be a demon like our dog. *Hyacinth. Hyacinth! Give me that needle. Dammit, what did I tell you about shooting heroin, Hyacinth?*

Stacie also did her share of vetoing, crushing my hopes of bestowing a comic book superhero name on our hypothetical child. Stacie vetoed Peter Parker Hemery, Bruce Wayne Hemery, Ghost Rider Hemery and Professor Xavier Hemery. And despite my perseverance, she vetoed my name suggestion for twins: Luke and Leia.

"But when they're born, I can stand at the end of the hospital bed and say," I breathed deeply to conjure up my best Darth Vader impression, "'Luke and Leia, I am your fawtha.'"

"Is this all a joke to you?" Stacie asked. "I mean, would you really name our children…"

"Hypothetical children," I said, interrupting her.

"Fine. Would you actually name our *hypothetical* children Luke and Leia?"

"Yes, and then I'd have them sent to different parts of the galaxy to shield them from my evil ways."

Nearly all of the names on our imagined hypothetical list were for girls, but we struggled to find any boy names we cared for, let alone agreed upon. Stacie actually wanted Luke to be included on the scant boy side, but I refused to allow Luke to materialize unless she agreed to his sister, Leia. I was vetoed.

Despite our lack of boys' names, I wasn't concerned because I didn't consider the name game any indication that we were making a sincere decision about parenting. I likened it to the "what would you buy if you won the lottery" game. The entire prospect remained in the realm of the theoretical. After a year of names, most of which were vetoed, I'd never bothered to consider that Stacie was serious in her desire for a child. I figured it would pass like most of her whims. Four summers ago Stacie bought all the gear to knit, but so far has produced only two scarves that sit on the top shelf of the closet. Her year-long gym membership was used for six months. Stacie owns more cookbooks than Martha Stewart, but most of the dessert baked in our oven is squeezed out of a Pillsbury tube.

So despite the frenzied nature in which Stacie fired off names, I was perfectly content with naming our hypothetical child Magneto. There was nothing *real* about the process until I noticed a list tacked to the refrigerator door. On one side was the word "Girl." Underlined. On the other side, "Boy." Beneath "Girl" was a list of the half-dozen or so names that we mutually agreed upon. Hyacinth topped the list. I unclipped the list and held it up in the living room where Stacie was reading.

"What's this?" I asked, waving the list.

She looked nonchalantly at the list and said, "What does it look like?"

"You tell me."

Domestic disputes are fantastic because perfectly intelligent adults revert to elementary school retorts: *No, you tell me. Tell yourself.* And on and on.

"It's the list of child names," Stacie said, returning to her book.

"*Hypothetical* child names." Stacie ignored me and continued to read. "Why is this written out? The rule clearly states that nothing was to be recorded, written, or mentioned to outsiders until we held another meeting about this."

"What's your problem? You've been resisting this since I brought it up. You haven't taken any of the names seriously. If you don't want to have a kid, you need to tell me, because I need to know. I'm fine with that, but I need to know how to think about the future."

"I don't know," I said. And I meant it. "This list just makes it real."

"Well, this is real. We don't have forever to make this decision. You've been avoiding this by suggesting names like Frodo and Captain America."

"I sort of like Captain America," I said. Stacie shook her head. I read through the names again. "You know we don't have any boys' names."

"I know."

"Are we not going to have a boy?" I asked.

"I don't know."

"We should probably figure this whole baby thing out now, huh?"

There was a brief moment of silence. "Do you have any feelings about this?" Stacie asked. "I mean, do you really even want a kid?"

I thought for a few moments and said, "I see this like dinner. I'd rather you just tell me where we're going, and then I'll figure out what to get from the menu. I can always find something I like and leave satisfied. But you know I can never decide where to go. So I'd rather you just tell me what we're doing, and I'll make it work."

And so began the first official meeting to set forth a hypothetical timetable to make our hypothetical child less, well, hypothetical. We decided to begin "trying" when we were both finished with our master's degrees. I always chuckled when people said they were "trying" to have a baby. One year at a Super Bowl party, friends of ours, Jake and Michelle, announced to everyone in attendance that they were going to start *trying* to have a baby. Everyone "ooo'd" and "aaa'd." The women surrounded Michelle to begin commiserating on the details. I asked Jake if he was looking forward to *trying*. He blushed. They'd basically announced to a sizable room full of people, which included all four of their parents, that they were going to begin having a bunch of sex. Just because people call it something else like "trying," they're still informing the world that nearly every evening when we're all eating dinner or walking our dogs, they'll be sweating it out in the bedroom.

We began a list of bylaws and policies regarding this new stage in our decision-making process. First on that list was not to tell people when we began "trying." We also insured that we were in agreement on several key details of the child-rearing process: Stacie would breastfeed the kid and stay home for the first two years (as long as the school would give for maternity leave). No football or wrestling—we worried about broken necks. And vegetarian, until it was old enough to make the decision for itself. Herself. Himself. I also promised to stop calling our possibly not hypothetical child "it." The most important resolution set forth in that meeting was the creation of a clause—a fool-proof exit strategy that stated if either party (still Stacie and me) had a change of heart, not wishing to go through with this, there was the opportunity to cancel all baby creation. We'd share the rest of our lives together alone. No children. No questions. No regrets. It was aptly dubbed the "Pull-out Clause."

The Pull-out Clause enabled me to assess the possibility of being a father much more clearly. I have a tendency to say "no" anytime I feel I'm not being given options.

Mike, we're going to visit my family over Spring Break.
No.
Mike, we're going clothes shopping this afternoon.

No.

Mike, we're having a child.

Begin tantrum.

But if I know there are options, my infantile male brain hushes, so I'm capable of engaging in an adult discussion. I no longer felt like I had to resist Stacie's nudges with such adamant resistance. I even allowed myself to have meaningful conversations, out loud, about which room we could convert into a nursery. She let me commit to the idea, with a no-strings-attached opt-out policy.

"You're almost acting like you enjoy the idea of having a kid," Stacie said one day.

"Well, maybe I am. But remember, there's always the clause," I reminded her.

Stacie will complete her masters in four months and I'll be finished in a little over a year. We still aren't sure if we're making the right decision. But I think that's part of it, too. Maybe parents are never entirely sure they made the right choice, even after they've been at it for a while.

Recently as we walked Cherry around the block on a snowy winter evening, I said, "Sometimes I worry that we shouldn't bring a child into this world."

"I do, too," Stacie said. "But, I think we'd be good parents."

"No, not just that," I said. "I think we'd rise to the occasion of parenting. But it's more that I worry about the state of the world. It's a shitty place. There's wars, STDs, drugs, and global warming. I mean, the whole environment thing alone is disturbing—there may be no planet at all for little Hyacinth. Or she'll have to wear a special, shiny heat-repellent suit or something."

"I don't have the answers for that one." We walked in silence for some time. "We haven't committed to anything, you know? You can always implement the Pull-out Clause."

"I could," I said. Cherry tugged on her leash, burying her nose in yellow snow. She sneezed and lifted her leg to pee on a tree stump—she's taken to peeing like a male dog recently. I pulled her forward. "We still don't have a boy's name, you know? We're screwed if we have a boy. We'll just have to shout, 'Hey, you, it's time for dinner.'"

Stacie laughed, kicking the snow with her boot. "I actually have one, but I know you'll veto it."

"Oh no, is it Pine or Oak or something horrid like that?"

"No," she said, shaking her head. "Since all we have are girls' names, I came up with one that we could use for a boy or a girl."

"Is it Cherry? Because we're not naming our kid Cherry."

"Are you going to be serious?"

"Okay," I said, "what is it?"

"Phoenix."

The snow was falling harder now and Cherry shook the flakes from her coat, jingling the tags on her collar. The neighborhood was silent except for the sound of our boots compacting the snow. The wind was kicking up and the sun was setting, now masked by the gray Cleveland clouds that seem to be ever present in the winter.

"Well?" Stacie asked.

"It's actually not bad," I said, grabbing her gloved hand in mine. "Phoenix Hemery is pretty good, actually."

"And we could call her or him 'Finn or Phoeni' for short," she said.

"Did you pick this name because of the movie?" I asked. We'd just recently watched the third X-Men movie—a film based on the comic book where Jean Grey (codename Phoenix) assumes the lead role. She is reborn as a highly powerful, intelligent, yet confused woman who can only obtain ultimate freedom by dying at the hand of her true love, Wolverine.

Michael Hemery

"Well, that made me think of it, but that's not who we'd be naming our kid after. It would be for the right reasons. The traditional Phoenix."

"Of course," I said, nodding my head. "Rising from the ashes and everything."

"I'm serious," she said. "I'll only name our child Phoenix if you promise not to think of her or him as a comic book character."

I promised, pulled up the hood on my jacket, wondering how soon we could begin trying to create a superhero.

Contusions

Scavengers

The entrance to a nudist colony. The last place contestant in a marathon race. A Mail Pouch Tobacco barn. A military tank. Road kill (not a rabbit or squirrel). Fire (not in a fireplace or from a match or lighter). A homeless man. A stranger crying. Laughter. A police officer sleeping in his car. A cow's eye. Rain. A music stand. An accident. Wind. Falling. Something broken. Someone in a bear costume. Someone who doesn't want to see you. Safety. A weapon. The outside of a slaughterhouse. Rules. "Toilet on a tree lawn, toilet on a tree lawn," my dad shouted, waving for me to take the freeway exit we were about to pass.

The toilet on a tree lawn was the last item I needed to complete the assignment entitled "Scavengers," a contest for my high school photography class that required us to snap pictures of twenty-four items in as few shots as possible. For example, shooting a homeless man wearing a bear outfit running last place in a marathon while holding a music stand would fetch some serious points. As Mr. Bodin explained the project, announcing there would be a reward for the student who took pictures of all twenty-four items in the fewest number of frames, he mentioned that quality also counted. "I will deduct points if you cram everything into one mess of a shot. Don't set up the shots—I won't count the shot if you force it. It needs to occur organically. I'd prefer you have twenty-four shots, rather than one, trite train wreck of a picture." He flipped through the leather portfolio on his desk and said, "Speaking of train wrecks, here is an example of 'Something broken' that a student turned in several years ago." He passed around a black-and-white picture of a human body split in half on a railroad track. The train had severed what looked like a teenage boy into two clean pieces, except for the neck and the head, which the left side of the body won rights to. Each student that held the picture recoiled, the girls passed it on quickly, barely looking, while a few of the boys lingered too long. "A student took that shot right before he called the cops," Mr. Bodin said. "That's the kind of dedication I'm looking for."

Early in the week, I drove the rural streets near my aunt's farm, resting my elbows on the post of a road-side fence, where I waited for a cow to wander close enough so I could snap a shot of its eye. I found the barn, an opossum road kill, a broken telephone pole, and the entrance to the nudist colony with tiny cameras in the trees following me as I approached. Although pleased that the trees swayed in the background of the slaughterhouse picture, earning me double points, I couldn't help but feel remorse as the cows lined up one after the other in the fenced entry, awaiting their systematic deaths.

The following Saturday my dad and I drove to downtown Cleveland where I took pictures of a sleeping police officer, his shotgun in the background (a weapon), with his radar gun resting in his lap (rules). I became more obsessed with winning and cared less about my subjects. While I wondered how the student who took the picture of the boy on the tracks could stomach the shot, soon after hours of shooting, I grew less sympathetic with my subjects. I used my telephoto lens to shoot the homeless man warming himself near a rusted oil drum. Right before I opened the shutter, I clicked my tongue against the roof of my mouth so he'd notice me. The man scowled, as if he didn't want to see me. "That's three in that shot," I whispered to my dad as I handed him the camera. "I wish he were crying, because there would have been four."

After my dad spotted the toilet, we slowly crept down the street in the notoriously poor, Hispanic neighborhood. As we approached the toilet, my dad reached over and took the wheel so I could lean out the window to take the picture without stopping the car. Even though the street was empty, my dad said that as white folks, we shouldn't linger. The houses on the street looked fragile, porches held up with bricks, siding slipping to the dirt yards. I opened the shutter twice, taking two pictures, just to be sure my movement didn't blur the image. I quickly gave the camera back to my dad and pushed the gas to leave the neighborhood with its grassless front lawns.

But the street was a dead end. I pulled into a driveway, backed out, returning the direction we entered from. As we worked our way out of the neighborhood, dozens of Hispanic boys and men emerged into the street, as if they'd been watching us, waiting for us to take the toilet bait. A few carried bats and many wore loose-fitting jeans with white, skinny-ribbed t-shirts tucked in. I pressed on the brake, bringing the car to a stop several yards from the gathering crowd.

"Where the hell did all these people come from?" I asked my dad. "What do they want?"

"Hell if I know," he said. "Just go." I'd only been driving a year and was still unsure how to handle myself in a car.

"What if they don't move?" I asked.

"They will when the front of the car hits them."

I eased my foot on to the gas, then flicked my ankle, pressing down, hard.

The car lurched forward, but the men stood still until the hood nearly clipped their legs. Bodies jumped from our path. Someone shouted in a language I couldn't understand. My dad shouted back in one I did. I eyed the on-ramp a few yards ahead, forgetting to look back to see what'd happened to the men.

The following week, Mr. Bodin inspected our rolls of film. He held his tally outstretched in his arm, so he could read it without having to put on his glasses. I'd won the contest by six points. "Mike found his stride on the second half of the roll," he said. "That's when the shots got interesting." As the winner, I automatically received an A on the project and was exempt from developing any of the pictures into prints. "But it looks like you have some good stuff on this roll," Mr. Bodin said after the class trudged into the darkroom to begin the enlargements. "You may want to see what this shot of the homeless guy looks like blown up."

I thought about his suggestion. It was easy to take the pictures, scavenging like a buzzard, tearing flesh from my subjects, then departing without a second look. But I didn't know if I was capable of studying the homeless man's face, steadying my hand long enough to dodge the shadows from his eyes. I feared an unnoticed face in the window of a house behind the toilet or a cow at the slaughterhouse who glanced into my lens right before the shutter opened.

I thanked Mr. Bodin for the compliment, but decided instead to sleep at my desk, leaving the negatives tightly wound together on the roll.

Scapes

"If you'd just listen to me and grow marijuana," my Aunt Cathy said, "we'd all be much happier." She, like the rest of us, sat outside of Uncle Larry's barn—straddling a picnic bench with a beer in one hand and a bulb of garlic in the other. Bob Dylan's *Greatest Hits* was playing as loud as the mud-splattered, crackling cassette player inside the barn would allow.

My grandpa turned around on his bench and said to Cathy, "Did you just say mary-ju-wanna?" He chuckled, deepening the crow's feet under his eyes. He stretched out his hand, retrieving the metal clippers he'd rested on the bench.

"What?" Larry hollered, emerging from the barn with a plastic washtub filled with Music—a particularly large variety of garlic.

"I said," Cathy began shouting, tossing another cleaned and trimmed garlic bulb into a wicker basket resting at her feet, "if this was a thousand pounds of pot, all we'd have to do is cut it down on our way to our summer homes in Hawaii. But no, you had to be a garlic farmer."

"And instead of beer," Stacie, my wife, said, "we'd have champagne."

"Served by hookers," I added.

It seems that most families retain a series of commonly practiced rituals and rites that are cause for gatherings—religious holidays, baptisms, graduations, or even funerals. I have a friend whose entire extended family flies to their beach house in Key West each December for Christmas cookouts and a swim in the family's pool. Another helps coordinate her annual family reunion, which has been recently held in Hilton Head, the Outer Banks, and Ocean City. My family has something very similar—we converge for garlic.

At the conclusion of every summer, Uncle Larry and Aunt Vicki hold an end-of-the-summer garlic-cleaning party on their organic farm near Cleveland. I've suggested renaming the event the "End-of-the-Summer Garlic-Cleaning Cheap-Labor Day," as the event more resembles a merry work camp than a traditional social gathering. I can think of no other party where guests work in the scorching summer sun all afternoon and are then treated to (or paid in) cold beer and lukewarm pizza.

But despite my compelling suggestion, the event remains a party that is well attended by nearly all members of the family. My mom's cousin Jim, a man who'd slip cloves of raw garlic into his shoulder bag, chewing on them like candy for an afternoon snack, flies 2,500 miles from San Francisco each year for the soiree. But regardless of our motivations for being there—we are there. For Stacie and me, two born-and-raised suburbanites, the occasion is an opportunity to feel like authentic farmers, covering our jeans with a thin layer of dust and, if we're lucky, working up a blister or two to show our friends back home.

For my uncle, this party is the culmination of a year's worth of work and toil with this odorous root. Uncle Larry worked for the gas company, installing and checking lines, but as soon as he returned home from his eight-hour day job, he'd rush into the fields of his farm, tending to his organic garlic. Larry dabbles in other vegetables, growing thousands of additional individual plants, including broccoli, corn, and squash. But the garlic occupies the majority of his space.

In order to make the garlic more aesthetically pleasing for sale in grocery stores and markets, farmers peel away the first layer of skin that has been in contact with the dirt, trimming the hairy follicles at the end of each bulb. By the time we gathered for that year's party, Larry had cut, cleaned, and trimmed most of the garlic (1,000 pounds or 7,500 garlic plants). We cleaned the remaining hundred pounds, which we tended to in the early afternoon. Our efforts were only thwarted by the constant refills of beer, which slowed production considerably by 3:00 p.m.

We worked in pairs like a small-scale assembly line. Stacie peeled off the skin, while I sat on the picnic bench with a plastic laundry tub between my legs, cutting the hairs into the tubs, placing the clean bulbs into wicker egg baskets. Larry didn't do any of the physical labor that day, but instead managed us guests (workers), ensuring we always had a basket of bulbs to clean and a bottle of beer to drink.

Larry brought Stacie and me a new basket of bulbs and removed his baseball hat, wiping the sweat from his forehead onto his shirt sleeve. He began, "Cathy's right, you know. Garlic is actually one of the most labor-intensive crops to grow. You measure the amount of labor based on the number of times you actually have to touch the produce. You'd think that would translate into more money, but it doesn't."

As a child, I'd been to the farm hundreds of times to play with my cousins Mat and Kathleen, but we rarely left the comfort of their farmhouse, unless it was to search for some reprieve from the summer heat in the sprinkler. In my twenties, I grew more appreciative of the process, curious about the logistics of my uncle's life-long passion.

"So you don't have to touch other produce as much?" I asked.

"Right," he said. "For something like broccoli you just dump it into the ground after starting it in the greenhouse, and then pull it out of the ground, wash it and you're done."

"How many times do you have to touch garlic, then?" Jim asked, tossing another cleaned bulb into the basket.

"Well, as soon as we're done cleaning the rest of this, a third of these bulbs will get split into individual cloves and put back into the ground for next year's crop," Larry continued. He explained that he could only really sell about two thirds of the crop. Each fall he fertilizes the cloves with organic seaweed, mulches the plants to repress weed growth, waters the hell out of the fields if it's a dry summer, pulls any weeds that encroach on the garlic's space, and then trims any of the scapes (seedpods) because they suck the energy from the plant, leaving anorexic-looking garlic bulbs. Then he has to harvest the bulbs, dry them, cut them, and finally trim and clean them. Only to shove a third of those bulbs back into the ground for next year.

"Like I said," Cathy said, "we'd be much better off selling pot."

Having never much cared about Larry's farm, I'd never given much thought to our minor role in this garlic producing process. In fact, I typically left the party imagining that I was a critical component in providing the organic garlic supply to the Cleveland population. At the end of the party, Larry would announce how many pounds of garlic we cleaned, ushering everyone into the garage for pizza and some manifestation of roasted garlic. We'd applaud, dust off our pants, and enjoy every morsel of our seemingly hard-earned meal. But this particular year I couldn't help but feel like a fraud on that picnic bench. Comparatively, we'd essentially accomplished close to nothing that day. I was delusional in thinking that I'd actually done something more than witness the final stages of one man's year's worth of arduous work.

The following summer Larry retired from the gas company to dedicate all of his efforts to expanding his garlic business. After filling his fields, he rented several acres of land from a retired farmer across the street, replanting almost half of his previous year's crop to utilize the expanded space. The new fields were experimental, as he was unsure of the soil's potential. This was the first year his daughter Kathleen, an English major at American University who'd landed a long-term internship, wouldn't be returning home for the summer to work in the fields.

This was also the first summer in which Stacie and I had no work commitments. We'd returned to night school to obtain our high school teaching licenses and obtained positions at the same school—so we had no pressing financial pressures to take on summer employment. Of course our afternoons were still filled with vital issues like, *What should we have for lunch?* And, *Is it too warm to nap in the hammock or should I stick to the couch by the air-conditioning vent?* Books and video games occupied most of my time, so it came as a complete surprise to Stacie when I announced at the dinner table one evening, "I think I'm going to help Uncle Larry with those new fields of garlic this year."

She began laughing and then realized I wasn't joking. "You're serious?" she asked.

"Yeah, I think I need to be connected to the process." The decision was even less noble than that. It wasn't an internal desire to connect with nature, but more of an exterior desire for people to see me as connected to nature. I wanted to farm because I thought it would bolster the credibility of my carefully crafted image as a naturalist. Because I don't just feel like a fraud at the garlic cleaning party, but actually live a fairly overarching fraudulent existence. I'm vegetarian for purely ethical reasons, read fervently about living a "green lifestyle," and even own outdoor gear. One winter my wife and I each purchased a pair of top-of-the-line, Gor-tex hiking boots. As the salesman laced up my boot, he said, "If you're planning on spending that sort of cash on this high-tech of a boot, you must be a serious hiker." I nodded, handing him my credit card, knowing I needed the best boot man could make to keep my feet dry as I walked my dog around the block or embarked on daily treks to the end of my driveway to retrieve the mail.

"But," Stacie began, "you don't like to sweat."

Amongst my closest family members, there is an ongoing joke regarding my complete disregard for all manual labor and the outdoors in general. My father adoringly recounts the story of my college graduation party, held in his backyard, when I questioned when he'd planted all of the full-grown pine trees lining the perimeter of his property (I lived at home during college and commuted to the nearby school). To the amusement of my family and friends he said, "If you'd left your room or, better yet, even looked out your window once since the seventh grade, you'd have noticed the dozen trees I planted *ten* years ago." Despite his mocking tone, his assessment of my apathy for the outdoors was accurate. During my teen years I sequestered myself in my bedroom and could more readily identify with the glow of my computer screen than the light of the sun.

That's not to say I was entirely inexperienced with outdoor manual labor. When the environmental organization I interned with during my junior year of college announced they were downsizing their marketing budget, so my grant writing position would be cut back from five days a week to three, I was offered a spot on their landscaping crew to complete my internship requirements. On those two days a week, it was my job to drive around downtown Cleveland in a bulky box truck with two landscapers who'd recently graduated high school, watering trees and hanging petunia baskets planted in the median of busy urban throughways. Granted, on most days, we found ourselves in the driver's basement playing video games and eating Doritos. The only monitoring our supervisor conducted was checking the water level of the tank to ensure we did our job. So while I napped or fought off electronic zombies, we let the hose from the truck empty into the sewer to make it look like we'd depleted our allotment of water. But, at the very least, the experience gave me the general idea of what it was like to get up every morning for work.

"Honey," Stacie said, touching my hand, "you know you don't have to prove anything. Your allergies haven't been too bad this year. Don't do anything to irritate them. I still think you're a man." And with that final comment, an obvious statement that she or someone may question my "outdoorsiness" and now my manhood, I called my uncle and told him I'd be more than happy to help him mulch his new fields of garlic the following morning.

Standing in the doorway of our house, Stacie slathered sun block on my face and helped me to run through the list of items I needed for my manly day outdoors: Work gloves were in my pocket (Stacie reminded me to remove the price tag)—check; tennis shoes double knotted (I decided not to wear my new hiking boots because I didn't want to scuff their pristine finish)—check; extra deodorant to protect against excessive perspiration—check. Now I was prepared to connect with the natural world.

"Dammit," I cried, removing one of my newly purchased, padded leather gloves to swat at a particularly enormous and pestering fly that circled my head. Standing in the bed of my uncle's 1984 pickup, I waited to stack the bales of hay he was heaving at me from the loft of the two-story barn. The black flies were dive-bombing my scalp. During my burst of inspiration the previous night, Uncle Larry said we'd be mulching the garlic rows with dried alfalfa hay, so I'd envisioned the afternoon resembling the quaint farming scenes in *Of Mice and Men*—the 1992 Gary Sinise version—my uncle swinging a scythe or something while I hauled and hoisted bales of hay against the waning blood-orange sun. In retrospect, that film is fairly misleading, due in large part to the surprising absence of pterodactylian-sized insects.

Flailing the glove around like a propeller, attempting to thwart the mischievous critter's attempts to make any sort of cranial landing, I'd missed Larry shouting "incoming" as he tossed the bale down from the loft. The dried alfalfa sliced my ankle and the fly immediately began swarming the tiny tributaries of blood.

"Are these sonofabitch horseflies dangerous?" I shouted to Uncle Larry as he readied the next bale to be stacked in the truck. He didn't wear any type of work glove, trusting the layers of calluses to defend his hands from the jagged blades of hay. I struggled to fit my cumbersome gloved hands underneath the taut binding wire to organize the bales into neat stacks— maximizing the number of bales we could transport to the acres of garlic across the street.

Larry didn't hear (or ignored) my fly inquiry and dropped another bale onto the tailgate for me to lift and stack. I convulsively flailed my head around as the fly unremittingly attempted to land between the spikes of my gelled hair, nipping out small chunks of flesh. By the time I retrieved the next bale from the tailgate, Larry had dragged three more from the stock in the barn and was waiting for me to make some space in the bed of the truck.

"What's the matter with your head?" he yelled down to me.

"It's those damn flies, they won't leave me alone. I don't know how you stand it out here," I said between huffs, hoisting the bale into place.

"You got shit in your hair?" he asked.

"Shit?"

"Yeah, you have some sort of hairspray or something in your hair?"

I ran my now bare hand over the finely sculpted points of my hair. That morning I applied a little more than my typical palm-full of gel because I knew the wind or physical activity may soften my style.

"Because you don't want to have that junk or any perfume on when you come out here," he said. "The flies love that stuff. You don't see them around me, do you?" He used his hands like a *Price is Right* model to confirm his fly-free hairdo then tossed another bale into the truck.

As we ventured to the garlic fields, the truck lurched and bounced on the uneven terrain. A thermos of ice water sloshed between my legs; I snatched the two paper cups from the dashboard just before they fell to the floor. When we left the house, he figured we could both take swigs out of the same jug, but Aunt Vicki insisted that we take along the cups just in case. I shrugged off the predicament, declaring that it didn't matter to me, but ran back to the house before we left for the fields to thank my aunt for watching out for me. By 8:30 a.m. the temperature in the shadeless field was already in the mid-eighties according to the thermometer in the truck. Sweat coursed from my face as I bent over to spread the hay underneath the stalks of garlic.

Despite the taxing nature of the work, there was plenty of opportunity for conversation. Even when accompanied by others, I'd assumed that farmers worked in silence—concentrating on their connection with nature. But Uncle Larry was considerably verbose, discussing vacations he'd taken in his twenties to the mountains of Colorado, the lifestyle of his Amish friends, and general theories of existence.

I broached many topics, including man's role in nature and our evolutionary limitations. Larry had a response to each of my inquiries. "I actually think it's not us that have evolved," Larry said. "I mean, how have we really changed or grown in thousands of years? But look at these vegetables." He walked to a green, leafy field next to his garlic rows, snapped the fruit off of a small plant, and returned with two, petite brown tomatoes. He offered me one, blew the dirt off of his and placed the whole thing in his mouth. I repressed my inner desire to bolt to our water thermos to rinse off the tomato, but figured this act was the first of many in my transcendence into a rugged, natural man. "Sure, man has created a lot of new produce—take for instance these chocolate tomatoes." There is nothing more flavorful than an organic tomato right off the vine. Most of the produce in the grocery store is comparatively bland, the result of large-scale factory farming (something Larry later explained). But a real tomato, free of pesticides, preservation waxes and sprays, is blissful.

"I think the produce is actually evolving to taste better," he said. "Because if you think about it, if humans like the taste of something, they'll continue to grow it. And if we continue to grow it, then the plant will continue to propagate its species over and over. Humans are like bees spreading pollen to the plant. I actually don't think we control the plants, they're actually controlling us. They're the ones who've evolved. We're just the mindless idiots who spread their seeds." He spit the stem of the tomato onto the ground, covered it with dirt, and returned to the truck to gather another bale of hay.

The significant increase in temperature reminded us that the morning was gradually slipping into early afternoon. The increasingly irritating itch in the back of my throat reminded me that I had no business being anywhere near the outdoors. I felt like a cat attempting to hack up a hairball as I used the back of my tongue to scratch the back of my throat. I also began sneezing into the sleeve of my shirt. During one of my numerous water breaks, I did the "farmers blow" to clear my nose—plugging one nostril then firmly blowing out the other so the snot projected to the ground. There were flecks of dirt floating in my water glass, yet despite my best attempts to drink around them, I inevitably swallowed chunks of dust, which only further goaded my throat.

Thrill junkies say they need to engage in extreme sports and activities to remind them they're alive. There's extreme wakeboarding, extreme skydiving, and extreme skateboarding. I engage in a similar life-threatening activity known as extreme allergic reaction to nearly everything in the natural world. There comes a certain buzz in knowing with one wrong move I can die, or at the very least, render my body useless for a few hours. I believe I suffer from every allergy known to man. Some of my more prominent allergies include fall allergies, spring allergies, grass allergies, and food allergies. I've been afflicted by hay fever since I was a child and resort to bathroom cabinets full of medications and nasal sprays, which only slightly numb the symptoms. I spent a great deal of my youth on my parents' couch with a wet washcloth draped over my face to filter out the ragweed and pollen from reaching my nose.

Then there are the skin allergies. I can't come into close contact with the ornamental grasses that sway in our backyard when I'm mowing the lawn because one brush of the grass and my arms break out into intolerably itchy hives. My all-time favorite allergy, one that many can readily identify with, revealed itself in my fourth grade science class. My teacher devised a wonderful culminating activity for our botany unit and led the entire class into the woods behind the school to conduct leaf rubbings of the many leaves we'd been learning about. The teacher handed us each a leaf that we placed underneath a sheet of paper, rubbing furiously with the flat side of a crayon. When we returned to the classroom we were to compare our leaf to the chart hanging in the classroom and identify its name based on a series of prescribed characteristics. Adam was handed a flawless oak leaf and

John scored a maple. I was unable to identify my leaf based on the chart in the classroom. The teacher was baffled as well and instructed me to explore the leaf with my fingers, searching its ribbed texture for clues to its identity. I tore it slightly and held it to my nose searching for any faint hint of spearmint or lavender.

Finally, after many scientific trials, my teacher concluded that I'd discovered a new leaf and named it "Hemery." Unfortunately, that evening I determined that I wasn't the first person to discover this leaf so the science community was probably going to have to stick with its more commonly known name, *Toxicodendron radicans*, or poison ivy. Some people are immune to the effects of poison ivy. I'm not one of those people. A painful rash promptly appeared on nearly every patch of my body. All ten fingers swelled with the oozing rash that made it impossible to fit a pencil between my enlarged phalanges. Heading off a lawsuit, my science teacher excused me from all written assignments for the remainder of the quarter.

And I can't ignore my slippery food allergies, which continue to transform on a daily basis, making any meal an exciting game of Russian roulette. I can recall the specific day in college when my food allergies became slightly more intricate. I was eating lunch in the school's literary magazine office, rifling through submissions, when I bit into a peach and my throat suddenly began to swell. The dangly thing in the back of my throat, which I later learned is called the uvula—a term I'd always associated with the female reproductive system—grew to nearly three times its normal size; breathing suddenly became awfully difficult. Since that day, my food allergy has morphed to include a variety of foods, such as walnuts, apples, melons, and cherries. The situation grows a bit more complex because my uvula seems perfectly content with ground walnuts, baked apples, and chocolate-covered cherries. The list continues to change as I age, as items are added, but never subtracted, to the list with new dining experiences. I'm too dense to remember all of the included foods, but I'm fortunate that my wife carefully examines my intake at each meal, reminding me what I can and cannot consume.

I realized that Stacie was correct again that I should have remained inside my air-conditioned house, because as Uncle Larry and I headed back to the field, my right eye began to cloud over with a yellow film of mucus. This too is one of the many allergic reactions my body has to the outdoors—a thick glaze coats my contacts like milky varnish, leading to complete loss of vision until I remove the contact, clean it and place it back in my eye, only to be recoated within twenty minutes. I attempted to muster up tears to wash the scum that clung to the contact so I could see where I was walking and not accidentally step on the garlic stalks. I also began incessantly itching the red welts that covered my arms—a result of direct contact with the hay. Between itches and scratches, I was squinting my eyes to produce tears and gagging slightly as my uvula began swelling.

The new fields were completely mulched by around 12:00 p.m. My shirt was sopping with sweat as the cloudless sky permitted the temperatures to peak beyond the predictions for the day. Uncle Larry said he'd call when it was time to cut the scapes. Seeing my reddened eyes, dripping nose, and welted arms, Larry promised there'd be less contact with the plants next time. I drove home with the air conditioning on maximum, pulling to the side of the road every ten minutes to remove my contact, clean it, and place it back in my eye. That afternoon, after an extended shower, I slept on the couch for four hours while Larry mulched the other 3,500 garlic plants in his old fields we didn't get to that morning.

Over the course of that summer I returned to the farm a few more times to cut off the scapes, which was a fairly painless, allergy-free procedure, and once more to pull the garlic from the ground. The day we dug up the garlic, I drove his truck to the rented fields while he crept behind in his rusted tractor with an anchor-looking attachment that excavated the ground, freeing up the garlic bulbs that were compacted in the dry earth. Unlike other vegetables in which you can see exactly what you're going to get, there was a fearful anticipation to pulling up the garlic. If the fields were too dry or weren't draining properly, the entire crop could be wasted. It wasn't just the pain of losing one year's crop, but since a third of the garlic went back in the ground, next year's crop was threatened as well.

I ambled behind the tractor as the metal "anchor" burrowed between the rows, loosening the soil enough so that I could tug the bulbs out by their stalks then organize them in the truck according to their variety. It was an ugly day, not because of my allergies—I wore a long-sleeve shirt, overmedicated myself on nasal sprays, put no product in my hair, and wore my glasses—but because most of the garlic crop in this field spoiled and rotted. After Uncle Larry made his first swipe with the tractor, I began loading the garlic into the bed of the truck, but he told me to wait. He paced the length of the row, gathering the tiny, shriveled bulbs in his hand.

"This isn't good," he said, placing the bulbs back onto the earth with gentle reverence. He took a shovel and began digging up more garlic a few rows away. "I may have waited too long. I was tinkering around with my main fields too long this year. These probably should have been pulled last week. Or maybe it's the pitch of these new fields." He reached down and pulled up more rotted garlic. He bit his lip then took a long breath. "We'll dig them up anyhow. There might be a few I can save." Despite the loss and countless wasted hours of physical exertion, Larry never threw a single bulb. In a fit of anger, he never picked up a bulb, launching it into the nearby forest. He simply rested the garlic back onto the earth and moved on.

We spent the remainder of that morning loading worthless bulbs into the bed of his pickup. He insisted I still separate them by variety. Music was in the back, Fire in the center, and German Hardy in the front. After digging up the bulbs, they'd need to be hung in the barn for several weeks to dry before being cut, cleaned, trimmed, or, most likely, discarded.

He said these new fields were an experiment. His more reliable garlic fields yielded much hardier garlic, but none were up to his typically high standards that year. Larry said he hadn't decided what to do with this bunch yet. But he couldn't just leave them in the field.

As we packed up the truck with the remaining garlic stalks and I knocked out the dust from my gloves, Larry asked if I wanted to see "something sort of cool." We walked past the exhumed garlic fields, the broccoli and tomato plants, and a thick, concealing wall of corn stalks. Beyond all of this were rows and rows of stunning, brightly colored zinnias.

"I didn't even know these were here," I said, fingering the pink and yellow petals. "Do you take these to market and sell them?"

"No," Larry said looking at the rows of color, "these aren't for sale. These are for me."

"For you?" I asked, begging clarification.

"For me. I plant rows of zinnias in each of my fields every year simply so I can look at them while I work." He stroked the plants and continued, "Aren't they gorgeous? It just amazes me how something so beautiful can come out of this dirt." He kicked the dry soil with his boot.

"Do you have to tend to these, too—watering and mulching them?"

"No, they actually do this all on their own. I throw down some seeds at the beginning of the season, and they do the rest of the work."

"So do you let these stay out here until they die?" I asked.

"Well, I take some back to your aunt each week to put in the house, but most of these will grow brown in the field and dry up in the late summer. I gather up the seeds at the end of the season, dry them, and replant them each year. But I wait to pull them until there is no more color—until they are totally gone."

Although that was the only summer I worked on the farm, I still return each year for the garlic cleaning party, feeling a bit less like a fraud. I keep my picnic bench outside to avoid the cats residing inside the barn that cause my eyes to tear and my uvula to swell. Uncle Larry recovered from the disappointing crop of garlic the summer I worked, and his bulbs, even from the new fields, are larger and more flavorful than ever.

The experience never transformed me into a rugged out-doorsman who has aspirations and hopes of owning a few acres of my own. The only garlic that courses through my blood is the result of Italian dining, but that too eventually trickles out my pores. So in that sense I didn't grow any closer to the natural—in fact it may have pushed me a bit further away, as I'm even more leery to leave the comfort of my air-conditioned house during peak allergy season. But I like knowing his farm is there. I like knowing there are small farms like his tucked in the folds of the planet. Just as I like knowing we have rainforests, arctic glaciers, and sprawling desert wastelands—all locations I never plan to visit, but find some sense of peace in knowing these places exist. And I like knowing that somewhere behind a field of rotted garlic and overgrown corn stalks, hundreds of stunning zinnias flourish, never to be witnessed by anyone except a few buzzing flies and a solitary garlic farmer.

Mystery Hole

My wife begged to stop at the Mystery Hole as we drove through the curving, rain-slicked hills of West Virginia with failing brakes. "Mystery Hole" was written in uneven, block lettering on a red, yellow, and blue metal shack resting mere feet from the road. Stacie, I should add, was unaware of the minivan's condition, how the brake pedal would bounce under my foot whenever pressed, offering little assistance in stopping our van that took the snaking curves at sixty-miles-per hour. Only after pumping the pedal repeatedly could I coerce the van to stop, but I saw no point in sharing this information with Stacie, because there was no sense in both of us worrying we wouldn't emerge from these hills alive.

"For the love of God," I said as we shot past the gaudy monstrosity, "we're not going to some place called the *Mystery Hole* in West Virginia."

"What if it's the highlight of our vacation and we miss out because you're too stubborn to stop?"

"I'm pretty sure I don't want to lock myself up in some trailer on the side of the road while a bunch of West Virginian hillbillies from *Deliverance* explain the mysteries of any hole to me."

"No sense of adventure," Stacie said, laughing. She turned to look out the back window of the van and waved. "So long, Mystery Hole. Your hole will forever remain a mystery to us."

"I'd like to keep it that way," I said, feeling the brake pedal shudder under my foot.

We hadn't planned this detour, but a multi-car accident closed the freeway on our way home to Cleveland from our vacation in Florida. Police officers directed the freeway traffic to a steep, unmarked, two-hour bypass that caused the van to lurch forward as it downshifted up the inclines. Metal signs warned truckers to check their brakes before attempting the descents.

After driving for nearly an hour, traffic dispersed. It'd been raining for the better part of the afternoon and the sun was beginning to set, making visibility difficult when the road cut deeper into the woods.

Stacie turned our map over and over, declaring that we were lost.

I checked the digital compass on the console. "We're still headed north, which means we eventually must be taken away from this God-awful place."

After another hour, the trees thinned and the road opened onto a small town in the valley. Although a few homes clung to the mountainside flanking the town, most of the shacks huddled in small clusters beside a railroad, which ran parallel to the New River. A wooden fence surrounded each bunch of ten to twelve homes, not much larger than our living room, with narrow dirt driveways. Cars and pickups rusted outside the houses, but vehicles were sparse. Dozens of boxcars sat inert on the tracks, mounded with heaps of coal. A soot-covered coal shoot loomed just beyond the last series of homes.

"There's no mailboxes," Stacie said. "How can they not have mailboxes?" Nor were there any numbers on the houses. Every home was a shade of brown, some darker than others, more from wear than choice. The only sign of recent life was laundry hanging on lines in front of the houses and the few bicycles tossed on their sides.

"Where is everyone?" I asked. Stacie shook her head. "Isn't it a little spooky?" Not one man, child or dog stirred outside the homes. I pumped the brakes to slow the car so I could peer inside the tiny windows for any movement, but the curtains, torn or crooked, were all drawn closed.

I'd never seen this sort of poverty before—people who owned so very little, living next to train tracks, existing in a black haze of coal dust hovering above their homes. But just beyond the town, a sunset reflected off the ambling river and rolling mountains. "Can you imagine if celebrities got a hold of this land?" Stacie asked. "They'd build huge mansions that'd be tucked away from everybody. It's all beautiful and tragic."

"No one is even out looking at the sunset," I said.

As we approached the coal shoot, we saw one last collection of homes, the sides covered with soot. Hanging from one of the windows was a basket with yellow and red flowers, black dust outlining their petals. I pushed on the brake to show Stacie, but the van progressed forward, stammering only slightly as it continued away from the town.

Michael Hemery

Paul's Boots

The night Paul, our office building's janitor, leaped out my office window, he neatly set his work boots side-by-side on my windowsill. The police said the boots' laces were double knotted, with the toes pointed toward the open window leading to the alley, where Paul snapped his neck on the rusted edge of the blue dumpster. Brian, the building manager, who found Paul the next morning, said he didn't even recognize him. His six-foot-ten frame was doubled over, twisted, his neck bent back the wrong way. He didn't leave a note.

By the time I reported for work at the nonprofit that raised funds for children in Cleveland's inner city, the police had taken pictures of Paul's body, the dumpster, five stories below, and various corners of my office. They removed the boots, closed my window, and locked it. Before I began typing a foundation report I'd begun the previous day, an officer asked if I had any insights as to why Paul may have chosen my office as his point of departure, why he didn't choose the next room to avoid the collision with the dumpster. "Typically," the officer said, "if jumpers leave something behind, like shoes, it's some sort of message to the living."

I told the officer Paul and I spoke casually when he completed small jobs in my office, but we were never particularly close. "That's usually how it goes," the officer said. "Without a note, we'll never really know what goes through these nut jobs' heads."

The first time I met Paul he stooped to avoid the top of the doorframe. "I usually try to work in people's offices at night when they're gone," he apologized, replacing the bulb above my desk. Although I stand at six-foot-four, I would have required a ladder to reach the socket. "But I figured you'd want this light replaced as soon as possible, to see what you're doing."

"We both have jobs to do," I reassured him. "If anything, I'm in your way." I explained how my dad worked as a janitor for years in a school system. During dinner each night he'd speak of teachers who'd order him around, reminding him their job was more important than his.

"It's not that bad," he said. "Most of the people on your floor are okay. But you're right, not everyone's that nice. Sometimes people tell me to come back later, so I work pretty late."

"You can come in here whenever you need to—just tell me to get out of your way and I will." Paul laughed, replacing the plastic covering of the fixture and straightening the cuffs of his blue work shirt. Gradually, Paul began working more on our floor, servicing my radiator that clanked or helping Carla, our secretary, rearrange the filing cabinets in the front lobby.

One day I invited Paul to join us for lunch in the break room, and soon he ate with us at least once a month. He'd silently read the paper at the end of the table while we discussed upcoming projects in the marketing department. Shannon, my boss, told Paul she was sorry if we were boring him with our work chatter. He said, "But that's why I enjoy eating up here, the conversation is better than when I eat with Brian. And anyhow, I pretend you're talking to me."

When we'd ask Paul questions about his personal life, he'd explain bits and pieces, stops and starts, but never a story in its entirety. Over the course of the years, Paul mentioned two trips to rehab for alcohol and a brief stint in prison for a crime he wasn't willing to discuss. We never pushed Paul for more information, because he made it clear when he'd said enough. Once he said, "That's enough about me—I'm with myself all fucking day. I'd rather hear about your lives—that's why I'm here, to escape myself for a little while."

Carla openly flirted with Paul at the table, saying things like "I bet everything on you is big" and "I can only imagine what you can do with those huge hands." Paul never responded, but would laugh and turn the pages of the paper.

The longest conversation I had with Paul occurred several months before his suicide. He dripped oil into the perpetually squeaky hinge of my door when he asked, "Does your dad ever say anything about being a janitor?" He moved the door back and forth to make sure it was quiet.

"He said it's tough work, if that's what you mean."

"No, I mean, does he ever say he hates being a janitor?"

"My dad just sort of does his job and comes home. He hates people's assumptions about him, but he says he needs to be moving and doing something all the time. Why, are you getting tired of working here?"

"I don't mind the work, and hell, I don't know what else I'd do. I'm trying to save up enough money to buy this plot of land down in southern Ohio that this guy I know is selling. I have a few debts to pay off, but if I save up enough, I can get out of the city and work on a farm down there." I gestured for Paul to sit down, but he shook his head and continued to stand for the remainder of his half-hour lunch break.

In an unexpected moment of vulnerability, Paul told me about sleepless nights in public housing, when he'd listen to rats pillage cereal boxes then tear up underwear he'd left on the floor. The bloodstains he could never completely remove from the carpeting after he'd had enough and "let those rats have it with a baseball bat," the one he won at the county fair when he was seventeen. Some nights, too exhausted, he'd leave the carnage for morning, chipping blood off the carpet with a snow shovel before tossing the bodies into the alley twelve stories below.

He said he never wanted it to turn out like this. His wife handed him divorce papers two years before and said, "I refuse to live in this shit hole apartment and be married to a fucking janitor." She said he promised her the world, and she gave him every opportunity to give her something more. Now, she tired of his reasons why he couldn't get a better job. "How many fucking times do I have to make excuses why we can't go out with our old friends—we can only use the story that your goddamn grandmother died so many fucking times before I'm going to have to tell them we have no money to go out." She said this wasn't the life he promised. It wasn't even close. Instead of telling her he loved her more than life itself, he drank himself blind. Most nights it's better to be dizzy than to see straight.

"All I want is to blend in like everyone else," he said. "But at six-fucking-ten, that ain't so easy." He said when he'd wait for the bus after work kids will smack their mothers' legs, asking if that tall guy by the bus stop played for the Cavs. They'd beg their mothers to ask for an autograph. But their mothers looked at his uniform, "Paul" monogrammed on his chest, and said things like "You don't want *his* autograph."

"Do you have any idea how sick I am of hearing that?" Paul said. "I can forgive the kids, but you'd think their mothers would know better."

He checked his watch and gathered the can of grease. He moved the door back and forth one more time and said there was one more story he had to come clean about. "I lied to you guys a few years ago when I told you about rehab. It wasn't twice, it was more like eight times. I figured I should be honest with you, since you were nice enough to listen. But if you could just keep that between us, I don't want everyone around here to think I'm some sort of monster."

On the night Paul committed suicide, he held the elevator door open for me as I left for home. He asked if my door hinge was squeaking again. I said it seemed fine. He told me to have a good night. I said to do the same. The police officer said he escorted each female employee to her car in the parking garage across the alley just as he did every night. He'd carry their bags or hold their umbrellas when it rained. The alley behind our building was a notorious hangout for junkies; during my five years with that company, I lost track of how many people died back there. One night as Paul walked Carla to her car during a snowstorm, he refused to return to the building until he saw her drive away. Carla told him it was cold outside and he was going to catch a cold in his short-sleeves. When she told me the story, I hoped she touched his arm. She said he stood firm and said, "The world is a fucked up place—you never know what people are capable of doing to each other. I'll wait until you're gone." Carla said the night he killed himself, he waited for her car to clear the alley like he did every night.

For the rest of the evening, the police officer surmised that Paul carried on as usual. He vacuumed the carpets and dusted our computer monitors. The garbage bags in our offices were emptied into the dumpster then relined with fresh bags. He watered the hydrangeas on Carla's desk, straightened the chairs in the lunchroom, and recycled the newspapers we'd left strewn on the meeting table.

The police officer handed me his card and said, "So, you have no clues for us?" I shook my head, accepting the card. "It's not like it makes much of a difference, anyway. It won't bring him back. But just let us know if you remember anything because we'd like to close this case."

Years later, I attended a photography exhibition at the Cleveland Museum of Art in which a photographer took pictures of his apartment bedroom immediately after his wife jumped out the window. Light poured in from the open window of the tidy room, the bed sheets neatly tucked under the mattress, covered with a quilt, and the nightstand organized and dusted. The room lacked any distinctive characteristics that indicated suicide; it could have been mine. Except for the windowsill, where her shoes rested side-by-side, pointed outward, and slightly out of focus.

Bad Blood

Uncle Bob called from his burning car for advice. After work he knocked back a few forty-ouncers in his garage, passing out with a lit cigarette smoldering on the front seat. When the smoke woke him, he poured the few remaining sips from the Schlitz can on the flames. He said that only agitated the situation. Instead of finding a bucket of water or fleeing to the kitchen, Bob rolled down the driver's side window, reaching for the phone he'd installed in the garage.

My dad answered.

Bob explained that the seat was now cooking something fierce, beyond what he believed he was capable of extinguishing, taking into consideration his inebriated state. Bob said he didn't think he could squelch it all—a lingering spark might sneak into the gas line. My dad suggested calling the fire department, but Bob insisted there wasn't enough time. He figured it would take too long for the firemen to load their gear into the truck and then drive to his house. He said the whole damn car would blow to pieces by then. After the two deliberated for a few more minutes, my father told Bob to drive his car to the station, eliminating preparation time.

Bob said that wasn't a half-bad idea, hanging up before my dad could explain that he was kidding.

Bob turned over the engine and drove to the fire station three blocks away. Mr. Mackall, the elderly man across the street, said Bob drove all the way down the street with his head out the window, the haze thick inside. Smoke billowed from the open windows like streamers. Neighbors waved at Bob. They said he waved back, the car swerving into the curbs.

Later that night Bob called my dad, saying, "The bastards stuck a goddamn hose through the passenger window. After they drenched the car, some asshole ripped the whole fucking seat out to hose it off some more." My dad asked what Bob expected. Bob said a little less carnage.

Bob lived with his mother, Idella, and son, Bobby, in the house directly behind my grandfather. We'd visit on holidays, but never stayed too long. The house smelled like deviled eggs and cigarettes—a glaze of smoke slicked on lampshades and curtains. Aside from work, Bob didn't tend to leave the living room, a tiny space stuffed with a couch, recliner, and hard-backed chair. Idella, a morbidly obese woman who wore yellow muumuus even in the winter, worked on her jewelry by the window, concentrating on the beads she strung onto fishing line. Sometimes Bobby played his drums upstairs, the only music he could hear. During his mother's pregnancy, she visited a friend with measles. As a toddler, Bobby never responded to her voice, so she'd beat him with a two-by-four across the skull to get his attention. After doctors confirmed he was deaf, his mother sent him and his father packing, hanging on to the other six kids.

Whenever we'd visit, kung fu movies blared from the TV. The screen's color was off—always too red. Since Idella was losing her hearing, they cranked the volume, loud grunts and karate chops, cigarette smoke and drums smashing upstairs to no particular beat.

Bob called me "Jocko." He'd point to a framed picture of an orangutan that hung on the wall behind his chair and laugh. "You're Jocko," he'd say, his lips loose. He never wore his teeth when he was home.

I asked Mom why he called me that. She said she didn't know. She said Bob lived in his own world. She said that's what happens when you drink all day.

Bob drank his beer warm, a stack of five or six unopened cans to his right. Crushed empties to the left. Bob's bedroom was behind his chair, separated from the living room by a maroon curtain. One time my cousin Mat and I asked if we could play in the bedroom while Mom and Aunt Vicki visited. Mom agreed, but warned us not to touch anything. The room was narrow, only a foot between the twin-sized bed and the wall. At one end was a small dresser with a plastic model of the Duke's of Hazzard car. The walls were pasted with posters of women in bikinis. They washed cars and straddled motorcycles. Mat and I grew bored with the car, so we lingered near the entrance. Mat stuck his hand underneath the closed curtain, searching beneath Bob's chair. I asked what he was doing. He whispered that's where men kept their dirty magazines, under their chairs. He was right, because he pulled out two magazines.

Mom shouted from the living room, "You two all right in there?"

I shouted back that everything was fine. Bob told her to leave us alone.

Mat opened the magazines on Bob's bed—pages of naked women. "What if we get caught?" I whispered.

"They're not ours," he said. "We just found them. Bob's the gross one—they'll yell at him."

I watched the curtain more than I looked at the magazines, worried Mom would toss the curtain aside, dragging me out into the living room with the magazines. But between glances at the curtain I ogled the women. They were beautiful. After every page I thought I should stop looking. I thought if I stopped, I could walk back into the living room with a clear conscience, no shame. But with every girl I promised myself just one more.

After we finished, Mat slipped the magazines back under the chair. We returned to the living room—red-tinted kung fu flicks.

Mom asked if we had a good time. I nodded. I began to say too much. I said we were just playing with the car in the back of the room and pretending we were in the TV show and that's all we were doing. Mat pinched my leg, whispering for me to shut up.

Bob crushed a can, letting it fall to his left. He reached for another, pulling the tab open. I could barely hear the carbonated fizz over the TV and drums.

"Hey Jocko," Bob shouted. "You have fun in my room?"

I opened my mouth to speak, to tell him again about the car in the back of the room, but Mat poked me again. I said, "Yeah."

"You see anything you liked in there, Jocko?"

I nodded.

Mom and Aunt Vicki sat next to Aunt Idella, helping her choose beads for a necklace.

I swallowed hard.

"You put everything back where it belonged, Jocko?" Bob asked. He took a long pull from the beer. His eyes wandered the room as if they weren't attached to his head, each traveling in its own direction.

I nodded. "We didn't touch anything, Bob," I said. "Only the car."

Bob reached under his chair, moving his hand back and forth for several seconds. He spilled beer on the carpet. Hiccupped. Continued to search. I looked at Mom and back to Bob.

Bob stopped. He began to laugh. He pulled his hand from beneath the chair, empty.

"Good, Jocko, good. Just always make sure you return what isn't yours."

Bob smiled. No teeth. Just an empty space.

After my dad landed a job with a local newspaper as a pressman, he convinced his boss to hire Bob. My dad said Bob held it together for a year, but he began to show up drunk more often than not. My dad said he could only cover so long before management noticed the slurred words, the stink. Bob said my dad didn't try hard enough to defend him. My dad said there's not much you can do for a drunk.

Grandma and Grandpa didn't invite Bob to their Fourth of July picnic, but he came anyway. Mat and I had just finished a water balloon fight with the other men in the family that left us drenched. My shirt clung to my body like another layer of skin. Now we crushed caps—tiny strips of flint—with hammers, the scent of gunpowder gathering on the porch. I didn't identify Bob's misfiring engine at first—I thought it was Mat with a firework. Bob slammed his car door shut, the partly opened window rattling in its jam. He walked toward my grandmother, who stood by the grill, loading hotdogs onto the silver serving tray. It was windy. The flag behind her cracked as he approached.

"Thought you could have the party without me?" Bob hollered. "Thought I wasn't part of this family anymore?"

Bob grabbed her by the elbows and shook her. Grandma screamed, the tray of hotdogs slipping from her hands, crashing onto the cement driveway. My grandfather charged from the other side of the yard, where he was leading a tour of his garden for the family. Bob instantly knelt down to pick up the hotdogs that rolled into the grass and the cracks of the driveway. He kept saying, "I'm sorry. They're still okay. Just a little dirt." My grandmother knelt down beside him, taking the tray and loose hotdogs from his hands.

She said, "Bob, just go before there's trouble."

Besides my grandfather, none of us moved.

"I can't," he said. "Not until I pick these up. I'll make it right." He gathered more of the hotdogs, placing them back on the grill. He said he was sorry a few more times.

I don't remember how hard my grandfather hit him. I recall the way Grandpa's elbow cocked back thirty-degrees, then extended forward into a straight line. But I don't remember what it looked like when Grandpa's fist struck Bob's face. Grandpa was strong; he served with the Marines during World War II. My cousin and I figured he'd killed at least one hundred enemies. I worried Grandpa would forget he was home now, not in the Pacific. I shouted, "Don't kill him!" I was cold. The wet clothing and shifting wind made me shiver.

Bob didn't fall, but staggered to the hood of his car. Grandpa hit him again. He told him to get lost. He said he wasn't welcome.

"I'm part of this family," Bob yelled, holding his face. "I'm part of this goddamn family, too, whether you like it or not."

My dad and uncle held my grandfather back now. My dad told Bob to leave. He said, "Not today, Bob. We didn't need this on a holiday."

"I thought you were on my side," Bob said, opening his car door.

"There's no sides," my dad said.

"None of you are any better than me," Bob shouted. Grandma was crying next to the grill. Bob's son sat with his back to the driveway. He didn't hear a word. I whispered to my cousin that I never wanted to drink, that I never wanted to be like Bob.

"We're all the same." Bob crawled into the car and started the engine. It popped and groaned. He shouted again, "We're all the fucking same." He tore out of the driveway, leaving tracks where his tires had been.

I thought of him when I drank my first beer, first bottle of rum, first slug of whiskey, the first time I puked into a toilet. A case of beer during a poker game in college. Forty minutes. Finished. I giggled into the toilet, how I could vomit sitting down. How easy it all came out. The room spun. My dad calls the spinning the "swirlies." The walls, the ceiling, the floor moving, but never full circle. Just a perpetual pull to the right. When I flushed, the water spun, straightening my spinning vision. I thought of Bob. How I swore I'd never drink. Disappointed in myself, I closed my eyes. But there was no respite. Even the darkness moved.

Bob's gone—a state-run nursing home somewhere downtown. A place for people like him. After Idella passed, he sold the house, her jewelry, his car, the TV. He wandered from shelter to shelter. We lost track. No, we stopped looking. We let the answering machine pick up, incoherent requests for money. Just this once. Just one more time. We never called back. There was no number to call.

Bobby visits him on Christmas. His wife knits Bob a sweater. He won't allow his four children to know his dad. At the last family wedding Bobby signed that his dad's sober now. He said the home won't allow the drink. My grandfather said Bob's life was a tragedy. He said the sauce killed his own dad and two brothers. Said it would have gotten him, too, if he hadn't sobered up. My dad shook his head. Mom said at least Bob's better now. He's comfortable and safe. There wasn't one of us at the table without a highball inches from our lips.

When I was born, the doctor left some of the placenta inside. Mom nearly bled to death. Back then patients had to either pay for the blood or donate it back. Several members of the family offered donations. But Bob was the first. As soon as he heard of Mom's condition, he rushed to the hospital to make a donation. He stopped in Mom's room before stomping off to the lab. He told her he'd offer up as much blood as they'd take. But after a few minutes, he returned. He said they'd rejected him because of syphilis. He'd spent the afternoon sobering up just to donate. Mom said his head hung below his shoulders. Before Bob left, he said he probably picked it up from the blond at the bar with the heart tattoo on her ass. He said he knew she wasn't right. Bob apologized to Mom again. He said he wanted to help, but his blood was no good.

Michael Hemery

Combustion

Because of my dad, I purged every *shit, piss, bitch, goddamn,* and *motherfuck* from the book. It took me two days. Toiling in my bedroom, I blackened each profane word with permanent marker, the felt tip raising the fibrous grain of the pages. Although I attempted to read the other words, the ones framed by the blasphemous, I was too drawn to the vulgarity to appreciate their significance. I sacrificed theme, character, and plot for *damn, hell,* and *fuck.* But after unremitting determination, I owned what was most likely the only self-censored copy in existence of *Robocop: A Novel.*

I began expurgating the book after my dad lost his mind in our basement. I'd often perch on the top stair to watch the old man fiddle with various mechanical devices. He said I wasn't permitted downstairs on the odd chance something went amiss. He said he didn't want me to get hurt. I didn't mind the restriction because I was disinterested in the work itself. I didn't much care how to router the edge of a bookshelf or replace a sparkplug in the snow blower, but simply enjoyed my dad's company while I read comic books and ate granola on the top step. One day my dad struggled for hours with a broken generator his father asked him to repair. He began taking the whole machine apart in the early morning—screws, nuts, and wires organized into dozens of piles on the cement floor. Late in the afternoon he finished reassembling the unit, every screw, nut, and wire back in place. I'd just begun to nod off, my head resting on the banister, when the sound of metal on metal jarred me awake. My dad reeled back to strike the generator again with a large hammer. The head of the hammer struck the casing of the machine, metal caving. He didn't swing the hammer with the gentle accuracy he always demonstrated. Instead, he clenched the rubber handle with two hands, pounding haphazardly, as if it didn't matter where his blows landed.

After he transformed the mustard yellow metal casing into wrinkled paper, my dad began swearing clusters of phrases— *fucks* coupled with *cocksucking goddamn pieces of shits.* Soon his entire monologue was void of any words I could say in my fourth grade classroom without receiving a vicious spanking from the principal. He lifted the large generator, awkwardly raising the mass above his head, wires torn from their sockets, dangling in his face. Like one of the heroes in my comic books, he heaved the generator across the basement. The unit quickly made contact, skidding across the cement floor. On impact the metal came alive, showers of sparks and burning raw heat. It was magic. Alchemy. He picked up the machine again and again, hurling it with grunts of profanity. It crashed into walls and folding chairs. Shrapnel flaked off, ricocheting off walls and the furnace. As he raced to recover the apparatus, he accompanied his physical attacks with a barrage of verbal assaults, commanding the once lifeless contraption to "fucking die."

Finally, he gave the mangled wreck one last heave. The generator sparked to a stop at the base of the steps, wires and guts exposed, pieces of metal blistered in shards. With that last lob came one final "fuck." The "fuh" thrust the generator forward, while the "ck" brought it to a halt, the click of a lock, the generator motionless.

My father surveyed the remains at the bottom of the steps before glancing up. He must have forgotten. He didn't flinch or recoil or apologize when he saw me, but stared without saying a word, without blinking. I'd stopped breathing; my father's heaving shoulders and deep breaths were enough to sustain us both. His blue work shirt was drenched with sweat, his hands sliced open from the torn metal. We held one another's stare. I craved permission to breathe again, but didn't dare ask. I wanted to retreat to my room to transcribe every word he screamed, bottling the most raw display of emotion I'd ever witnessed. I wanted to tear down basketball hoops, overturn tables, and manufacture fire from concrete and metal. I wanted to repeat his cry. I wanted to say *fuck* just as he did—like a bullet. No, stronger than that. More unpredictable. Like a god.

For the first time, I wanted my dad to invite me down the steps to take a swing at the generator. To make it spark.

But he didn't.

He only stared at me. He smeared a cut above his eyebrow with the back of his hand. The gesture aggravated the wound, blood now trickling down his eyebrow, under the temple. He looked at the back of his hand, then back at me.

Finally he opened his mouth, his lips sticking together as he struggled to say, "Go to your room." I didn't move, unsure my legs could support the new weight. My dad dropped his head to look at the generator. Without looking up he said quietly, "I was so tired of dealing with it." He paused. "Promise you won't say anything to your mother." I nodded, even though he couldn't see. I began to breathe again.

I'd never loved my father more than that afternoon. When he tucked me in at night, my dad would explain that words failed to express how much he loved me. He held me instead. He'd embrace me so tightly I could hear his heart thudding against my ear. He wouldn't let go because he said when he did, he'd have to use words again. He said words were bound to fall short. But at the top of the steps, I learned that *fuck* didn't fall short. Those words perfectly embodied the tributaries of blood that ran down my father's cheek.

I ran to my room to retrieve *Robocop: A Novel* from my bookshelf, a gift from my father. Each week at the grocery store I was allowed to choose one comic book. But after my tenth birthday he said I could pick a book instead. I was immediately drawn to the cover of *Robocop*: a cyborg with a gun. But after I'd read the first few pages, cluttered with profanity, I filed the book on my shelf. The words scared me. I now returned to the book, blanking out every profane word. The words were destroyed not because they frightened me like before, but because I wanted to be the sole owner. I didn't want to share those new words with anyone. They were a secret between my father and me. I thought the intertwining of their letters could create heat.

Although I desperately wished to say *fuck*, uttering it over and over until I mastered the delivery, I worried if I used it, the moment would fizzle. I thought the words would lose their force if stolen from my dad's mouth. To prevent this fate, I forbade myself to even think of cussing. I told the boys at school not to say *damn* when they didn't toss the basketball through the hoop. I held my pillow over my ears when my parents rented *Good Morning Vietnam*. Robin Williams was supposed to be Mork from the television, not the foul-mouthed voice I heard through my bedroom door. My dad's words remained pure for years. Unsaid. Untouched.

Although it was common practice for my dad to call the ants that infested our house *cocksuckers* or the neighbor a *worthless piece of shit*, I hadn't witnessed another onslaught of language like that afternoon in the basement until I was eleven. My dad needed to pick up a part from the printing shop where he worked. He invited me along for the ride. I loved the smell of ink inside the pressroom—it was intoxicating, like gasoline. The smell coated all surfaces—the tables, railings, and dim fluorescent lights that hung from the exposed rafters. Once inside the shop, my dad hurried me into the break room while he stood outside the closed glass door to speak with his friends. Although he'd shut the door to protect me from the conversation, the air vent near the floor betrayed their every word. I crouched next to the wall, pressing my ear to the metal slats. I could no longer see the men, so their words melded together into a language spoken by one man or millions.

"Did that fucker expect me to fix this shit on my goddamn day off?"

"He doesn't give a flying fuck if it's your day off or not. He said that shit needs to be done before we do the goddamn run for Thursday."

"You're his bitch ever since you fixed that web last month."

"It's still not my fucking problem."

"You could tell the old man to fuck off, but it won't matter much, he knows you need this job, man."

"This is some bullshit is all I know."

"Hey, at least you get some motherfucking time off. Us fucks are here for the rest of the night until this job is done. So quit your fucking moaning."

Then they laughed.

I couldn't believe my dad spoke this way outside of our house. But even more surprising was the legions of men who said these words. At first I thought it was the language that unified them. But I soon understood rage brought them together. The words expressed an anger I never experienced. I began listening to the stories my dad told at dinner after work. These men worked long hours for little pay. Their bosses took advantage of them. So they held tiny protests of language. The syllables rallied in anger. The words allowed for the respite of laughter.

My dad hardly ever let this anger slip in my presence. We'd play in the yard together or he'd sketch cartoon characters for me at his drafting table. But his language and gestures were always gentle, although never watered down. He never spoke to me in "baby talk"; I was always addressed as an adult. But this adult conversation didn't include a language of anger. The day I pressed my body against the air vent, I realized my dad led two lives. He balanced a world where he assisted me with math homework, built Lego castles, and allowed me to sleep in the crook of his arm with a darker existence. One where an alter ego inhaled ink and grime, spoke like the R-rated movies I wasn't permitted to watch, and created fire from his bare hands. To me, this other persona was the action hero, his costume a blue work shirt and steel-tipped boots. This man was rough, vengeful, and angry. I liked that. I wanted to be angry, too.

During a game of dodgeball in eighth grade, Shamus Kennedy whipped a red rubber ball at my groin. As I doubled over I thought the word *fuck*. My lips didn't move, but my mind fluttered. That evening, still a bit sore, I apologized to my parents.

"Did the teacher hear you say it?" Mom asked.

"No," I explained, "I didn't say it aloud. I just thought it." I began to cry. Between sobs I begged for forgiveness. I swore it'd never happen again.

But it did.

A few Saturdays later I stumbled to the kitchen table for breakfast. My dad asked me how I'd slept.

I said, "Freaking great." The kids at school used the word "freaking" every day, a safe replacement for my father's language.

My dad stopped eating his cereal. He said to repeat myself.

I swaggered a bit as I passed him, reaching for the box of cereal in the cupboard. "Freaking great, I said. I slept freaking great."

My father seized my forearm. He held it tight, pulling me toward him. My dad had never struck me or used any type of physical restraints on me. The box of cereal shook in my other hand.

"That's not appropriate language, do you hear me?" he said. His eyes were focused and narrow.

"It's not a bad word," I explained. "Freaking is not a bad word."

"Everyone knows what word you mean. Never will you say that again. Do you understand?"

"It's just a word," I said. "It's just like the rest of them."

"It's trash," he said. "Only poor trash talks that way, and you're not trash."

"But you say those words. You say them around the house. You said them in the basement. I heard you say them to those guys you work with. And they laughed when you said them."

His brow remained wrinkled and folded. He leaned forward and said, "That's the language of trash. And you're not trash." My arm ached.

"But neither are you," I said. "I just want to talk like you."

"Never again," he said. He let go of my arm. Red marks burned where his fingers had been.

But his directive was too late. I couldn't return the words. But unlike my father or the men he worked with, my profanity didn't possess any anger. I'd never been wronged. My parents provided more love and support than any child could want. I never went without. School came easy to me. I scored a four-point with minimal effort. My teachers adored me. Yet, despite my idyllic life, I yearned to be like my dad. I craved the smell of ink, the torn wires, metal sparked to life on cement. I taught myself anger.

I began by collecting profanity. I devoured it. Every CD I purchased had a parental warning sticker. The more profane the better. But I wasn't drawn to music that arbitrarily spewed profanity. I searched for a controlled burn. I didn't care if the music was punk, rap, or metal, as long as the singer said *fuck* like he wanted to change the world. Like the way my dad said it that afternoon to his friends in the shop. The bands said fuck the government, fuck racists, fuck meat eaters, fuck big business, fuck authority. I quickly learned there was much to hate. I read *1984* and *Brave New World*. I couldn't believe I'd been content so long. Once I began to actively seek anger, I realized it was everywhere. It had been waiting for me.

But the words weren't enough. In order to transcend into this new world, I required a costume. But I couldn't wear a blue work shirt like my father. My entire life I'd been preened for white-collar work. Mind over labor. My dad never even made me take out the trash. Instead of chores, he said I should concentrate on my studies. So instead of donning the blue collar, I grew my hair long, wore piped-leg jeans that covered my shoes and sagged low around my ass, latched a heavy dog chain from my wallet to my belt loop, and covered my backpack with patches, each secured with dozens of safety pins. I learned to skate. I tucked my skateboard into my locker and hung out with kids who pissed on the sides of buildings after school. My dad loathed my outfit. He said people wouldn't take me seriously. I said those sort of people weren't worthy of my respect.

I began to ebb back and forth between the two worlds with ease. I remained section leader of the marching band, concert band and orchestra percussion sections; four-point honor roll student; and manager of a local movie theater. I received a standing ovation for my *Flight of the Bumblebee* marimba solo at the spring orchestra concert. But on my days off I frequented The Red Eye, a rundown bowling alley converted into a dingy concert venue for local punk bands. The place was dangerous. Mohawks screamed revolution, while boys tucked heat under their shirts, believing the metal on metal of a gun was magic. At six-foot-four, I governed mosh pits, swinging my fists, heaving bodies into bodies into bodies. When the lead singer said *fuck*, we said *fuck*. But louder. Hundreds of voices in a chorus of anger.

When I crossed the street, car doors locked. I received looks from strangers. The biggest thrill was opening the door for old ladies. Instead of clutching their purses they thanked me, their faces pleasantly shocked by the politeness of the angry young man. I always went out of my way to be courteous—hoping to eliminate prejudice against the angry youth. Bring the two worlds together in one gesture.

As I left school one day, my headphones strapped securely to my head, Mr. Hertle, my physics teacher from the previous year, waved for me to stop near the vending machines. "What are you trying to prove?" he asked, gesturing to my clothes with his coffee mug.

I shook my head, pretended like I didn't understand. He pulled the headphones off my ears. "Last year you looked like a respectable young man," he said. "Now you look like some kind of goddamn vagabond. What're you trying to prove?"

"I'm still getting straight-A's," I said.

"But you look like the rest of the dumb shits walking around here with their heads up their asses."

He shook his head and walked away.

I smiled, placing the headphones back on my ears.

I began writing for my high school's paper—editorials and music reviews. I introduced the general populace of my high school to angry bands they'd never heard of. Bands that didn't get any airplay on MTV or the radio. I followed up the reviews with editorials exposing injustices that went unmentioned. I wrote about how cattle were tortured to make our hamburgers, suggested that alcohol and drugs were actually encouraged by the government to keep us in line, and encouraged women to arm themselves against oppressive men. Every month when the paper was released teachers and students alike would engage in a discussion. One girl I'd never spoke to before asked me to be the lead singer of her band. I told her I'd never sung before. I asked her why she'd want me. She said she'd read one of my articles in the paper. She said she liked the anger in my words.

In college I joined the newspaper staff. All freshmen were placed in the general news department. I was assigned a story on college tuition rate increases. It ended up being a call-to-arms, encouraging students to riot, demanding lower tuition so all social classes could receive an education. My editor told me the story was too biased. She said this was not how journalists write. She said I was being cut from the news staff, but she'd made a recommendation for the editorial department to pick me up. She said they needed new blood to shake things up on the quiet campus.

After writing for two years for the paper, I quit after an editorial change that refused to print controversial articles. My friends and I started an underground paper that we printed on campus copiers using stolen passcodes from the official newspaper. One night when my friends couldn't help me staple the paper together, my mom and dad helped me assemble the papers. They said they were proud of me. My dad said he was "fucking proud of me." I don't remember the first time I said *fuck* in front of my dad. But now we said those words in each other's presence without hesitation. That night as we stapled sheets of paper together, he said I just might change the world.

After college I took a job with a trade magazine, teaching myself to write without bias. After a month on the job, the editor told me I'd be fired if I didn't cut my hair, which now stretched down my back. I wore a shirt and tie to work every day, but she felt my hair sent a bad message. I filed a discrimination case against the company and won. I made the editor cry. I was happy.

After working corporate for five years, I returned to night school to obtain my high school teaching license. I cut my hair, and now teach English to sophomores and seniors. I teach the same thing I wrote about in high school—equality, the meat industry, the government. When my sophomores read *Fahrenheit 451,* I teach them how to be angry. Inevitably there are sparks.

One day a fellow teacher said I should Google my name because one of my former students had written about me on his Myspace page. The student didn't do much work the first quarter. But after we read *Fahrenheit* he came alive, asking questions nearly every day about how to make change, how to pull the veil from his eyes. On his Web page he recommends several books: *Fahrenheit 451, Slaughterhouse Five, Clockwork Orange,* and *To Kill a Mockingbird.* Under his heroes he's written: "My Dad, Mike Hemery, and anybody who is a thinker."

I'm glad he didn't write *Mr.* Hemery. His blatant disregard for the authoritative title that I enforce in my classroom shows he's learned. I still feel like a fraud some days in front of the students. I wear a new costume—shirts, ties, and close-cropped hair. I find myself moving between two worlds again. Although I'm now authority, I stage quiet rebellions. I hang stickers on the wall behind my desk of current punk bands who sing about politics. But now I write detentions when students are late. I send students to the office when they act up or swear. The worst time occurred my first year on the job. I'd called a boy's mother the previous day about his failing grade in my sophomore English class. Just before class started I said good morning to him. He responded with clusters of profanity. He flipped his desk and said, "You think you're a badass motherfucker?" Notebook paper soared about the room. He wore his pants several sizes too big, riding low, well below his ass. "Suck my motherfucking dick. C'mon, get on your fucking knees and suck my cock." He pointed to his crotch. I walked toward him, placing my body between his and the rest of the students. I didn't want anyone to get hurt. He thought my move was an act of aggression. He screamed, "Hit me, pussy. C'mon. Hit me in the motherfucking mouth, bitch."

The classroom of kids, mostly wearing Abercrombie and Fitch clothing, stared wide-eyed at the scene. They didn't move. Or breathe. I stepped forward. He stepped back. I moved to my desk to call the office, asking for the police officer to be sent down.

"Please leave," I said calmly. He threw his bag at the door. It shook. I stepped forward again. We exited the room together. He heaved his backpack at the lockers across the hall. The zippers clanked against the metal doors. I could hear the rush of students in my classroom, clamoring to see what they could through the tiny slatted window in my door.

"Fuck you," the boy screamed. "Seriously, who the fuck do you think you are? Why the fuck did you call her? Why the fuck?"

A teacher down the hallway looked out her doorway, shook her head, and closed her door.

"Because I ultimately want what's best for you," I said. "You know that."

"You don't fucking know what's best for me. How the fuck would you know?" He buckled, collapsing to the grimy tiled floor. I cracked open my door and told the students to return to their seats.

"My fucking mother is leaving us. The fucking whore is leaving my brother and me at the end of the month with my stepdad. She said she's fucking done with it all. And we're stuck with this motherfucker who hates us. This is my third fucking dad. And without her there, I don't know what the fuck he'll do to us. So, did you know that? Did you?" I shook my head. "So how the fuck can you know what's best for me? Explain that to me."

"I'm sorry," I said. The school's police officer jogged down the hallway with his cuffs in hand. I waved him off, but the student turned to see the cop. The boy stood up, punched his fist into the locker, bending back the metal. He faced the cop and screamed, "Fuck you." The *fuck* echoed in the empty halls.

I tried to explain to the officer that the cuffs weren't necessary, but he told me to go back to my classroom. I heard the metal click of each cuff locking into place as I shut my classroom door. When I entered my room, two of my A students were at the front of the room reenacting the incident. They stood where the two of us stood, said what we said, but in this rendition they censored our words. The one boy pretending to be me said, "Now, just calm down," while the other waved his fist in the air and said, "F you, homeboy. Hit me, you P. C'mon mf-er."

"That's enough," the real me said. "Let's just forget about that and get back to our discussion." But I knew we'd never return to the lesson that day. My body still shook in tiny tremors, adrenaline surging. I breathed hard. I knew while I discussed their research papers, they were rehearsing the scene in their heads, trying to remember every word so they could retell it to their friends during lunch. I hoped they managed to capture the energy of every *fuck* and *goddamn*, giving the boy's anger the justice it deserved.

Fractures

Michael Hemery

Blind

Our sixteen-year-old bodies slid past one another's in the blackness of Michelle's basement. The knees of my jeans glided easily across the glazed concrete as I crawled on all fours, stopping only to tug on my pants creeping off my body. I attempted to adjust my belt several times, but I couldn't manage to pull it any tighter around my slightly protruding gut. Fumbling about in the darkness, I made broad, sweeping motions with my right hand, searching for walls, chairs, or the back pocket of a girl's pants.

I don't remember who made the suggestion at Michelle's birthday party to play blind hide-and-go-seek, but I was the first to shout "not it." Although I'd never played the game before, especially not with a room full of girls smelling of strawberries and vanilla, I understood the loneliest predicament would be to wander about in the darkness by myself. If I joined the masses, I'd repeatedly collide into the girls, especially Michelle, the brunette with blond streaks in her hair who played flute in our marching band.

Earlier in the week as I hauled my quad drums to the band room after a three-hour autumn practice, Michelle jogged beside me, asking if I'd be interested in coming to her birthday party that weekend. My face flushed as sweat began to run down my body. While most of the members of the band only had to carry their trumpets or saxophones during practice, we drummers heaved fifty pounds of equipment around the asphalt parking lot, the harness leaving damp sweat stains on my back and fleshy stomach even when it was cold outside. At first I thought Michelle's request was some kind of joke, as we'd only spoken once before, when I accidentally ran the shell of my front drum into her hip. I apologized repeatedly until the band director shouted for me to quit socializing and play the drum break. I asked one more time if she was all right, but she said not to worry about it, rubbing away the pain.

Although this was our first real conversation, I'd been watching her from the back of our formation for months—the slight curve of her arm when she lifted her flute to her pursed lips.

"Yeah, sure," I said. "I can't imagine I have other plans this weekend. Well, not that I couldn't, because I'm sure I could. But, right now, I don't have anything planned, so it works out for both of us. Well, mostly just me. This Saturday, you said, right?" I forgot to breathe and choked a bit. She laughed, reaching into her front pocket to retrieve a slip of paper. She took the drumstick from my right hand and replaced it with the slip of paper that had directions to her house. Her hand lingered on mine. She tapped one of my drums with her painted fingernail, the head holding its pitch for several seconds, before handing the stick back.

Somewhere near the school a fireplace was burning, filling the air with the scent of cider and leaves.

I labored for the remainder of the week to find the perfect birthday gift for Michelle, eventually choosing a pair of fifteen-dollar gold-plated earrings from the jewelry kiosk in Sears. When she opened the front door I handed her the tiny box, wrapped in excessive amounts of blue paper and secured with wads of Scotch tape. She said I wasn't expected to bring a present. "We haven't done presents since I was in elementary school," she said. "I should have said something, but I figured you knew." The other fifteen or so kids mingled in the background, the girls sipping Cokes while the boys tussled on the couch, knocking over stacks of magazines, trying to pin one another down. "Should I open it now?" she asked. Dawn, one of the flag girls, stood next to her and made a dramatic, "Awwww" that raised in pitch the longer she held it. I intentionally wore three shirts to the party, and casually put my hand near my armpit to ensure the sweat hadn't penetrated the layers.

"Later," I said. "Maybe when there aren't so many people around."

After pizza and cake, Michelle's mom ushered us downstairs, requesting only that we didn't break anything. A cement wall divided the basement, with a door at either end. One half of the basement was relatively open, except for a couch and a television, while the other side was further sectioned into two separate areas—one for the washer and dryer and the other furnished with an overstuffed chair, a wooden coffee table, a floor lamp, and a brown, shag rug in the center. I mapped out the lay of the rooms before the lights were snapped off, because once the game began, we survived on silence and touch.

Just before Fred, the boy who failed to shout "not it," began counting down from twenty, Michelle announced another twist in the game. She said if you were caught, you couldn't make a sound, but instead had to crawl to the couch until everyone was found.

"But that could take all night," Fred insisted.

She smiled and said, "I know."

When Michelle turned off the lights, she grabbed my wrist and pulled me to my knees. "Stay with me," she whispered as we began to crawl in the direction of the back room. "Eighteen, seventeen, sixteen." Our hips bumped repeatedly as someone collided with a filing cabinet. I let Michelle feel her way through the doorway first and I followed, extending my hand to brush her calf. "Nine, eight, seven." When we passed to the other side, Fred seemed much further away.

As we crawled into the room with the rug and chair, suddenly the lights snapped on.

"Why were the lights off down there?" Michelle's mom shouted from the top of the basement steps.

"We're just playing a game, Mom," Michelle shouted back. She was still on all fours, but faced me. She wore a loose black top with a wide neck that sagged low to reveal her matching black bra.

"Well, be careful down there," her mom shouted. "Don't get hurt, because I don't want to be responsible for calling anyone's mother to explain this."

"We will," Michelle responded. "Just shut the lights off and close the door."

When the room went black, we insisted Fred begin counting from twenty again, to give us more time to find new hiding spots. But it didn't sound as if many of us kids moved. On the far side of the basement I heard rustling near the washing machine. Each second that ticked away was the loss of guaranteed darkness and isolation. Michelle grabbed my hand, navigating me past the sounds of cotton shirts rubbing against fabric, lips, and breath. My side grazed someone as Michelle led me to the corner of the room, behind the chair. She pulled on the base of the chair, bringing it closer to us, offering less space to be discovered.

"Twelve, eleven, ten." The back of her hand tapped my knee, but she held it there, slowly turning it over. Her hand was warm, conforming to the bend of my leg. She moved her hand toward my shin, but stopped when she reached my ankle. Our bodies were turned around in the darkness; I was half sitting, my legs crossed under one another, my t-shirts riding up my back. In the light, I would have been concerned if my hair was sticking up or if my shirt was pulled down enough to cover my underwear. But not in the blackness. I raised my arm and felt my forearm gently brush past what was surely her chest. I touched her neck, while her hand rested on my thigh. I touched her ear, her hair. "Three, two, one. Ready or not."

For the first time the entire basement was silent, except for the sound of fabric and flesh. Michelle ran her other hand up my arm and we both leaned into one another when someone's head jabbed into my kidney. I flinched. Michelle released my thigh. "Sorry, sorry," said the voice, followed by the sliding sound of jeans on cement, the sound fading from the room.

I laughed and whispered, "Sorry." But Michelle made a hushing sound before placing her hand back on my thigh. A boy's voice from the other side of the basement shouted, "Oh, Fred, stop touching me there."

"Jackasses," Michelle said. Her breath was mint, her lips sounded moist when she spoke.

Frozen in the perpetual shadow, her hand remained on my thigh, mine on the back of her neck. I'd never touched the back of a girl's neck before. The skin seemed softer, perhaps protected by the hair. I ran my thumb from her ear to her hairline. My fingers registered the shift in her neck muscles before my mind realized she'd begun to lean into me—I could taste her berry lip-gloss, even before our lips touched. In the darkness, I didn't bother to adjust my wrinkled shirts that now strangled my stomach, my belt that cut into my waist, or my pant leg that somehow became tucked into my sock. The darkness smoothed out the imperfections.

The basement door squeaked open. There was a pause of silence. "Hey, guys," Michelle's mom shouted. "I think you need to find something else to do. In the light." The lights snapped on, but I instinctively closed my eyes to keep it out. But I didn't need to open my eyes to know that Michelle had already left. Her body slipped away from mine the moment the basement door opened. I blinked opened my eyes, letting in shutter snaps of light, Michelle by the doorway already, my shirt slightly damp, a room full of teenagers twisted into one another, jutting out, unable to be concealed by the tables and lamps.

Michael Hemery

Ah, Nuts, I'm in Love

What a tragic day in the history of young romance when you can't win a girl's favor by calling attention to her equine stride. After all, Rachael Black, the brown-haired, pouty-lipped girl who sat next to me in seventh-grade English class, did sound rather horse-like that day, approaching our classroom nearly twenty minutes late, her black, high-heeled shoes clipping loudly down the empty, tiled hallway. The class giggled as the footsteps grew louder and louder, clip-clop, clip-clop, then stopping abruptly and settling, clipclipclipclip, in the doorway. We turned in unison to see who'd been making such a racket for the past thirty seconds down the hall. Rachael offered a yellow pass from the guidance office to Mrs. Adams, our portly English teacher with stringy gray hair who was attempting to introduce the importance of Huck Finn to our thirteen-year-old lives, then trotted her way to the seat next to me in the back of the class.

I'd been madly pining away for Rachael's attention for the entire school year. When Mrs. Adams assigned Rachael the seat inches next to mine the first week of school, I began to memorize her gestures and features so I could be with her, even when we were apart. I had a prime spot to study Rachael's body because the classroom didn't contain the typical, solitary high school desks, but instead had long rows of interconnected tables. My vantage point next to Rachael allowed me to notice the small birthmark on her shoulder that was only visible when she'd reach down for her purse to retrieve items such as the blue-green case for her dark-rimmed glasses. I surmised she was self-conscious of how she looked in glasses, because she'd only resort to wearing the spectacles after squinting incessantly at the board, her nose scrunching up in a series of adorable ripples while her cheekbones raised to reveal shallow dimples. She favored blouses made of rougher fabrics—not silk or even polyester. Her shoulder would scratch and scrape the abrasive cloth when she wrote in-class essays, the back and forth driving me wild. I didn't give a shit about the theme of *Flowers for Algernon*, but could only concentrate on the rhythm of her shoulder as her pen traveled the length of the paper.

Our imagined relationship was strictly physical. Although her responses to Mrs. Adams' questions were consistently insightful and she seemed to possess a likeable personality (based solely on conversations that I'd overheard her having with students who weren't terrified to open their mouths), I knew more about the slight dip in the back of her neck than her feelings, fears, or desires. Despite this minor setback, I knew we had a future together as she dragged me out of boyhood adolescence. I spent most of my time trying to be "cool" with the guys—searching the local stores' inventories for Air Jordan shoes to gain approval. But now I was smitten with a female, yet entirely unsure how to win her attention. I'd sometimes intentionally bump my pencil off the desk, waiting for her to casually look to the floor, reaching down to retrieve it for me. I'd become lost in the neckline of her shirt, counting the goose-bumps that formed on her chest from the morning chill of the room. One time when she placed the pencil back on the desk I muttered, "Thanks for the pencil getting." After stumbling over my words, I could feel my ear beginning to warm up in embarrassment. This peculiar oddity began in sixth grade—whenever I grew nervous, my left ear would burn with heat, glowing a peculiarly disturbing incandescent red. I never understood why it was only my left ear, while my right had been spared, but I'd quickly cover it to hide my humiliation. That year, I often heard Mrs. Adams' lectures in mono, spending much time covering the ear facing Rachael.

During the seventh-grade winter dance my buddies told me to ask Rachael to slow dance, even though she appeared to be content standing on the other side of the gym with her friends.

"But she probably doesn't want to dance with me. I'm just the creepy guy who sits next to her in English class," I said.

Marty, my best friend at the time, said, "I tell you what, just walk over there near her and if she looks up to make eye contact with you and smiles, you'll know that she wants to dance. If she ignores you, don't say anything and just come back over here."

Couples swayed back and forth under the darkened lights of the cafeteria when I finally agreed to test his theory, walking toward her. Rachael was talking with her blonde friend, back turned slightly toward me. Her friend whispered something into her ear before she slowly began to twist her head in my direction. My ear began to warm as I slowed my stride to read the expression on her face. Just as our eyes almost met, I was suddenly pushed in the back by the force of many adolescent boys, my body crashing into Rachael. She managed to stay upright after the collision, but my gangly body hit the floor. I was devastated. I snapped my head around to see my friends laughing hysterically, running back to the "safe" side of the gym. I held my ear with one hand, hoisted myself back up with the other, and chased after them, assuming Rachael wasn't standing before me with a welcoming smile upon her face.

As the year progressed I became more infatuated with Rachael—the way she held her pens between her pointer and middle finger, leaving her thumb entirely out of the equation; how she'd answer Mrs. Adams' questions in a low, smoky voice, like an old-time jazz singer; and how she'd cross and uncross her legs, unknowingly resting the heel of her shoe against my shin. In the last month of school, I'd grown more bold, not by actually speaking to Rachael, but by "accidentally" brushing my leg against hers when I reached down to get paper or books from my bag on the floor. Surprisingly, she never cried out in repulsion or retracted her leg away from mine. Instead, day after day, she let my calf and tube sock press against her smooth leg.

On the day in which Rachael entered the room late, I couldn't help but notice the way her short skirt teased her thighs as she walked toward me in the back of the room. The room itself was cramped with poorly positioned desks, so in order for Rachael to squeeze into her seat, I had to stand up in the aisle, push in my chair, and allow her to pass. As she wiggled her way past me, I whispered loud enough for the students sitting around me to hear, "Nice of you to show up for class every once in a while, Mr. Ed." I surprised myself, unsure of where this repressed vocalization had even come from. I grabbed my ear in anticipation of its inevitable flaring. I'd spent the past nine months in near silence, not wanting to embarrass myself in front of the girl that I surely was going to be with someday, but of course my unconscious longings found it necessary to manifest themselves in the form of equestrian comparisons.

Craig, the curly-haired boy who sat in front of me and earlier that year taught me the words to "There once was a man from Nantucket," turned and said, "Actually, it was nicer here without you and your loud-ass horse hooves." I laughed a breathy, forced chuckle, returning my attention back to Rachael.

Rachael slammed her books onto her desk and asked, "What the hell are you two trying to say?"

Mrs. Adams continued to write words like "Tom," "racism," and "equality" on the chalkboard, ignoring the rowdy spat brewing in the back of the room.

"You know," I said, "clip-clop, clip-clop."

And then I neighed.

I realize now that thirteen-year old boys often lack the maturity and finesse to declare their interest in the opposite sex and resort instead to tactics such as "pulling the girl's hair on the playground." The reaction is beyond our control and determined by something more primordial, probably in our pants. But girls are supposedly the more observant gender, so you'd think Rachael would have picked up on my subtle flirtation in the form of public humiliation.

God, she had great lips. I focused on them as Rachael squared up to me and cried, "Fuck you." In the next few seconds I lost track of those lips, most likely because I lost consciousness. Rachael clenched her first, socking me in the nuts with the force of, well, a bucking bronco. I immediately blacked out. Seconds later I awoke on the floor in the back of the room near my desk, writhing in pain and curled up in the fetal position. I was sure both of my testicles had been permanently shoved into my stomach. I clung to the cold metal leg of my desk searching for some sort of relief from the throbbing in my groin. The boys in the class collectively groaned, while someone clapped on the opposite side of the classroom.

Rachael picked a crumb of lint off her white blouse, smiled, and tucked her hands behind her knees to hold her skirt back as she slipped into her seat. I couldn't see Mrs. Adams, but heard the chalk stop scraping across the chalkboard. From the front of the room she asked loudly enough so I could hear from the floor, "Is everything all right back there?"

I coughed out, "Hit…in…nuts," which was received with nervous laughter from Craig, who refused to look me in the eye. The remainder of the class stared, horrified as my body continued to twist and contort itself on the floor. I'd accidentally nipped "my boys" a few times in gym class during dodge ball and along the crotch-level rail in the cafeteria lunch line that we rested our trays on, but I'd never felt pain this intense in my young life.

Mrs. Adams now stood over me and crouched to feel my forehead with the back of her meaty hand. "No fever," she said.

"Just take all the time you need down there; no hurries." She returned to the front of the room, continuing to write on the board.

The pain actually subsided more quickly than I'd expected, but as some sort of prepubescent protest, I remained sprawled out next to my desk like a middle-school tragedy. For the next half-hour I remained on the floor, resting my head against a chair rung. Remarkably the class either forgot about my body in the back of the room or simply chose to ignore it. From this lowly perspective, I could see the stunning lines of Rachael's legs and the red imprints of her thighs right above her knees when she crossed and uncrossed her legs. In fact, the initial bout of pain was worth my new perspective of her legs. She opened her notebook and began studiously copying the lecture notes, ignoring my occasional coughs and murmurs from the floor. When Mrs. Adams handed out worksheets that correlated with the previous night's reading, someone flung a paper at me, but I simply let it settle into the grit and dirt scattered about the tile.

While the remainder of the class diligently followed Mrs. Adams' instructions, I wondered how this recent turn of events would impact my relationship with Rachael. Had I completely ruined my chances of slow dancing with her at the next dance? Would she ever speak to me again?

Again. I realized that we'd in fact spoken, albeit not in the way I'd fantasized for the previous nine months (none of those scenarios ever involved me getting socked, close-fisted, in the nuts). But we did speak. There was always the chance that she could run late again, so maybe I could find some other clever way of commenting on her tardiness to continue the heated conversation that we'd started that day. I smiled, returning my gaze to the back of Rachael's calves.

When the bell finally rang, Rachael gathered her books into her arms, pressed her knees together as she stood, and gingerly stepped over my body to exit the room. The heel of her shoe landed inches from my ear and continued to echo across the room, down the crowded hallway, and into the white noise of my youth.

French Kiss

Despite my grandfather's persistent and not-so-subtle suggestions that I learn French, ("If you cared about the country where I lived for forty years, you'd learn to speak my language.") I met his requests with indifference. I made a feeble attempt to acquire his native tongue in junior high, but cheated my way to a passing grade. My dad, who lived in Fécamp, Normandy, until he was twelve, completed most of my homework. All I can really recall from class was the overweight, always-perspiring teacher who would begin each afternoon session by changing his socks, like some sort of grotesque Mr. Rogers. While he picked the brown sock fuzz from his toenails, he'd ask us several questions in French, which none of us understood or exerted any effort to understand because we were attempting to divert our eyes from the display of vulgarity in the front of the room. He'd shake his head, pull his shoes back onto his feet and sing off key in English, "I talk to the trees," a gesture to the only thing paying attention to his lectures.

Although I assume most of the responsibility for my language deficiency, my grandparents were of little assistance in the learning process. Each time I'd practice my limited vocabulary with them, they'd correct the pronunciation of each and every syllable.

We.
No, Oui.
Wuh-hee.
No, Oui.
Wha-ee.
No. Oui.
What-ever.
No. Oui.

The only genuine connection I had to my grandparents' previous life was a love for French baguettes with soft Camembert cheese and the knowledge of the traditional French greeting—a kiss on both cheeks. I'd never given much thought to the way I kissed my grandfather until fellow fifth grader Shane Barty witnessed the exchange between the two of us after my elementary school's performance of *A Christmas Carol*. Grandpa told me I was a convincing Scrooge, leaning forward to touch his cheeks against mine, making kissing sounds. The sweet odor of his aftershave lingered on my flesh long after his skin slid away from my face.

After observing the kiss with my grandfather, Shane announced to the class, "Mike kisses boys!" I struggled to clarify that we were French, but fifth graders are none too interested in ethnic heritage. For the remainder of the year it was understood amongst the ten-year-olds at Muraski Elementary School that in my spare time I made out with old men.

My earliest memory of the kiss involved a thorough elucidation of how Grandpa's father and his father's father conducted this salutation ever since he could remember. He likened it to an American handshake. He said the kiss was an imperative part of my heritage, defining me—the first American-born child in the family with deep-seated French roots. My dad disregarded the European customs when he moved to the United States in order to better assimilate into society, so the ethnic rite was strictly reserved for my grandparents.

Although I never fully abandoned the kiss, during my junior high years I did accelerate its speed in public, swooping in like perhaps I'd tripped or accidentally fallen into my grandfather's face. Twice. On both cheeks. As I grew older (and taller), I became more comfortable with the social perception of our kiss, but worried more about the logistics of leaning my six-foot-four frame down to reach my grandpa, who stands at five-foot even. The kiss has always been an incredibly awkward but necessary component of our relationship.

So it was no great surprise that I suffered an insatiable and profoundly nagging guilt when I made the conscious decision to terminate the kiss, completely, as a result of hyper-paranoid hygienic concerns when Grandpa began to lose control of his bodily functions.

My grandfather has accumulated a series of devastating health issues over the past ten years, including a brain aneurism, blood clots, and a multitude of strokes. Evidence of his decline is made apparent by the contorted position of his lips when he smiles, the loss of strength in his legs, and the smattering of food, mucus, and dried blood (from botched shaving efforts) strewn about his face at all times of the day. Although my dad still pressed his cheeks against his dad's face when we'd visit their house, I'd lean over the brown, stained couch that he parked himself on each day, hold onto the wooden couch arms, keep my face several inches away from his, and make obnoxious kissing sounds without actually making contact. As I'd straighten up, his eyes seemed to search the air, as if wondering why he didn't feel my face against his. Or worse yet, maybe he knew that I avoided contact because I feared the germs and illness that reside in the gloss—as if this particular brand of slow, haunting death could be transmitted through physical contact.

Some days, depending on the severity of the slop on his face, I'd avoid the couch completely, simply waving as I entered and exited the room. I was aware that denying my grandfather this greeting was abandonment—severing our one connection and demoting our relationship to that of casual strangers. As I'd drive away from their house, I pictured the old man sinking into the cushions of the couch, grieving the loss of his grandson. Each visit I promised myself I'd make things right by making contact with his cheek. Yet every time I'd leave with regret and lasting pangs of guilt.

After years of focused efforts to care for my grandfather in his own home, the family concluded my grandmother lacked the physical and mental strength to tend to his needs, making the decision to have him admitted into one of the finest nursing homes in the area, as determined by the local hospital. My dad researched and visited over a dozen homes and verified that this particular facility, located mere minutes from our homes, would be the best location for Grandpa to live out the remainder of his days. Although the facility was a bit clinical with its white, tiled floors, long hallways, and fluorescent lighting, it was immaculate and exceptionally sterile, lessening the chances of Grandpa acquiring some sort of illness. The attendants ensured he was always in clean clothing and dressed him in adult diapers, in case they weren't available to assist him into the bathroom.

The nursing home was a definite improvement to his physical environment—the cream, wallpapered walls were adorned with lavishly framed replicas of famous paintings and each room contained decorations for each approaching season (pine wreaths at Christmas, cardboard cutouts of fall foliage for Thanksgiving, and bat and witch displays for Halloween). Despite the new environment, Grandpa hadn't undergone much of a facelift—the glossy sheen of food particles and mucus still clung to his face. I'd try to make the trek to visit at least once a week. I'd lean over Grandpa, offering my faux-kiss, bracing myself on the arms of the wheelchair to make the stretch down near his face. When I stood up, his eyes still wandered about the room, anticipating the contact that I was unable to make. Even though the nursing home was always sanitary, retaining a permanent, biting stench of bleach, I made contact with as little as possible. I reacted to the nursing home in the same manner as I did airplane rides and hospital visits: I immediately returned home to bathe under scalding shower water to eradicate any germs that may have embedded themselves in my flesh.

Despite my unreasonable fear of the nursing home, I remained true to visiting on a frequent basis because I wasn't comfortable with the knowledge that we'd left him in the company of perceived strangers. But it didn't take long for my grandpa's thick French accent to attract the attention of hordes of women in the facility. I'd sometimes find him cornered in the window-lined lunchroom, surrounded by herds of women in wheelchairs, asking him dozens of questions, hoping he'd slip into his romantic native language—a language at age thirty I still couldn't understand.

Some of the women worked harder to separate themselves from the nameless faces in the lunchroom. The first time I met Grandpa's friend Ruth, she slinked up next to his wheelchair while he and I were engaged in a rather sentimental conversation about Fécamp. Grandpa wore a pair of ill-fitting, saggy gray sweatpants and a scratchy blue and gray flannel shirt. We were located near the front entrance next to an arboretum. A receptionist sat at the front counter, checking in guests, assisting with nametags or finding family members. There seemed to be a constant air of haste in the home—some resident or member of the staff bustling by us to reach some critical destination. There was no opportunity for solitude in the home, unless Grandpa spent his days in his room, but even that was a shared space with another resident. I'd repositioned a metal-backed chair from a nearby table so I could sit at a safe, germ-free distance, next to my grandfather. I inspected the chair, banging the legs onto the ground to shake free what I hoped were food crumbs on the flowery vinyl seat cushion.

Grandpa hadn't noticed Ruth's presence so he continued to offer details of the time he pilfered Benedictine, a sweet French liqueur, from the factory where he worked so he could celebrate his engagement to my grandmother. I'd heard the story dozens of times, but tolerated the retelling because the tale gave him great delight. Frantically waving her hand next to Grandpa, Ruth caught my attention, scrunched her eye to form an overly exaggerated wink, and mouthed, "Watch this." She raised her wrinkled arm, brushing the back of her hand on Grandpa's face. Grandpa had lost most of his physical ability to dozens of strokes, so his body wasn't able to react to the surprise, but his face certainly still possessed emotion. His eyes widened, his mouth formed a lopsided "O" and he stopped mid-story to slowly crane his neck to discover who was sitting beside him. When he met Ruth's eyes, his lips grew wide with pleasure, revealing several missing teeth. He reached out with his "good" hand to hold her exposed speckled forearm. The sleeves of her blue snowman-embroidered sweater were pushed just above her elbows.

Grandpa nodded his head toward me, saying in his thick, French accent, "This is my grandson, and I'm very proud of him." To my surprise he recited the entire sentence in English. Since being admitted into the nursing home, Grandpa had begun speaking more and more in French. The nurse's station called my mother somewhat alarmed when he first began switching back and forth freely between the two languages. They explained that typically when they asked him to speak English he'd apologize (in English), continuing to answer their questions in French.

He'd also begun to ignore some questions in English, responding more frequently to French inquiries. One afternoon when I visited the home with my dad, Grandpa began to frown, hold his breath, and push rather incessantly on his groin. My dad asked several times, in English, if he was experiencing some sort of pain or if he needed to use the bathroom. I suggested calling the nurse when he remained unresponsive. Finally my dad asked in French if Grandpa wanted us to find the nurse to take him to the bathroom. Grandpa responded, *"Pas la peine d'appeler la nurse, on va dans nos cullotes ici."* He smiled his cock-eyed, stroke-damaged smile, and returned to breathing normally.

I looked questioningly at my dad. He leaned to me, whispering, "'No sense calling a nurse, we go in our pants here.'"

During my solo visits to the home, most of our exchanges became hybrids where I attempted to discern the meaning of the French words based on the context of the English. But it wasn't too difficult, as he said things like: "This place is like a [French word] prison. [French phrase or sentence.] Your grandmother put me in here so she could [French word] the plumber."

Recently Grandpa had concocted this notion that my grandmother orchestrated his stay in the nursing home so she could solicit various home repairmen to "service" her in my grandfather's absence. If she didn't arrive exactly at 11:00 a.m. each day, he'd ask where she had been. When she explained that she'd overslept or that traffic was congested, he'd call her a "whore" in French, ordering her to return home to have torrid sex with the roofer. She'd rush out the front doors in tears. My dad would have to explain to her that Grandpa's reaction was simply another symptom of his dementia. After his fits, the nurse would report that he'd sobbed himself to sleep at night, asking where his beautiful wife had been all day.

"We call him Romeo," Ruth said, straightening the collar of her sweater.

"Sounds like you have quite a way with the ladies, Grandpa," I said. Grandpa gave a crooked smile before obsessively rubbing his hands together on his lap. Although his health had declined, he still maintained a full head of puffy white hair that women cooed over.

"I really enjoy making your grandfather smile," Ruth said. "I don't know his whole story, but I know that he's been through a lot. It can be lonely in here by yourself, so I try to make sure he smiles a few times a day. I know his family can't always make it. All I have to do is touch his face and he lightens up. Don't you, Jean?" Grandpa smiled, muttered something in French, and stared at his writhing hands. Ruth explained that she tried not to spend too much time with him in the public spaces, because there was a lot of gossip in the home so she didn't want anyone to think they were an item.

As Ruth continued to explain how she and my grandfather weren't like Betty and Ron in Wing C, who smooch by the therapy room between walking lessons, another woman shuffled toward our party in a walker, introducing herself as Joan. She wore a matching lime green pantsuit with daisies printed on the legs of the pants. Stone-faced, Grandpa looked up at the woman and then returned intently back to his hands.

"Ask me where I was today," Joan said to me.

"Okay, where were you today?" I asked.

"I don't remember, but it must have been pretty damn good," she said with a chuckle. She placed both of her hands on her hips and said, "Because I feel pretty goddamn good today, so I must have been somewhere other than here. Not that here is so bad. But I just know I went somewhere. That's what I do—I go on every damn trip they offer. My son pays extra so I can go anywhere I want. We've been to some amazing places, but the thing is, I never remember where the hell we went. I just know I feel better on those days when I get out of here for a little while."

Grandpa refused to raise his head, so I forced my hand onto his shoulder—attempting to offer some sort of comfort from the obvious depression that had overtaken him. I hoped the layer of thick flannel between my hand and his flesh would protect me.

"Well, that doesn't sound so bad," I said. "This place sounds all right. There are things to see and places to go. That's more than you were doing when you were at home, right?" Grandpa couldn't walk on his own any more, spending most of his days incontinent, making failed attempts to stand when Grandma left the room. He'd chipped several vertebrae in his back during a recent spill. He didn't look up or even acknowledge my question. My smile slowly faded to mirror his indifferent expression.

From the pink plastic basket wire-tied to the front of her walker, Joan lifted a patchy stuffed monkey that suffered from the mange. She wound a metal key protruding from the creature's back. The scraggly beast began to make "ooo-ooo-ooo, aaa-aaa-aaa" sounds as its cracked plastic eyes rolled around in circles. The creature shook like it was suffering from a seizure. Grandpa looked up and smiled, gesturing toward the monkey to ensure I didn't miss this performance.

"I see it, Grandpa." He continued to point and smile. "That's pretty funny, huh?"

It pleased me that Grandpa had made friends in his new home, even if they were a bit addled. Although most days Grandma stayed with him for six hours and my parents, wife and I made visits at least once a week, I felt some comfort in knowing that when Grandpa was alone, he wasn't really alone.

After the monkey stopped whirring and shaking, Grandpa returned his eyes to his hands. Ruth explained that she used to be a nurse, possessing a special knack for caring for those who needed it most. She sensed my grandpa needed happiness. She said happiness was her specialty.

"I used to deliver babies, too," Ruth said.

"No one cares what you used to do," Joan snipped, winding her monkey back to life.

Ruth, still positioned directly next to my grandfather, covered his ears and said, "I just want his grandson to know I'm

146

taking good care of him." Grandpa was slow to respond to her touch, but painfully turned his head toward Ruth to smile. She returned his smile, fixing the neckline of her sweater again.

"I don't think I could deliver babies," I said, trying to continue the conversation so Grandpa knew I liked his friends—his surrogate family that provided what I was not capable of offering. "I'm too freaked out by the blood." A nurse scuttled by, squeezing Ruth's shoulder as she passed. She nodded to the group of us. The receptionist at the front counter clicked a pen open and closed, rocking slightly in her chair.

"Actually," Ruth responded, "the vagina doesn't bleed as much as you'd think."

"I'm sorry?" I said, hoping I'd misheard her. It wasn't just the word vagina that irked me; it was the fact that it was loudly being delivered by a woman my grandmother's age in a crowded room.

"The vagina," Ruth pointed at her crotch, "it doesn't bleed."

"Not anymore," Joan said, placing her vibrating monkey back into its basket.

"Well, no, not anymore. But I mean during childbirth," Ruth said. My eyes darted about the room to ensure no one had heard Ruth's boisterous pronouncement. Still resting my hand on Grandpa's shoulder, I must have clenched up, because he turned to me and said something in French.

"English, Grandpa, I don't know French," I said.

"Oh, I'm sorry," he began slowly. "Are you okay *mon petit bezot*?"

"I'm fine."

"Bon," he said. "You know your grandmother [French word] [French word], and I love her very much."

"She knows you love her, Grandpa." I discovered from the nurses that he'd told my grandma to leave that day. "Have you met my beautiful wife?" he asked Ruth.

She nodded, offering a polite smile like she was thinking about something else. He returned his gaze to his hands.

"I don't know why people think that birthing a baby makes a lot of blood come from the vagina. But that's not how it is," Ruth began again. "Because I've seen a lot of vaginas in my days as a nurse. And I've only seen a few bleed. And that was because the babies were so big. And you know, it," she pointed to her lap again in order to clarify exactly what she meant by *it*, "is not always wide enough for a baby's head. But it's the afterbirth that grosses some people out when it slips from the vagina."

Joan let out an exasperated sigh and snapped, "Will you stop saying *vagina*."

Ruth shook her head, "I'm just saying it because that young man said he couldn't deliver a baby because he wouldn't look at a bloody vagina."

Joan petted her monkey and said to me, "So, you're the vagina man?"

"The what?" I asked, caught entirely off guard and searching for the right words to respond.

"Don't play stupid, vagina man," Joan said, almost singing the words "vagina man."

"I never said anything about," and then I whispered, "vagina."

"You're right, Ruth," Joan said. "There he goes again. That boy is always talking about vagina. It's like it's the only thing he thinks about." She covered her monkey's ears. The receptionist had taken an interest in our conversation and ceased rocking in her chair and now leaned forward. I shook my head, mouthing to the woman, "I'm not the vagina man," while nervously waving my hands about. The woman reclined back slightly, clicking her pen.

My grandfather, who'd been ignoring the conversation, looked back to me and said, "I want to go home and see my wife and my dog. I miss my beautiful wife. She's so wonderful because she's classy and modern." My grandmother brought most of her current wardrobe with her from France in a crate when they came to the United States in 1960. There have been very few updates.

"And she loves you very much, Grandpa, you know that, right?"

His eyes grew watery, his nose dripping. I stood up to snatch a Kleenex from the receptionist's desk, daintily holding it out to him, careful not to make contact with the snot that had dripped onto his hand. He stopped ringing his hands long enough to mop up his face. He shrunk back into himself.

"I'm so stupid," he said.

"Why, Grandpa? You're not stupid. Grandma loves you, and she knows you love her." I sat back down.

"You come to visit and [several French sentences.]"

"English, Grandpa. I need English."

"I'm sorry," he said, focusing on his hands.

Ruth touched his face again and said, "Joan, what's for dinner tonight?"

"How should I know?" Joan leaned over to me, pretending to whisper, but spoke loud enough for everyone to hear, "You know, I don't know what the hell she's talking about half the time, but I'm fine with that, because it's not like I'd remember it anyways."

Ruth waved her hand at Joan and began laughing. Ruth continued to stroke Grandpa's face until his eyes dried. He stared blankly at the wall, just to the right of where I was sitting. He ceased to answer any of my questions or engage in any sort of conversation. I announced that I had to leave to make dinner for my wife. I promised I'd be back next week to sit with Grandpa to watch the staff erect the Christmas tree in the large common room. I waved goodbye to Grandpa, without a kiss.

Ruth promised to take good care of him. Joan shuffled next to me in her fuzzy, green slippers as I walked toward the exit, insisting she was coming home with me for stir-fry.

"I don't know if I should bring you home," I joked, "because my wife might become jealous." She laughed and said she understood. She wound up her monkey, waving his arm at me, its eyes spinning uncontrollably.

Locating Grandpa in the nursing home each visit isn't a simple chore. The nurses wheel him around quite a bit in order to give the patients new perspectives, preventing them from clawing at the walls. The following week when I returned, I checked his room, the common room, and the therapy room but still hadn't found him. I ran into Ruth and Joan in an annex adjacent to the secondary cafeteria, hoping they'd seen him. They were both sitting at a small table tying green ribbons around candy canes for the holiday party. The room had a small, black television set in the corner that a woman in a wheelchair stared at without blinking. Her head was cocked to the side, her mouth open. The nursing home positioned birdcages throughout the facility. A particularly rowdy green parrot flapped about in a white cage next to Ruth and Joan, squawking and preening its feathers.

"I'm sorry young man, but I don't think I know you," said Ruth.

"Oh," I said, confused, having spent over an hour with the duo less than five days ago. "I'm Jean Hemery's grandson. I was sitting with you last week near the entrance."

Joan turned to look me over. She said to Ruth, "If that is one of my boyfriends, tell him I'm tired and I can't go out right now."

I tried to rehash some of the previous week's conversation, but Ruth shook her head and said, "I'm sorry, but you may have us confused with someone else. But it's very nice to meet Jean's grandson. I've heard Jean's been through a lot. I don't know his whole story, but I know he's been through quite a bit."

Joan slowly reached over to the basket of her walker, sliding the monkey onto her lap. She dropped some blue plastic shopping bags that were anchored in the bottom of her basket to the floor.

The cafeteria doors swung open and a procession of wheelchairs began gliding through the annex. Half-a-dozen attendants began wheeling the residents to their next prescribed station in the nursing home. Near the end of the line Grandpa waited, glaring down at his hands. I spoke with the nurse, who agreed to release him into my custody to watch the tree being set up. Grandpa looked through me, expressionless.

"It's me, Grandpa, Mike." I willed myself to lean forward, thinking perhaps I'd make contact today. But as I approached his face, I noticed a wet, slobbery gleam to his cheeks and some gelatinous pudding stuck to his whiskers. As usual, I forced kissing sounds from my lips from a safe distance on each side of his face.

No response.

I had envisioned my mere presence bringing sustained elation to my grandpa. I thought by logging in my thirty-minute visits once a week, Grandpa could find the joy and peace to carry on another week. But many visits resulted in the same stoic, expressionless mug. It's not that he didn't enjoy my company, but he didn't reveal the exuberant delight I expected. He shrugged his shoulders when I told him the plan for the morning. No smile.

Grandpa pointed to me and said, "Ruth, I'd like you to meet my grandson."

She nodded at me and said, "Watch this, I can make him smile." Despite the old lady's charm, I grew impatient and annoyed by the redundancy of this exchange—she touched his face, he smiled, and I attempted to divert all conversations clear of the word "vagina." I got it: she was magic and brought him happiness; I was wasting my time by even making the visits, because before my car even pulled out of the parking lot, he'd probably forgotten I'd even been there. I considered wheeling Grandpa from the room, wishing the ladies a fine day, but supposed there were worse things than seeing an elderly woman comfort my grandfather by touching his face.

I was correct. There were much worse things.

Ruth pulled up next to Grandpa, facing him, locked the wheels on her chair, and leaned forward to encroach upon his personal space. She rested her hands on his thighs, tilted her head and let her lips sink into his, opening her mouth a bit. She held the wet kiss for several seconds. I grew short of breath and felt the sweat begin to collect on the small of my back. Joan, oblivious to this tawdry event, scolded her stuffed monkey for tying one of the ribbons asymmetrically onto a candy cane. When Ruth finally pulled away from the kiss, my grandfather smiled, leaning back in his chair, as if he forgot I was even there. How could I compete for Grandpa's attention with a move like that? In silence she unlocked her chair, wheeled herself back to the table and resumed her afternoon craft. The parrot unleashed a guttural scream.

While stretching out a piece of precut ribbon, Ruth said, "I try to make him smile. He always smiles when I do that." She said some more, but I quit listening. I'd never seen Grandpa kiss my own grandmother on the lips. Hell, they'd slept in separate beds for as long as I could remember. I was sure my father was the result of some sort of stumble, rather than any sort of passionate evening of procreation. When I regained my wits, I could hear Ruth talking to Joan, saying, "Because I used to be a nurse. And I have this ability to make patients smile."

Joan huffed and said, "Oh, will you shut up about the nurse business already?"

I checked the locks on Grandpa's wheels and pushed him out of the annex into the common room where the tree was being decorated—as far away as I could take him from this horrible, horrible scenario. I parked Grandpa by the oversized windows. A maintenance man hoisted himself into the air on a gas-powered hydraulic lift platform to string ribbons and decorations of golden angels and silver birds on the Christmas tree that stood over fifteen-feet tall. I'm usually quite adept at making conversation during my visits, but we sat in silence for some time as the image of Ruth kissing my Grandpa on the lips played over and over in my head. This wasn't the first time something like this had happened. My dad recounted an incident earlier in the week when Ruth noticed Grandpa's hair was sticking up, so she licked her hand to flatten his locks. She repeated the process, leaving a streak of moist slobber across his forehead.

I then began to obsess about Grandpa's well-being. I wondered if I should report this behavior to the nurses. I began to fear for Grandpa's health, remembering my undergraduate sociology professor who explained that HIV cases were rapidly increasing amongst senior citizens because very few used birth control. And furthermore, he looked just a little too happy when Ruth leaned into him. I expected him to share my repulsed reaction. Maybe he'd forgotten he was married. Maybe Ruth took advantage of his mental decline, convincing him that she was his wife? Maybe his dementia had totally disrupted his logical pattern of thinking?

Or maybe for ten seconds in a day of confusion and loneliness he found solace in her kiss.

Grandpa was ignoring the trimming, staring just past the tree into the window of the tiny chapel across the hall. I asked him if he visited there often. He whispered his response in French. I asked him to repeat it in English. He shook his head and closed his eyes.

"The tree is beautiful, isn't it?" I asked.

"It's the most beautiful tree I've ever seen. [French words.] [More French words.]" At that moment his face grew tired, so I stopped asking him to repeat anything in English.

"You look really good. You look healthier than you have in a long time," I said. When he was at home, his falls and spills painted deep purple bruises on his face and crusted cuts on his arms.

He nodded.

"We'll all be here for Christmas Eve," I said. "We'll have a wonderful Christmas Eve around this tree. I know it's not like being at home, but some things are like home. You have a nice tree, after all."

He nodded again, pushing his hand against his groin.

"Heck, it might even be better," I said. "At least you won't have to eat any of Grandma's burnt meatloaf."

He smiled, sniffing quietly. He said, "But, I didn't mind it so much."

When the maintenance crew plugged in the lights of the tree, Grandpa lost himself in their warm glow. We spent the rest of the morning trying to figure out what the other was saying. I spoke too quickly and repeated myself slower, while he continued to speak mostly in French. When I saw Ruth rolling down the hall, I gathered my jacket, stood up, and suggested that I take him back to his room, because perhaps he was growing tired. I thought it wasn't healthy for him to be in the presence of these kinds of senior citizens with their unrestrained libidos and filthy, psychotic monkeys.

"I'm happy right here," he said. I understood.

Michael Hemery

Ruth used her legs to maneuver her wheelchair next to his. For the third time he introduced me to Ruth. She nodded, fearlessly reaching for his hand. She tenderly caressed it with her thumb. In eighth grade my best friend told me I could hold her hand in the movies if I bought her ticket. Without hesitation I forked over the cash and an extra three bucks for popcorn and soda. During the film I moved my thumb over the soft part of her hand, where the thumb meets the pointer finger. She leaned over to whisper in my ear, "If we were dating, I'd be yours tonight. All a guy has to do is rub right there with his thumb, and a girl will melt." The expression on Grandpa's face reflected this same euphoria.

Ruth allowed her arm to twine with Grandpa's. The flotsam that clung to his flannel shirt now wedged itself into the weave of Ruth's blue knit sweater. Her thumb continued to slowly move back and forth over his hand. Grandpa's eyes went soft, his body lay quiet, and his hands no longer worked into each other.

I placed the chair back under the table and zipped my jacket closed to prepare for the icy conditions outside. I told Grandpa that I loved him, would be back soon, and leaned forward to kiss him goodbye, lingering on each cheek, allowing his rough, gray stubble to scratch and pierce my skin.

Ovations

Mom originally coerced me into playing the piano under the guise that it would increase my popularity. She said, "When you're older, you'll be able to play songs at parties, on Christmas and before our Fourth of July picnic. Everyone will love it when you can just sit down and play the piano." Well. She forgot to mention everyone would love it when I played the piano *well*. That four-letter adverb certainly makes a significant difference because my first piano teacher, Mrs. Straubanion, most definitely did not *love it* when I played the piano.

Mrs. Straubanion was one of the most highly respected piano instructors in the area. She and her husband both taught at a local private college known for its conservatory. Mr. Straubanion did not accept students, as he dedicated his efforts to composing classical arrangements for the college. Only Mrs. Straubanion offered private instruction, but the chances of being accepted as a student were slim. Applicants and their families were forced to undergo a rigorous interview process to determine their commitment just to be included on her waiting list, which was several years long. The arts section of the city newspaper always seemed to be running a blurb about one of her former students now studying at Julliard or NYU or some school that viewed the piano as more than a clever form of party entertainment.

But somehow Mom slipped me past the waiting list by cashing in favors with several friends who served on the local PTA—our suburb's local branch of the Mafia. Close connections with these cookie-making heavies insured last-minute strudels you forgot to order for Easter breakfast from Mertie's, the most popular strudel shop in town, front row seats for the elementary school's performance of *A Christmas Carol*, and piano lessons with the best piano instructor in the Cleveland area. Mom told me not to ask any questions, but just to be ready for my first lesson at 2:00 p.m. the following Saturday. "And Mrs. Straubanion said it's essential that you use the door in the garage, and do not ring the front doorbell because it will disturb her husband," Mom said. She was emphatic about this. "I had to do quite a bit to get a lesson with her, so be sure you listen to what she says and don't use the front door."

"What if the garage door is closed?" I asked.

"She said it wouldn't be. And if it is, we'll just wait for it to open."

I enjoyed the implied secrecy of my first lesson. My boy-hood-imagination hoped there was also some sort of secret knock. Maybe a bald-headed muscle man in a tight black shirt would ask for a password, leading me through secret corridors to my lesson. To my disappointment, the following Saturday I was greeted by a rather round woman with a purple scarf tossed over her shoulder. She masked her thickness with a loose-fitting, lavender linen pants suit that perpetually appeared to be wrinkled. The large, brown curls of her hair spilled from her scalp like someone had accidentally dropped them there and was too lazy to pick them up to organize them properly. Mrs. Straubanion was rather nondescript, the sort of woman who could blend into any crowd and go unnoticed, except for her nose. Extending from the soft flesh of her face was a long, severe nose that was squeezed together so tightly at the end it appeared to lack openings from which to breathe. It seemed to even sag at times, like a piece of dough pulled to a point and left to gradually succumb to gravity.

"You're awfully old to be starting lessons now," she said, closing the door behind me.

We stood on a small landing with flower-printed linoleum. I removed my shoes, placing them side-by-side in front of the door. "I'm really just tall for my age," I said. "I'm eight."

"Most of my students have been playing for at least four years by that age. You're behind already." She repeatedly flicked her fingers towards the poorly-lit basement stairwell, as if rushing me to the practice room would help make up for four years of frittered time.

"I'm sorry," I said, when I reached the bottom of the stairs, "but there's not much I can do about that now." She briskly walked past me, motioning for me to follow her into an open door to the immediate left of the stairs. There were two other wooden doors, one facing forward and the other to the right, but both were closed.

The small room we entered had cream, speckled wallpaper and thick, green, shag wall-to-wall carpeting. Having only hardwood floors at home, I was immediately taken by how smooth and soft the carpet felt under my socks. I enjoyed dragging my feet back and forth on the rug, charging my body with electricity, shocking the hell out of Mrs. Straubanion every time our fingers touched when she attempted to hand me a book. There was a closet to the left, a brown upright piano pushed against the wall, a bench, and a metal folding chair. In the corner was a stack of what appeared to be music books. The walls were empty—no pictures, no paintings, no windows, no shadows. The exposed fluorescent tube lights that hung from the ceiling only added to the starkness of the room. I thought perhaps this woman was a sham, because this did not appear to be the practice room of greatness, nor did it match the elaborate exterior of the sprawling house with wrought iron fences and pink and purple flowers in the wooden boxes attached under the windows.

I sat down at the bench as she squatted in the corner to rifle through the stack of books. The loose curls of her brown hair bobbed as she hastily shuffled the stack. Her scarf began to slip so she heaved it back over her shoulder with one hand while still pulling books from the stack with her free hand. She stood up, set a few books on top of the piano and slipped the bifocals, which hung around her neck by a thin, gold chain, onto the pointed end of her nose. Just as soon as she had the glasses adjusted on her face she removed them, pointing them at me. She held one of the arms between her thumb and pointer finger, saying, "What I'm trying to say, Michael..."

"Mike," I interrupted, "is fine."

She put the glasses back on her nose. "What I am *trying* to say, *Michael,* is that you have quite a bit of work to do in order to remain one of my students. I don't normally allow older students to skip my waiting list entirely, but I'm doing your mother a favor. If we waited any longer you might as well just take up the drums." She removed a small notebook that had been sitting on the piano before beginning to read the words written across the lines. "When I spoke to your mother on the phone she mentioned that you wanted this badly, so I'm assuming your passion for music will elevate you to high levels of achievement. At the very least, I'm hoping you'll be able to play like my four-year-olds." I wondered exactly what Mom said to her on the phone. All I wanted was Mark Hooster, a fellow third-grader who already possessed muscle definition, to stop punching me in the arm during recess. I hoped that playing the piano, as Mom promised, would make people love me. Or stop Mark from leaving bruises on my arms.

Mrs. Straubanion continued, "You owe it to her to follow my very strict instructions in order to remain on my weekly roster. If you fail to follow my practice schedule, I will offer your spot to another deserving student. My contract with you can be ended at any moment. If we're in the middle of a lesson and I feel you're not worthy to be here, I'll call your mother, ask her to immediately come and get you, and send you on your way.

Do you understand?" I nodded and shifted my butt on the hard bench, which creaked and twisted underneath me.

Mrs. Straubanion then launched into a rather lengthy speech outlining the required practice schedule: twice a day (one hour immediately when I returned from school and one hour after I'd completed my homework and finished with dinner). She handed me three books, receiving a small shock from my charged hands. She said I could borrow them for the week, but was expected to purchase my own copies by my next lesson. She talked about posture, attitude, and the finger stretches, which I needed to execute every morning and evening in order to keep my fingers "limber." "Each finger," she explained, "requires in-dividual attention." She demonstrated how to wiggle my fingers in a repetitive motion, in circles, up and down, and back and forth, for ten to fifteen minutes each day. I giggled. She didn't. I was beginning to wonder if my daily beatings at school were less torturous than Mrs. Straubanion's daily regimen.

She continued to lecture about her fundamental philoso-phies of piano, but I quit listening and began inspecting the shabby excuse for a piano that was sitting before me. The small upright was missing hunks of wood on the top of the box and the white enamel of the keys was yellowing and chipped in spots. I remembered my dad once mentioning that pianos shouldn't be stored in basements, because the dampness warped the wood or stretched the strings or something that caused the entire piano to go out of tune. If this woman was truly the best teacher this town had to offer, I wondered why she possessed this sorry excuse for a musical instrument in her dank basement.

When she finished her speech, she asked if I had any ques-tions before we began to play.

"Is this your only piano?" I asked. "Because I don't think you're supposed to have it in the basement, are you? My dad said it's no good for pianos to be in basements."

"This is the beginner piano. All of my *new* students begin down here and must earn the right to move upstairs and perform on one of our two baby grands. And of course, the grand piano in the performance room is reserved exclusively for Mr. Straubanion and myself."

Although I'd only seen the garage, the landing, the basement stairs and this crappy practice room, I could tell as we pulled up the driveway they possessed a massive home that extended into the woods at the back of their property. I imagined the other pianos were in grandiose rooms with halogen lighting and colorful art splashed on the walls. It was almost as if this room was designed to be intentionally degrading—some sort of psychological mind manipulation to arouse increased motivation to practice more than the required two hours a day in order to get the hell out of there. Despite the oppressive, drab nature of the room, I continued to joyfully slide my socked feet up and down the silky shag of the carpeting.

"Finally," she said, removing a pen from one of the many curls on her head to write in the small spiral notebook, "what sort of piano will you be practicing on?"

I proudly smiled and said, "A Korg synthesizer." She didn't write anything down. Instead, she closed her eyes, placed her now-closed fist to her forehead, and breathed deeply.

During the '80s synthesizers were gaining popularity among many rock bands so my dad thought playing on a synthesizer would be much cooler than playing on a traditional piano. I agreed. We also purchased a large amplifier that stood nearly as tall as me. We cleared off the spare keys and vases that resided on the dry-sink in the living room so the keyboard could rest on the flat, tiled surface—the mass of electronics and cables were the first thing you'd encounter when you walked in the front door of our house.

"So," I continued, "if I get bored with the sound of a piano, I can choose from eighty-eight other sounds. I can even make the keyboard sound like a duck." I figured I'd just cemented a place on her permanent roster because I was so cutting edge in the musical world. I bet she didn't have a synthesizer room upstairs.

She set the notebook back on the piano, opened a book of scales, and placed it on the piano's music stand. She left her bifocals on her nose, managing to whisper, "Let's begin."

And so began my association with one of the finest classically trained piano instructors in the Cleveland area. The week after my first lesson was the closest I ever came in our entire relationship to satisfying the requirements of her strict practice schedule. But even by Wednesday of that week, I grew bored with scales and warm-up exercises. I spent more time tweaking the sound effects of the keyboard than running my fingers up and down the scales. I discovered how to make the keyboard sound like an airplane engine. By pulling on the whammy stick, I could make the synthesizer a fighter jet firing off rounds of ammunition at imaginary enemies. Simulated warfare sure beat scales.

After a month any lingering inkling I possessed to practice the piano was exclusively to please Mrs. Straubanion and my mom, rather than for any inherent love of the instrument. And even that stimulus quickly dissolved. At home, Mom lost her patience with my apathy and would tell me I couldn't watch TV until I practiced my scales and songs each day. Every other day. "At least once a week, for the love of God," Mom shrieked. "We're paying good money for these lessons; you'd better change your attitude about this, now." I told her I didn't want to play stupid scales; I wanted to play rock songs on the synthesizer like Pa promised I could. She said rock stars started off by playing their scales. I highly doubted that. After each week of sobbing and screaming and foot stomping and tantrums (and that was just my mom's reaction), I'd lug my books through Mrs. Straubanion's always-swept garage and slump myself onto the rickety splintered bench. I had become quite comfortable in the cavernous practice room in the basement of Mrs. Straubanion's home and feared a shift upstairs would mean a loss of the soft weave of the carpet that I'd grown to love underneath my feet.

"Now your mom said you practiced more this week, so I'm looking forward to hearing what you've accomplished." Mrs. Straubanion would say something optimistic of that sort at the beginning of each lesson. She'd then follow up her words of encouragement with a grinding insult regarding the previous week's performance: "Because last week you had the rhythm of a shoe in a dryer" or "I've heard dropped pans that sounded better than you."

During my weekly scoldings, I'd focus on the white, marble bust of an ancient-looking man that rested on top of the piano. I thought perhaps it was George Washington, but Mrs. Straubanion didn't strike me as much of a history buff. I figured it had to be some famous pianist, but I didn't know any of their names. I couldn't help but notice how his curls were very similar to Mrs. Straubanion's hairdo. The old sport had the same nose as Mrs. Straubanion, but a more angular face with clearly etched lips and no apparent traces of neck fat. It looked like his shirt had some sort of frilly lace spilling out from underneath his carved jacket. The man looked stoic, dignified and proud—his chin pointing slightly upward—with one exception: the eyes. It appeared as if the sculptor caught the pupils of the eyes in a mid, sarcastic roll. The eyes may have been a mistake at the factory, or perhaps it was the sculptor's quiet gesture to something greater—to the thousands upon thousands of students like me who'd be disgracing the instrument this man so skillfully mastered.

In addition to the verbal insults, Mrs. Straubanion derived great pleasure in whapping me with the end of a metal pointer-stick. The first time she extended the metal rod, which looked like the antenna of a radio, I assumed it was to keep time. She clicked the metal on the wood casing of the piano and said, "You have the most preposterous posture I've ever seen. I swear, you're the laziest young man that has ever sat on my bench." She then gave my back a quick snap on the spine with the antenna. When I flinched, arching my back, she smacked my left hand and said, "The only reason I even keep you as a student is because of those long slender fingers of yours. It's a shame you refuse to use them properly." Each week I was subjected to increased beatings with the pointer. Granted, these attacks could easily have been lessened if I'd opened a single piano book during the week. But, to my credit, I was excelling in the art of sight reading.

In the middle of a particularly brutal lesson, I interrupted her mid-finger-beating to ask who the old guy was on the piano. "Why, that's Wolfgang Amadeus Mozart," Mrs. Straubanion exclaimed. "And he was *not* old. He was a brilliant young man who passed from this world much too early."

"Am I going to ever play any Mozart?" I asked.

"Not at the rate you're going," she said.

All I played were scales and exercises packaged as "beginners' songs," which lacked any sense of song whatsoever.

Week after week I fussed and whined about practicing on my synthesizer. Mom tried to convince me to practice my lesson with the guitar sound, number 47, to make the scales more interesting. I informed her only fiery explosions from my butt could possibly make scales more interesting. I lost TV privileges, outdoor play time with friends, and the right to play records in

164

my room until I practiced. I did feel somewhat remorseful about my lethargy, as Mom said she'd never had the opportunity to play as a kid. She said no one ever pushed her to take up any sort of hobby, so I should realize how lucky I was to have a mother who wanted the best for her son. But despite these sincere speeches, I never felt guilty enough to actually practice. To occupy myself during the many hours when I was boycotting the piano, I honed my drawing skills. I'd sketch cartoon frames in my notebook, drawing exaggerated caricatures of Mrs. Straubanion smacking me with her pointer (which transformed itself into a large, wooden stick in my renditions). My renderings often revolved around her nose, which usually was as long as the entire length of the frame. I'd draw buzzards perched on her beak, waiting for my beaten carcass to stop moving. The bubble from her mouth read things like, "You are worthless" and "I've never seen such a horrid excuse for a human being in all my years of teaching." The next frame always involved me turning my head to shout something uncouth back, like, "I've never seen a submarine stuck on someone's face in all my years of playing piano." The subsequent frames were consistently the same each time I'd draw out the scenario—I'd stand up, grab the stick from her hand, break it over my knee and taunt her with the mangled fragment as a symbolic declaration of my revenge. The only element to change in the last two frames was the object I'd beat her with—the Mozart bust, the door I tore off its hinges, her own nose, and sometimes even the entire piano itself.

The piano lessons were taking their toll on all of us. The irritability was most evident in my family's daily squabbles. My elementary school talent show was approaching, but there was only one more day until the deadline to sign up. My parents and I had been fighting madly about the performance for two weeks, as I insisted on lip syncing the Howie Mandel song, the "Watusi," with my neighbor Andy. My parents demanded that I choose a song to play on the synthesizer. "But that's so boring," I insisted. "None of the kids want to hear me clank away at some old boring song on the piano. They want something funny." My mom told me there was no way she'd spent that much money on piano lessons for me to move my mouth open and closed while someone else sang. She and my dad left for the grocery store instructing me to come up with a song by the time they returned.

I sulked and pouted, refusing to look through any of my beginner music books because I didn't want to face the embarrassment of playing lame piano music. Mark would probably interrupt the performance to pummel me in front of the entire audience. And they'd probably applaud, pleased the horrific performance had ended. When my folks returned from the store, they handed me *Amadeus*, a movie they'd rented. I was less than inspired by the film and more confident that I would be the joke of the entire school if I played that *boring* music. "We just want you to realize that it's not stupid to play classical piano; it's something that you should be proud of," Mom said. "Not all kids have the chance to play the piano like you." She gave me a 45-record of Falco's "Rock Me Amadeus" and told me to go play it in my room to let her know what I thought. Expecting another tiresome rendition of some classical song, I was pleasantly surprised when the European-sounding rock song began with poppy synthesizers and an edgy male vocalist recounting the history of Amadeus only to be joined by a sultry female who sang, "Baby, baby do it to me, rock me." Now this is what I'd been talking about all along.

I emerged from my bedroom and hugged my mom, apologizing for being such a brat for the past few weeks. "You were right," I said, "classical music can be pretty cool. I will play the synthesizer for the talent show." I marched to school the next day and signed my name in the final slot for the show. Under "Type of Performance" I wrote: "Synthesizer: Amadeus."

"I won't do it," Mrs. Straubanion protested. "I won't. It goes against every piece of my moral fiber."

"But I've already signed up and everything," I said. "I can't go back now that I've signed up."

"I don't care if you signed up to be the King of England, I will not teach you to play 'Rock Me Amadeus.'" She said the name of the song like each syllable stuck to her tongue. "It's a disgrace to such a brilliant composer and I'm offended you even asked me to teach you such trash."

"Then what am I going to do?"

"I will teach you a novice version of 'The Magic Flute,'" she said. "And that is what you will perform for the talent show."

"I hate this," I said.

"Good."

I heaved myself into my mom's truck after my lesson and protested, "I don't want to take lessons any more."

"What else is new?" Mom said, backing out of the driveway.

"No, I'm serious this time. She said she won't teach me to play 'Rock Me Amadeus,' and I told her you said I could, and she said…"

"You asked her to teach you to play *what*?"

"'Rock Me Amadeus,' like the record you gave me," I answered.

Mom looked away from the road and glared at me. "I never told you to play that song for the talent show," she said.

"You did, too," I protested. "You gave me that record and said I should listen to it."

"To learn to appreciate classical music," she said. "To see that even rock stars thought classical music was cool. I never expected you to play that for the talent show."

"But she wants me to play some stupid flute song and I just want to lip sync the "Watusi" because everyone will laugh with me instead of at me."

We yelled at each other a lot more that afternoon. I was sent to my room. I was told to come out of my room to get yelled at by my dad. And then sent back to my room to think about my lousy attitude.

"Mike," Mom shouted from the kitchen. "Get out here, pronto."

I dragged myself from my room, slipping my socked-feet across the hardwood floors, offering no indication of "pronto."

"I'm going to make you a deal," Mom said, pulling out the kitchen chair for me to sit on. She stood up, left the room, and returned with a wet rag from the bathroom to wipe off the tear streaks that were etched into my cheeks. "I just got off the phone with your music teacher at school, and if you promise to learn to play 'The Magic Flute' from memory, I'll promise that you won't be embarrassed."

"How can you be sure of that?" I asked.

"Trust me," she said. "You are going to be the last performance of the talent show." That spot had always been reserved for the best performance of the night.

"Mom," I begged, "please don't do this. I can't play the piano that well and definitely not the last act. The kids will be expecting something great."

Mom winked, explaining she had a compromise to make me wonderful, but I'd have to take piano lessons twice a week—once with Mrs. Straubanion and once with Mrs. Chmelik, my elementary school teacher. I also had to promise not to tell anyone her plan, especially Mrs. Straubanion.

The high school loaned us their theater for our talent show. I peered around the curtain as the student emcees began my introduction at the end of the night. I used my hand to shield the stage lights from my eyes, locating most of my family in the audience. Seated a few rows from the front was Mrs. Straubanion, who made a point of attending all of her students' recitals, adorned with a black scarf and her glasses dangling around her chest. I straightened the white, curly wig on my head and fluffed the ruffles on the chest and arms of my shirt. I pulled a piece of fuzz from my black pants and took a deep breath. I trusted Mom's promise that my performance would be well received and felt no real sense of panic. My synthesizer was on the opposite side of the stage, so I'd have to make a grand entrance, walking across the stage in my Amadeus outfit.

"It's time for a journey back in time," the student emcee said into the microphone. "With Amadeus Hemery, err, I'm sorry, Mike Hemery. Let's hear it for him." There were a few claps—mostly from my mother.

I stepped onto the stage, my black shoes clicking across the wood, each step more pronounced than the next. Someone in the audience shouted, "Nice wig, idiot!" When I reached the end of the stage I sat on the stool in front of my keyboard and turned up the volume dial. I flicked my wrists in front of me, as if that would better prepare me for the performance. I checked the keyboard sound effect—it was set to classical piano. Ignoring all proper rules of posture and finger curvature, I pressed down on the plastic keys to play "The Magic Flute" from memory. After pushing each key, I raised my hand in an exaggerated manner, over-emphasizing each stroke. The audience was quiet and polite. Someone coughed in the back. As I reached the end of the song, I held the final note with my right hand, and changed the sound effect with my left, pulling on the "whammy key" to give the new distorted guitar sound a wavering reverberation.

Using my free hand not sustaining the note, I whipped off my wig and tossed it behind me so hard it hit the black curtain. I stood up and kicked the stool aside, allowing it to fall over, clapping against the wooden stage. I tugged at the Velcro strips Mom sewed onto the shirt to hold it together and stripped it off to reveal a black Harley-Davidson t-shirt. I switched hands to free my other arm from its white ruffles, and reached behind me to turn up the amplifier's volume, causing the sustained note to scream to life. The podium near the front of the stage rattled on the wooden floor.

I held my free hand in the air, leaving it there for increased drama, then released the distorted note that had been sustaining me throughout the transformation. I then launched into a keyboard rendition (with a distorted guitar sound effect) of "Rock Me Amadeus" that my elementary school music teacher transcribed for me from the record. I rocked my head forward to the beat, smiling each time I heard a "whoop" or a whistle from the audience. The stage lights flickered and swirled to the beat of the song, preventing me from seeing the expressions of the audience. But it wouldn't have mattered much, because I never really looked up. Instead I watched my fingers as they clunked across the keyboard, belting out the repetitive rhythms of the pop song.

As I unleashed the final note and stepped away from the keyboard, the audience broke into wild applause. I walked to the front of the stage, bowed at the waist, and when I straightened up, I noticed the entire crowd was standing on its feet clapping. Kids and parents and grandparents whistled and hooted so I took another dramatic bow, catching a glimpse of Mrs. Straubanion, who remained in her seat and gathered her program, stuffing it into her purse.

Mrs. Straubanion's refusal to join the ovation was an obvious snub; I saw no reason why she couldn't have joined every other person in the audience, and stood up to congratulate me on a well-done performance. I spent the following week drawing cartoons of the incident—Mrs. Straubanion thinking what a horrible student I was while I beat her with my synthesizer, the podium, and the entire stage. At my lesson the following week Mrs. Straubanion didn't mention the talent show. I felt awkward bringing it up, so instead relied on the memory of the applause to sustain my confidence. After I played that week's repertoire, which I hadn't bothered to practice, I asked what I should not practice for the following week.

"Since this pretty much sucked," I said, "I'm sure you want me to play these scales again, right?"

Mrs. Straubanion removed her glasses and said, "Michael, I am dropping you as a student. This is your final practice with me. I told you our first day this could happen and it has happened. The only reason I kept you this long was I hoped you'd change. I gave you the benefit of the doubt, but after that embarrassing performance last week, you told me loud and clear that you cannot change."

I played with the chip of enamel on the middle-C key and said, "But I played the stupid 'Magic Flute' song. Are you mad that I played the other song, too?"

"Michael, it's not just the talent show. You and I have two very different ideas of what it means to be a pianist. I think you're wasting my time by being here each week."

"But," I began, trying to plead for a second chance—part of me worried my mom was right, that the piano was my ticket to popularity. But I also fretted about Mom's disappointment when I told her I blew it and wasn't allowed to take lessons any longer.

"And I believe I am wasting your time," she said. "You don't want *this*; I witnessed that at your talent show. You don't want to be a fine pianist. You want something very different." She retrieved her music book from the stand and took the tendollars I'd placed on the top of the piano, next to the Mozart bust. "I've already filled your slot with another student. So there is nothing more to discuss. But I'd like it if you'd come back at this time next week. But instead of coming to the garage, please just ring the front door bell."

I didn't understand what more this woman wanted from me. After such a successful performance at school, I was humiliated that she didn't find me worthy to even be in her presence. I thought my initiative to take lessons twice a week deserved some sort of praise. But instead, she seemed to feel that I undercut her authority, defiled her name. She wanted "Straubanion" to be associated with Julliard, not Falco. I left the practice room, trudging up the stairs to my mom's truck waiting in the driveway. I told her what happened. She said she wasn't surprised. She asked why I had to show up next week, but I told her I didn't know—probably so the old bag could embarrass me in front of her new student, *If you don't practice, you'll end up like this reject.*

The following week I walked up the long walk in front of the Straubanion house. Rows and rows of flowers and green, leafy hedges flanked the cement walkway. The double doors in the front entrance were constructed of dark wood and twice the height of a "regular" front door. I eyed up the doorbell and reached to push the button, which, of course, played three or four seconds of some piano song—Mozart, I'm sure.

The doorknob turned and the door crept open. A small, frail-looking white-haired man slowly edged his way out of the shadows within the house and held out his hand, saying, "Michael, I presume." I thought perhaps he was their butler. He said, "Won't you please follow me?" As I entered the foyer of the home, I was met by dazzling colored chandeliers and a staircase that wound spirals to the second floor. The man shuffled his feet across the dark-tiled floor. We walked past a kitchen with pots and pans hanging above an island in the center, a library with more books than the local library, and room after room of closed doors. Finally, we entered a grand room with dark, hardwood floors and large windows stretching to the ceiling. In the center of the room was a black piano that shined and glimmered under the bright recessed lighting miles above me in the high, raised ceiling. The piano was huge, though proportionate to the vastness of the room.

"Have a seat, won't you?" The man gestured to the bench pulled out in the front of the piano. I looked about the room, which was void of any furniture or chairs except for this oversized piano. Victorian galas could easily be held in this room that offered enough space for the dozens of guests and their round, oversized, twirling dresses.

"Is Mrs. Straubanion coming in here?" I asked after the man let the awkward silence consume us.

"Oh," he said, scratching his balding white head, "I'm so clumsy with introductions. I'm Mr. Straubanion, your new piano teacher. My wife decided that we may perhaps work together a tad better than the two of you."

I wondered why she offered me to a man who publicly announced in an interview with the local paper that he refused to give piano lessons because he hadn't that sort of time.

"My wife tells me you are a bit unconventional. She says you remind her of me when I was younger."

I watched his thin, wrinkled fingers reach for the chair next to the piano, pulling it closer to my bench so he could sit down. "How do you feel about composition?" he asked.

"I'm not sure I know what that is," I said. "But is it better than playing scales?"

The old man chuckled. The lines in his face deepened as his mouth stretched across his face.

"It *is* better than scales," he said. "A lot better. But those scales never really go away; we just think about them differently in here. We listen to their sound. No rules. Just their sound."

For the next hour Mr. Straubanion talked about the sound of a piano, the way notes sounded together. He asked me to play certain keys. I pressed them, arching my fingers the way his wife tried to teach me for months. I listened and hung on his every word. "No rules," he repeated when he stood up, pushing his chair next to the piano. "Look in there," he said. I pushed my bench back and stood on the chair, staring into the heart of the grand piano. The wires and pads and metal were beautiful, shimmering in the light. "Drop this on that string," he said, handing me a quarter. I took the change from his outstretched hand and held it out as far as my reach would allow. "Go ahead," he said. I opened my fingers to release the slug of metal. I watched it make multiple bounces on the strings, ringing and clanging, stirring up a ruckus inside the piano, eventually slipping between the strings and falling through.

That afternoon we dropped several dollars of worth of change into the piano, like we were making wishes in a musical fountain. Mr. Straubanion offered me a notebook filled with blank treble and bass clef staffs. "We're going to learn piano backward," he said. My homework for the week was to go home to write down the notes that sounded good together—the ones that made me happy. "Discover your piano or your synthesizer or whatever it is that sounds good to you," he said, his voice cracking slightly. "Then write it down. Come back next week and we'll see what you've discovered."

On the way out of the house, I passed the closed doors, the kitchen with its hanging pans, and the entryway, where Mrs. Straubanion straightened the front rug. She smiled, asking how everything went. "It was a lot of fun," I said. I asked her how her new student was and she smiled and said, "Much more obedient."

My mom's truck sat idly in the driveway. I thanked them both again for a nice afternoon, running to the truck, asking Mom to drive home as fast as she could, so I could sit down at the piano and practice, before I forgot everything he untaught me.

For the next two months we wrote music together. Our lessons weren't about posture or the way things *should* be done—but they were about music. I practiced each day for hours—begging to leave the dinner table early to work on my compositions, putting together strings of notes, testing each one with different combinations, hoping to discover the perfect combination.

After two months of lessons, Mr. Straubanion regretted to inform me that our time together was coming to a close. He said he needed to return to his work, but wished me luck in the future. I hugged him gently, not wanted to crush his thin frame. I also hugged Mrs. Straubanion at the front door, only getting my arms halfway around her waist.

"Thank you," I said to her, as I released her to slip on my tennis shoes.

"None of this excuses your behavior," she said.

"I know," I responded.

"I still despise that song you played for the talent show," she said.

"I know." I ran to the truck, flipping through the pages of notes to show Mom what I'd written that day. Two months later, after some serious begging, my parents purchased a new, upright piano for the living room.

For the next five years, I bounced from teacher to teacher. None of the instructors were interested in composition; they insisted upon returning to scales. My last piano teacher, a middle-aged mom of three girls, gushed over my sight reading. I'd returned to my old habits of not opening a book for the entire week. She said I possessed a raw talent, placing stickers on the pages that said, "Way-2-Go" and "Out-Stand-Ing!" Sometimes she'd answer the phone during the middle of a lesson and gab with her girlfriends about which mothers on the block were having affairs or what time they'd be getting together for drinks that night. While she chatted away she'd spin her finger around, indicating for me to continue playing. When I'd glance over at her on the couch, she'd give me a thumbs up and a smile.

I never realized how much I craved Mrs. Straubanion's strictness. I wouldn't go so far as to say that I wanted to play piano, but I didn't want to get away with not practicing. After becoming disenchanted with the whole process, I discontinued my piano lessons and packed up the synthesizer in its box. The piano soon became a storage shelf for pictures and random junk. I eventually took Mrs. Straubanion's advice and purchased a drum set. I quickly worked my way up the ranks of the percussion section of the junior high band, so by the time I reached high school I was first chair in the orchestra, wind ensemble, jazz band, pep band, and marching band. I was one of the only percussionists who could read music, so for the last performance of my senior year, my orchestra director pulled me out of photography class to ask me if I'd be willing to memorize the marimba solo for "Flight of the Bumblebee." She said I'd be "perfect." I borrowed my drum instructor's marimba to practice each night until I could hit every note with precision.

On the night of the performance, when the director announced my name as the featured soloist, I stepped onto the stage, the same stage I'd walked across to play "Rock me Amadeus." I walked the same route I had traversed years before, except without the white wig or the snide comments from the kid in the back. I straightened the sleeves of my tuxedo shirt, picked up my mallets, and delivered a nearly flawless performance of the piece. The mallets nimbly raced up and down the bars, scales layered upon scales. When I finished, I stepped out from behind my instrument, bowed at the waist, and was met with wild applause and yelps. I shielded the lights from my eyes, casually searching the audience, but failed to find one person who remained in her seat.

Like it Mattered

"The trees are aware of us," my wife Stacie said, walking through the park.

I entertained her statement for a moment. Stacie said trees are conscious of movement, the squirrel skipping its tail on a branch, the wind from our strides brushing tips of bark. She said they sense vibrations from our words. As we move through their space, they're whispering. They know about us, even before we arrive.

The late-March afternoon was still brisk, my breath visible as I stirred in thought.

After less than a mile, I asked what she thought about the baby nursery's color. I said maybe a muted green or a duo-tone with a bold border to separate.

Stacie hushed me. She said not today. She said she didn't want to talk about bumper pads or cribs anymore. She asked if we could walk like the trees knew we were there.

Like it mattered.

After a minute I mentioned the high chair with the highest safety rating in the *Consumer Guide* book.

Stacie shushed me.

I said we needed to add a bouncer to our registry.

She held her finger to her lips.

I said, "No baby talk at all?"

She shook her head.

I asked, "If they are aware, then don't you think they'd like to know? Wouldn't they be interested in the baby? In our lives?"

Stacie didn't answer, but continued to walk, her shoes displacing mud on the rain-soaked trail. Quiet utterances.

Abrasions

Michael Hemery

About Us

"No slack in the line," my dad said. "Otherwise we won't be able to feel if there's anything at the other end." My dad and I cast our lines off the cement pier, reeling them back a turn and a half. The red and white bobbers eased over the ripples on Lake Erie, making me believe each movement was a bite. I pulled on the line, but met no resistance. My dad dragged the plastic tackle box near him, searching for a weight to attach to his line. I waved my hands above our lunch bags, discouraging the flies from nesting on the food Mom packed: two plums, two peanut butter sandwiches, and two Cokes. I'd been fishing with my parents once before, but heaved the entire pole into the water when I cast out. After that incident I wasn't permitted to cast the line, but instead flopped the pole over the edge of the canoe, raising it out of the water every few seconds to see if I'd caught anything.

But on this afternoon I followed my dad's instructions to become a real fisherman. I flicked my wrist like he showed me to achieve maximum trajectory. My dad explained the word *trajectory* after he said it. He showed me how to tease the line to trick the fish into believing the worm speared on the hook was alive. I mastered the technique that afternoon, but still couldn't bait the line. When my dad handed me the worm, I couldn't bring myself to lance it. He held out his worm as an example, popping the barbed metal through the worm's skin. The worm twisted and thrashed when the metal pierced through. My dad pushed the hook into the worm again, to make sure it didn't fall off. Double knotted.

I didn't mind holding the worm. I liked the feel of its rubbery skin, how its body wiggled in many directions. But each time I placed the hook near the worm, I froze. The worm crawled over the hook, dangling like a limp, upside down U.

"Can't I just fling it this way?" I asked my dad.

"Not if you want to catch any fish," he said.

I fiddled with the worm a bit more. I even ran the point of the hook over its ribbed skin. The worm flinched, crawling away from me, but remained trapped in my hand.

"Does it hurt the worm?" I asked.

"It can't feel good," my dad said, taking the hook and the worm from my hand. He drove the hook through. Twice. He handed it back to me. The worm struggled, clumped in a ball, moving into itself. Years later my biology teacher forced us to dissect live worms. I'd always assumed the insects were hollow by the way the hook penetrated the body so easily. I hadn't realized there were hearts. Five of them that my partner and I watched slow to a stop.

While we waited for our catch, my dad and I talked about school. He reeled in his line and cast it again with the heavier weight. I did the same. The early afternoon sun shown through the cloudy water near the pier, overwhelming the green muck of Lake Erie with light. The surge of light made the lake look clearer, like we could see the sandy bottom if we tried hard enough.

That afternoon we fished off the most popular pier in San-dusky, Ohio. The locals said you never left without a bite. An array of people littered the pier, but most were scraggly old men with unkempt gray beards and meshed baseball hats. They didn't talk to one another like my dad and me. Instead, they concentrated on the water. I thought maybe they were taking advantage of the light, trying to catch a glimpse of the bottom, the fish that swam below. My friend Matt said he caught a Walleye the size of his thigh off that pier. He said he stuck his fingers through the fish's gills while it was still alive. He said the blood was warm and thick, remaining under his nails for almost a week. His dad took his picture, the fish wiggling by Matt's side. He said his dad hung the picture above his workbench at work because he was so proud.

The men on the pier hauled up fish, but most were too small to keep. They freed the hooks from the fish's mouths before tossing them back into the lake. Most of the men didn't watch the fish smack the water's surface, but turned to re-bait their hooks before the fish made contact.

Several hours into the morning, we still didn't have a bite. The sun was directly overhead now. The water failed to capture its glow, but regained its muddy composure. My dad pulled in his line to fasten a new worm on the hook. He said you had to keep the bait fresh. He asked if I wanted to bait my own line. I said I wasn't ready for that yet.

Each time a man pulled a fish from the water, I asked my dad if we should move near him. I thought maybe we were sitting in the wrong spot.

"There's no such thing as a right spot," my dad said. "The best we can do is keep our lines fresh and be patient, waiting for the fish to come to us. Our time will come."

My dad and I rarely spent the afternoon by ourselves. Mom always came with us to the museum or the park. But I liked being alone with my dad. I could concentrate on mimicking his movements so I could be more like him. He wiped his wormy hands on his shorts before he ate. I wiped my hands on mine, even though they weren't dirty. We left the lines in the water, the poles lying on the cement. I worried a fish might drag our poles into the water, but my dad said not to worry. He said we wouldn't catch anything that big.

We talked about cars and motorcycles. I told my dad about Amy Dunn, the girl who said if she wasn't dating her boyfriend when we came back from summer break that she'd kiss me in the cement tunnel on the playground. My dad said he thought I was still too young to be dating. I agreed, but said I wasn't too young for a kiss. He said maybe I was right, pulling me by the shirtsleeve towards him, giving me a loud kiss on the head. I laughed, wiping the invisible kiss residue from my hair. My black hair was warm, absorbing the sun's heat. My dad laughed, straightening the brim of his denim cap. He tilted his head backward to finish his Coke. I finished mine, too.

Something tugged my line.

The bobber surged under the water. When it was released back to the surface, the red top bounced to the left then right, trying to regain equilibrium. It went down again. I scrambled for the pole. Using his pole as a model, my dad showed me how to give the line a quick jerk, to ensure the hook bit into the fish.

I pulled on the line. It wasn't loose anymore, but offered resistance. My dad walked me through the process. I reeled the fish in slowly, making sure it didn't escape. After a minute or so I pulled a small bluegill, no bigger than my hand, out of the water. As I continued to reel in the line, the fish's tail flipped. The line felt heavy. I held the fish in the air; he turned slowly on the line. The sun reflected off his metallic scales. Streaks of blue ran down his side and scattered on his fins. I'd never seen a fish up close. Before, when I fished with my parents, my dad unhooked the fish before placing them in a wire basket in the water behind the canoe. He organized the fish in a cooler before we took them to Grandma's house to be scaled and cooked. But I was never allowed to see the fish up close. My dad told me there was nothing to see.

I held the rod away from me. I didn't want to touch the fish. It breathed hard, even though our air did him no good.

"Should we keep him?" I asked.

My dad said the fish was too small—wouldn't be much bigger than a potato chip after we scaled him.

"Go ahead and take out the hook," my dad said. "Before the poor thing dies."

I shook my head. I hated the way his body moved at the end of the line. Each time the fish shuttered, I could feel the movement up the line and through the rod. I was somehow connected to his every twinging muscle. When he flexed, so did I.

I made a face, sticking out my tongue.

My dad laughed and called me a wimp. He grabbed the line with his right hand, palming the fish with his left. He began working out the hook. The fish twitched again. My dad's face darkened. He balanced the fish on his thigh and opened the tackle box. The fish thrashed, falling from his leg. I lifted the rod before the fish hit the cement. He was suspended between us.

"What's wrong?" I asked. I'd seen my dad remove the hook dozens of times on the previous trip. It was a smooth process, like pulling a needle through silk.

My dad held a long, red piece of plastic. The tool was wide, with a notch cut at the end. He grasped the fish, brought it close to his face and pried the fish's mouth open. He tilted the mouth toward the sun. He squinted inside.

"Goddammit," he said.

I asked what had happened, but he didn't answer. My dad pulled on the line for slack. He pushed the piece of plastic inside the fish's mouth. The tool barely fit. He twisted it. Something made a wet, tearing sound inside the fish. The fish shook.

I asked again what was happening. My dad was sweating now. It ran from the rim of his hat. When he didn't answer, I asked again.

"He swallowed the goddamn hook," he said. "It's stuck inside of him."

I watched the fish's eye. It was large. I wondered if he could see me staring back. I wished he could close his eyes so he couldn't see my terror.

My dad worked inside of the fish for over a minute. He wiped sweat from his lip onto his shoulder. Each time he twisted his wrist the fish tore inside. I asked him to stop, but he didn't. He breathed deeply through his nose. The tip of his tongue stuck out, like when he concentrated on measuring a piece of wood at home.

He drove the piece of plastic into the fish, deeper than before. He yanked on the end. Something gave. Tore. When he removed the tool, the metal hook hung from the end. Bent. There was a chunk of sinewy blood wrapped around the point.

As soon as the hook was removed, my dad tossed the fish into the water. I scrambled to the edge of the pier to see the fish swim away, to see it cut through the water like the other fish I'd seen my dad release. The edge of the pier pressed into my chest. The plastic tackle box scraped against the cement behind me.

I watched for movement. But the fish didn't swim. It floated on the surface for a moment. Suspended. Then water slowly filled its mouth, which caved open and shut a few times. The sun was setting, clearing the water with a gentler light. It reflected off his scales, even as he sank. The light illuminated his slow descent. After a foot, the cloudy water consumed the body.

"I don't want to fish anymore," I said. I was still on my stomach, looking over the edge of the pier. I hoped the fish was momentarily stunned, that I'd see his shimmering scales dart by soon. My dad reeled in his line.

"Did he die?" I asked.

From behind me my dad said, "I don't know."

I bit my lip. I wanted my dad to tell me the fish was going to be all right. I wanted him to fix this. My dad always solved my problems. When the chain slipped from my bike, throwing me onto a gravel driveway, he greased the chain and reattached it while Mom wiped the blood from my knee. He touched up the scratch on the frame with red paint. My leg scarred, but the bike offered no signs of the accident.

"Did it hurt him when you took the hook out?" I asked.

He didn't answer. I turned on my side to look at my dad. The sun was behind him. His silhouette removed the bobber from his line, placing it back into the tackle box.

"Did it hurt him?" I asked again.

"Probably."

"Bad?" I asked.

"Can we stop talking about it? I didn't have any other choice. I did the best I could."

My rod was still on the pier, several feet of line strewn about. He'd wiped the bent hook clean.

"I have to know," I said. I crawled next to my dad. The cement scraped my knees. His eyes were wet. "Do you think we hurt him bad?"

The afternoon should have been about us—a father and son fishing like every other father and son. Not a stupid fish. But I had to understand what we'd done that afternoon.

"I had to get the hook out," my dad said. He secured his line back onto the rod. "I hurt him bad. It was stuck deep inside of him. I know I tore him. A lot."

He reached for my rod, reeled the line in, and clipped the hook onto the rod.

"We killed him?"

He nodded.

He put the red, plastic tool back into the tackle box. I put the Coke bottles back into the lunch bag. We walked our gear to the truck without saying a word. My dad handed me his rod, telling me to put it in the bed of the truck. He opened the small Styrofoam carton of worms we'd bought that morning, emptying the contents under the shade of a nearby tree. He knelt down to spread the dirt and worms evenly across the ground. He walked back toward the truck. I tried to lift the tackle box, but it was too heavy. My dad wiped his hands onto the front of his shorts. The dirt stained the fabric. We lifted the tackle box into the truck together. I wiped my hands on my shorts, but left no marks.

Paper Shuffle

Even though we'd never met, I composed a letter to Nathan Hinkle, my randomly chosen pen pal, each week for four months. On Fridays the students in Mrs. Pratt's second grade class shared our lives on wide-ruled paper with partners, strangers, at a neighboring elementary school. Mrs. Pratt said the assignment not only improved our writing, but also taught us about friendship, communication, and people.

I wrote Nathan about my parents, dog, and tree house with windows that opened and closed. I revealed my favorite color was blue and hinted at my sticker collection. Nathan wrote in his first letter that his great aunt worked in our cafeteria. I wrote back that I adored his great aunt, how she'd slip me an extra breaded cinnamon stick on Wednesdays without making me pay.

In the beginning, I enjoyed the correspondence, the distant friendship. Even though Nathan didn't write much, I thought it was nice to have someone.

For four months we wrote back and forth. Every Thursday we'd open our letters. Adam's pen pal sent him a baseball card and Katie's drew her a picture of what she thought Katie looked like. We all laughed when she held up the drawing because the hair was too dark and long, the glasses too big for the face. Brian said Katie's pen pal was a horrible artist. Katie said at least her pen pal cared enough to draw her a picture. We shut up after that.

In one letter Nathan wrote about football. He said he liked the Cleveland Browns. He said he'd rather play football than go to school. He said he hated school. I enjoyed school immensely, numbers cleanly adding together and stories about wars and love. But I didn't want my friendship with Nathan to become strained because of dissimilar interests, so I lied, writing back that I hated school, too.

In May, for two weeks in a row, Nathan didn't send a letter. In the previous message, I'd written that my favorite sport was soccer and my dad tried windsurfing on Lake Erie last summer. After the second missing letter, I began to worry that I'd said something wrong. I thought maybe he hated soccer or windsurfing. Mrs. Pratt said I was being paranoid because our pen pals were required to write back. She said if they didn't send a letter, they'd fail writing class. I hadn't considered that notion before. I thought we wrote because we wanted to, but now I understood this friendship was an assignment. Forced courtesy. Mrs. Pratt said maybe Nathan was sick or on vacation. She said I should still write to Nathan. She said he'd probably like to hear from me when he returned. And besides, she said, it was required.

I told Nathan I missed his letters, but understood that maybe he missed school because of the flu or a funeral. I wrote that my parents bought me a transistor radio for my birthday so I could listen to music when I was outside. I told him I'd sit in my tree house listening to classic rock. I asked if he liked Led Zeppelin or AC/DC. I said I liked AC/DC because when my parents took me roller skating at the local rink, they'd shut off the regular lights and turn on black lights. Then the DJ played "Back in Black" really loudly. I asked Nathan if he'd ever roller skated. I said maybe over the summer we could skate together. I ended the letter by stating that I looked forward to hearing from him next week. I underlined that part. I asked Mrs. Pratt to read the letter to make sure I didn't say anything that would upset Nathan. She said it was wonderful, placing it in the stack with the others.

Pen pal day was exciting in the second grade. The room went silent after we tore into our letters, slowly reading every word. The room burst with noise again as we talked about our pen pals, friends we'd never met, but became an extension of us. I felt like I knew Kevin, Marty's pen pal. His dad owned a real racecar and invited Marty to see it sometime. Brianna's pen pal had a dog that looked like Benji from the movies. Jenny's sent a picture of her whole family from their vacation to Myrtle Beach. In the photo, everyone was smiling.

The following week I received a letter from Nathan. I quickly ripped open the envelope. But Nathan didn't explain the missing letters, nor did he respond to the invitation to roller skate. The page was mostly blank, except for one sentence: "I ate a hamburger and popcorn for lunch."

I smiled.

I'd learned how to control my tears. In first grade I cried when I didn't receive a Valentine's Day card from the girl I loved. Shane Barty caught me crying at my desk. He punched me in the arm and screamed for everyone to look at the girl crying at his desk. Since that day I learned to cinch my eyes closed, pinching them with my cheeks. The gesture accidentally resulted in a smile.

I didn't shove the letter back in the envelope right away, but pretended to continue reading like the other kids. I didn't want anyone to know how short my letter had been. I laughed when other kids laughed. I was quiet when they were quiet. I needed the others to believe Nathan had just as much to say as their friends. When Adam asked if I wanted to trade letters I said I couldn't. I said Nathan told me a bunch of secrets that he made me promise not to tell. Adam said he understood, so he traded with Mark instead.

The next week, I received no letter. The same the following Thursday.

We only had one more letter left to write until the end-of-the-year picnic, when we'd finally meet our pen pals. In my last letter I wrote the usual amount. Mrs. Pratt read all the letters before she mailed them. I didn't want her to suspect my friendship had crumbled. I told Nathan my grandma's dog had fleas. I said Nathan could come over and play on my swing set or in the tree house. But only if he wanted. I said I was allergic to walnuts and wished it was summer so I could read comic books all afternoon.

In order to prepare for the culminating picnic with our pen pals at the local park, Mrs. Pratt instructed us to pack a lunch for ourselves and bring something to share with our new friends. I told Mom I wanted to give Nathan Cracker Jacks, because he'd not only get food, but a toy as well. She packed the box of Cracker Jacks, a salami sandwich for me, and a blanket so we didn't have to sit on the grass. She gave me the good blanket, the fuzzy checkered one that we'd take on our own family picnics.

On the bus ride to the park Mrs. Pratt distributed the final letters from our pen pals. A letter from Nathan was missing again. Mrs. Pratt said not to worry. She said if Nathan was absent I could eat with Adam and his pen pal. I told her I'd rather just eat by myself.

The other class was already at the park when we arrived. A few boys threw a football back and forth. Most of the girls wore dresses and some had pink and yellow bows tied in their hair. When we pulled up, our pen pals ran beside the bus. They began pointing and smiling. One girl whispered, "I wonder which one is mine."

Once we left the bus, the kids hushed. Mrs. Pratt read off the pairings. We were told to find a spot to eat and catch up with our pen pals. As each pair ran off, I gnawed on my lip. Adam left with his partner, a tall boy, about my height, but thinner, more handsome. When Mrs. Pratt called my name, then Nathan's, a boy with spiked-blond hair stepped up. He was chubby with dark circles under his eyes. Mrs. Pratt said the girls should hug, but the boys were to shake hands. Nathan paused when I held out my hand. He looked at his teacher. He said, "Do I have to? What if he has a disease?" A few boys from his class laughed. His teacher squinted her eyes. He looked back at me and shook my hand.

As we walked away I asked where he wanted to sit. He said he didn't care. I told him my mom packed a blanket for us to sit on, so we didn't have to sit on the grass, messing up our shorts. He said he didn't care about that either. Once we found a shady spot near a tree, I opened up the blanket, shaking it like I'd seen my mother do before picnics. But my dad always held the other side. Nathan didn't help. He picked up a pebble from the grass and threw it at a boy sitting near us. The boy winced when the stone hit him. He called Nathan an idiot and threw a stone back. I straightened the blanket by myself.

Nathan and I ate our lunches in relative silence. I said I enjoyed his letters each week. He said good. He looked around the field, not at me. I asked how come he didn't write a letter this week. I asked if I said something wrong. A crumb from Nathan's bologna sandwich stuck to his lip. He shook his head. He said, "This was a lame assignment, so I didn't want to write. When I finally wrote something, Mrs. Camdin said it wasn't nice, so I wasn't allowed to send it."

"What did you say that wasn't nice?" I asked.

Nathan picked up a rock and threw it at another boy. His teacher shouted for him to stop. I said I brought him Cracker Jacks. I handed him the box. "I didn't bring you anything," he said. "Our teacher didn't say we had to." All around us kids from Nathan's class were giving gifts to their pen pals. Adam's partner gave him a whole package of pudding—six small containers. They split the assortment and raced to see who could finish them the fastest. Marty's friend gave him a piece of chocolate cake and a miniature toy car. He said, "This is just like the one my dad drives. You still want to come and see it this summer?"

I told Nathan he didn't need to bring me anything, because I was full anyhow. I'd only eaten half of my sandwich. Nathan said he didn't like Cracker Jacks. He stood up and balanced the box in the grass, tall wise. Then he jumped, bringing his knees up to his chest and extending them, his foot crushing the box. It popped, the trapped air bursting from the cardboard, a tiny explosion. All the students looked over at us. I smiled, holding my cheeks in place.

Nathan picked up the mangled box of caramel corn and tossed it into the metal garbage can near us. He disturbed the bees hovering near the top for a moment, but they returned to their flight pattern.

Nathan said he was done with this crap, and ran into the field where a few of the other boys were throwing the football again. I wrapped up my sandwich, placing it back into my lunch bag. I folded the blanket in half. Then in half again, until it was small and manageable. I heard Nathan laughing with his friends, who invited the boys from my school into their game.

Mrs. Pratt spoke with Mrs. Camdin at a lunch table, so I slipped back onto the bus and collapsed on the seat, crying below the window. When my classmates returned to the bus, I wiped my face on the blanket, forcing a smile. I said what a nice time I'd had, too.

"Bryan Hample."
"Here."
"Megan Hander."
"Here."
"Mike Hemery."
"Here."
"Nathan Hinkle."

"Here."

Nine years later, when my junior English teacher read the name during roll call, I immediately looked up from the back of the room. I hadn't seen Nathan Hinkle since that day in the park. In a class of five hundred it was easy to get lost. He looked the same, but his hair was less blond, now combed to the side. He'd gained more weight. The teacher arranged us alphabetically, Nathan sitting immediately in front of me. She explained when we turned in assignments we were to pass them forward. Nathan would see my name. He'd recall that day.

I studied Nathan anonymously that year—the pimples on the back of his neck, the way he pulled down his shirt to cover his weight when he stood to write on the board. His body was large, moving like liquid beneath his shirt. On warm days he'd sweat, stains near his armpits. I gathered all the details that he never offered in his letters.

With each assignment I passed forward I thought my name would trigger a memory. But it didn't. Nathan never remembered. He was silent the entire year, only releasing an occasional cough or speaking when the teacher called his name for an answer. He never spoke to the other students. He never laughed. We remained strangers, shuffling papers back and forth, without resolve.

Two Lines Intersect to Make a Point

First came the convulsions—back arching, flopping, front two legs clawing asphalt. Its head heaved, trying to will crushed chest to the ditch, but wet organs pinned him to the road.

I'd never seen an animal move that way. Muscles don't flex that fast, that sharp.

My dad swerved to miss the groundhog on the way home from the beach, but the animal doubled back. The truck thumped. Twice. Something sounding like bone struck our metal underbelly.

Dad said *goddamn, stupid beast, sonofabitch.*

Mom held her hand to her mouth, eyes closed. She asked if it died. Dad said soon. He said it wasn't our fault. He said he did his best to avoid it. Nothing we could have done.

I thought if we'd only swum one more minute, paused at one more red light, taken another road home, he would have made it. If it wasn't for us. I began to cry, wondering if there were others who would notice his absence.

My dad said not to look back. But I did, staring in the rear-view mirror until the animal became a small flutter, a seizure of dust.

Bites

I was grading papers when she entered my classroom scratching a scarlet rash that ran the length of her arms with the motion of someone trying to warm herself.

"What happened to your arms?" I asked.

"Bug bites," she said. She sat on a stool near my desk. Momentarily she stopped itching to adjust her blond ponytail. The previous year when she came to class with a black eye and bruised throat, she swore she'd fallen while rollerblading. I told her she must have a special talent to injure only her right eye and neck.

"My dad. Again," she finally said, her chin shaking.

I reported the incident to the school counselor who called Child Services. They claimed these things take time.

Now these raised marks actually appeared to be bug bites, not welts from a cigarette or belt. "Where'd you get them?" I asked.

"Outside," she said.

"Did you forget they were biting you?"

"No," she said, adjusting her bangs that'd slipped over her eyes, "I willed them to do it."

She explained how her dad was stoned on the back porch, reading one of her poetry journals when she returned home from band practice. She asked why he'd been in her room. He asked, "What did I tell you about writing this shit?" She demanded that he return the journal, but he marched her into the house, forcing her to watch as he tossed it in the fireplace. She said she tried to save it or run away or fall to the floor, but he held her wrist until all that remained was the melting metal-spiraled edge. "And if you ever write again," he said, "I'll do the same thing." She said it wasn't the poems she'd miss, but more the record of the moment—her handwriting shaking when an-

199

gry or bubbling when she found peace. "I can never get that back," she said.

My desk is filled with her final drafts—the only safe place she can store them. When her dad came to the school's literary magazine release party the previous year—an issue featuring one of her poems—I shook his hand, telling him he should be proud of his daughter's talent. He forced a smile, glared at his daughter wearing a formal dress borrowed from her friend, and assured me he was. As they left, she said, her dad asked if I was "some kind of faggot."

After the notebook burned to nothing, her poetry now smoke and shocks of fire, she asked to be dismissed. He let go and said he didn't give a fuck. She said sorry to me for swearing. I told her it didn't count because the school day hadn't officially begun.

Not old enough to drive, she ran into the backyard, her dad back on the porch with his pipe, coughing after the hits. She lay in the grass because it was cool and soft and she felt like she was part of something. "That's when they started biting me," she said. "I flinched at first, because, it hurts, you know?"

I said I could imagine.

"But after a few more, I let them keep biting me," she explained. Her cheek moved slightly; she tried to gnaw her way out. "And that's when I had this really dumb idea." She shook her head. "It was so dumb."

She stopped. I said nothing. We both waited.

"I thought maybe if I stayed out there, they'd eventually take enough little bites until I was gone. I began counting bites, wondering how long I'd have to wait until there was nothing left. And instead of hurting, each bite felt good."

I looked down at the senior composition, because it was easier than watching her. "So what happened to that plan?" I asked.

"Well, the funny thing is, the whole time I had my eyes closed, I figured the bugs had to be taking part of me away. I thought about the hundreds of bugs carrying me away to their kids, making me useful. So I figured if it didn't work in one night, I could lay out there every evening, until eventually they picked me clean." She sighed, tracing the raised welts on her arm with her finger. "But when I woke up this morning and saw all the bumps, my arms all swollen and gross, I realized I was actually bigger than I was the night before. I'd made more of myself, more for them to carry away."

Save Often

"What the fuck, bitch?" the slightly digitized voice chiseled away at my eardrum. I fiddled with the tiny white ear bud to ensure my wife, Stacie, wasn't picking up any of this conversation as she sat on the loveseat opposite me immersed in W.S. Merwin. I stretched out my legs on the chaise lounge while intently staring at the small screen in my hand.

"I said what the fuck, mother fucker? Why didn't you bring me back to life, bitch? You got no headset nrhs15? Answer me! I said why didn't you bring me back to life?"

He was right. There was no excuse for me not to revive GangSta4Life818, my comrade in the campaign against terrorism; it was simply an oversight on my part. It was later explained to me that I could have pressed the square button as I tramped over the simulated, still-warm corpses of my comrades to revive them, allowing for continued game play. The truth was, I could barely understand how to reload the clip of my AK-47 or scale low fences and cement walls, let alone perform Christ-like miracles.

I was what is quintessentially called a "newbie" to the world of *SOCOM*, a military simulation game for my Sony PSP that I received for my twenty-ninth birthday. Instead of following the suggested strict boot camp procedures, outlined in the forty-nine-page instruction manual, to properly train for warfare, I grew impatient and wanted to experience the thrill of multi-player online combat against *real* people, not just the lifeless computer. My lame scrapping skills were only further compounded by my even lamer nickname. I lacked the polished handle of a veteran. In my haste to register for the online account, I named myself after the initials of the affluent, suburban high school where I taught followed by the date of my birthday, 15. Not exactly the sort of moniker that struck fear into my enemies. I regretted not trying a bit harder to achieve a name that contained some semblance of intimidation.

GREYKILL999, DEADMAN167, and Slap_Nuts_69 had obviously labored over their nicknames much more than me. In fact, I felt ashamed every time GangSta4Life818 had to take time out of his onslaught of profanities to sound out the letters n-r-h-s 15.

I was the only member of my squad to survive a barrage of attacks from the terrorists (other online gamers). Never mind that I outlasted my associates not as a result of intuitive survival skills, but because I never left our base camp because I couldn't figure out the correct keystrokes necessary to stand up my character and quit crawling around in the dirt on his belly.

Eventually my opponents systematically gunned me down, and it was in the post game chat room that GangSta4Life818 berated me with his insults. You can plug a headset into the PSP to shout commands at your fellow Seals during warfare, but I found most players didn't use the technology to converse about military strategies in the throes of battle. Instead, the soldiers carried on about their hatred for their science teachers and the hot girls who sat in front of them in their third period classes. The infrastructure of the Sony hardware is perfectly designed to stream audio across the WiFi connections, but affixes a slight digital tinge to the voices. Though sometimes a distraction, I was still able to undoubtedly ascertain that the only individuals who were playing this game were thugs with names like RealKillaz and fourteen-year-old boys. While GangSta, as I preferred to call him, ripped me a new one, Spawned4Killing22 and DeathMarcher10 clicked their headsets to life and began discussing in high-pitched cracking voices (not because of the technology, but because of puberty) where their friend Shelby had been all week. This secondary conversation didn't distract GangSta, so he continued to verbally slam me against the wall again and again.

"I don't get it, man, I was right there, you could have just revived my ass, but you was just walking around like some kind of dumb fuck or something," GangSta said.

In addition to my wretched nickname and poor combat skills, I also lacked a headset. As GangSta ranted, I feverishly attempted to respond using the onscreen keyboard that forced me to run the cursor over every letter and tap the *X* button to select it. This sluggish process allowed me to only squeeze out a brief, "Sorry," before the other inhabitants of the chat room started up again.

"I think she is staying with her mom this week, at least that's what John said," Spawned4Killing22 said.

"So did he tell her you liked her?" replied DeathMarcher10.

"I hope not, because if Jenny finds out she'll be so mad at me for not telling her first."

"I mean it bitch, what the fuck?" GangSta said.

My forlorn "Sorry" sat by itself on the screen so I typed in two quotation marks to repeat my apology. Finally IMWolverine13, the number clearly an indication of his age, but not his maturity, clicked his headset on to ask if we were going to play or sit around and bitch in the chat room all night. Slightly embarrassed, but seeking to rally friendship where I could, I typed in, "Yeah!" I had more to say, but that's all I could get out before the game began to load. I soon found myself overlooking a lush ravine with the sound of a waterfall raging in the background. With the game's instructions on my lap, I hastily read the keystrokes needed to stand up and followed the other Navy Seals in their quest to liberate Chile from terror lords. I proudly trotted about four steps before I heard a tremendous shriek and then an explosion from behind me. My character grunted, falling to the dirt; there I was, writhing around on my belly again.

Michael Hemery

Nrhs15 had been brutally murdered, but I could still observe the action taking place in my immediate vicinity. A Navy Seal in full camouflage fatigues slipped his smoking rocket launcher onto his back, switched his primary weapon to a smaller rifle and fired off two more rounds at my dead body. GangSta4Life turned on his headset again and said, "Now we're even, bitch." Using the analog stick on the control pad, I changed my perspective to gaze at the waterfall in the distance while I awaited to be revived. You can only gape at a simulated waterfall for so long before you go stir crazy listening to the distant crackle of gunfire, reminding you of the action you are missing. Lesson learned GangSta4Life818, lesson learned.

When my wife peeked over my shoulder to get a glimpse of my new game, she pulled away, saying how awful war was. She suggested that I read the article in *Newsweek* about some doctor who'd seen the horrors of battle. I sat on the couch, struck with pangs of guilt while I waited my turn to kill. It wasn't that I disagreed with her—a pacifist vegetarian, I loathed the idea of killing anything: human, ant, mouse, or cow—but there was something that drew me into the game. Some sort of boyhood fascination men have with strategizing and destroying. It's the same reason the Cleveland Browns can sell out a stadium every year without the faintest hint of a winning season—we men crave destruction. Like James Thurber, I wished that women would take over so that us men don't blow each other to bits. But in the same sense, I couldn't deny my compulsion toward the game. But Stacie killed my adrenaline high, so I resigned myself to bed as an evildoer who participated in appalling pastimes like video games.

I've had a longtime obsession with video games, despite my hippie parents' steadfast rejection of them when I was younger. They feared their bookish, Smurf-watching child would evolve into a mindless delinquent who turned tricks and snorted co-

205

caine as a result of increased exposure to *Frogger* and *Pitfall*. *All I know is poor Mike attempted to sprint across the freeway during rush hour after spending so much time with that damn frog! Tragic.* Our neighbor, Kevin, owned every video game system ever released (Intellivision, Atari, etc.). After successfully pleading with my mother to permit me to spend the night at his house, pledging we'd partake in a lively game of Parcheesi instead of video games, I'd return home in the morning with bloodshot eyes and twitching thumbs, swearing we hadn't really played video games all *that* long.

When my family invested in a Commodore 64 in the eighties, I convinced my dad "computer games" weren't in the same category as video games, especially if we programmed them ourselves. He concurred so we bought Commodore 64 magazines that contained hundreds of pages of code in the back for writing your own games. We'd sit together in the home office on Friday nights after grocery shopping creating games. He'd read strings of numbers, "gotos," "runs," and "ifthens" aloud while I feverishly typed in the values, all with the hope of video games penetrating the ironclad security of my parents' home. Usually the programs were successful so I was able to play baseball with block figures or race block cars on block streets. But too-often the authors of the code would accidentally print an eight where an "i" should have gone, eliciting a syntax error, forcing us to wait until next month's issue for the editorial correction.

Sometime after my patience of coding grew thin, Nintendo released their original gaming system. After Kevin moved to Florida, I became close friends with a neighbor named Marty in order to hunt Nintendo ducks with a red, plastic gun during the summers of my youth. Despite my pleas to be like everyone else, my parents still blackballed all gaming systems. On my high school graduation day I came home to discard my hat and gown on my bedroom floor when I noticed a small wrapped box positioned carefully near the pillow on my bed. I carelessly tore through the silvery paper to reveal a new Nintendo Gameboy portable video game system. My parents stood in the doorway. My mother looked defeated as she said, "We figured you were going to do it in college anyways, and we'd rather you do it in our house than in the house of some stranger."

But the floodgates had been opened. When I started earning enough money at my part-time college job, I marched to the local Target to buy a Nintendo 64 *and* a Sony Playstation the same day. While standing in the store, I resolved I couldn't decide between the two platforms, so I had to possess them both. When my college friends weren't at my house eating my parents' food and playing video games, I was hauling the system to their dorm rooms for *Mario Kart* tournaments that would engross the entire floor of students. I thought I'd hit the pinnacle of my video game mania during college until my wife surprised me with the Sony PSP for Christmas. This handheld unit had all the portability of the ancient monochrome-screen Gameboy, but the graphics and visual effects of the full-sized units.

She'd been making subtle hints about which games I'd like if I were to ever buy a PSP. To resolve this inquiry I turned to the experts: my fourth-period sophomore English class. These students had been raised on the more advanced video games and were appalled at the concept of *typing* in code to create a game. The most tech-savvy student in the class ensured his name was on a waiting list for the Xbox 360 so he could obtain the system before the general public because he "had connections." I pictured him knocking on the backdoor of a seedy warehouse, whispering, "You got the shit or what?" as he slipped hundred-dollar bills through the crack in the door.

There was a definite quorum in the class that *Grand Theft Auto* was the finest game *ever* created for this particular game unit. This cultural phenomenon created by RockStar Games began in 1997. The player doesn't don the persona of the "good guy," which is typical in standard video games: Cute little animated Mario trying to save the princess, etc. No, in this franchise of games you assume the role of the "bad guy," so it's your responsibility to accomplish a chain of decrepit and immoral tasks that include gunning down pedestrians in cold blood, beating the shit out of hookers to increase your bank, outrunning the police after stealing a paddy wagon, and racing ridiculously fast cars through the city streets. The game stood for everything wrong in this world. It was immoral, vile, filthy, demeaning to women, disgustingly vivid in violent detail, and against my entire moral fiber. I put it on my Amazon wishlist.

Stacie coordinated my Christmas gift with my mother and Mom conceded to purchase one game for me. Stacie relayed the story of their shopping experience as my mother stood in EB Electronics reading the back of the *Grand Theft Auto* box in utter horror. She marched the game to the twenty-something clerk demanding his thoughts. He assured her that this was their most popular title for the PSP to date, but she was absolutely correct in her assumption that it was very graphic and violent. It featured a mature audience warning label stamped on the front cover so that no one under the age of seventeen could purchase this title. Although he had played the game, he didn't think it was a fitting gift to put under the Christmas tree.

I only wish I could have been present for the argument that ensued in the store. As retold by Stacie:

"But he's almost thirty-years old," Stacie explained.

"And that's fine. If he wants to bang prostitutes, he can do it on his own dime," Mom argued back, catching the attention of the entire store.

"But that's what he wants. It's just a video game."

"And if he wanted a hooker, should I get him that for Christmas, too?"

The full version of the game for Playstation 2 contained a mission called "Hot Coffee" where your objective was to have sex with your girlfriend by controlling the thrusts with the "joystick." If you didn't satisfy your woman by slowly building up to climax, you failed and had to try again. There are some failures in life that we don't need to be reminded of.

But these warnings didn't concern me, because I wasn't underage. I was twenty-eight-years old. I could handle the mature nature of the video game, separating it from reality. But my mother still refused and bought me *Madden Football* instead. It was a splendid gift, amusing me for several hours on Christmas morning while Mom slept in the chair and Stacie watched a parade on T.V. But as I picked my offensive plays and punt faked to lead the Browns to victory over the Bengals, I still yearned for some good 'ol fashion prostitute banging. The next day I called my mom as I walked out of Target with the small bag in my hand.

"Thanks, Mom."

"For what?" she asked.

"The video game."

"The football game?"

"Well, yeah, and *Grand Theft Auto*."

"What are you talking about?"

"I just used the fifty bucks you gave me for Christmas to buy *GTA*." That's what all the cool kids called it, *GTA*. Well, the cool kids in my fourth period sophomore English class.

"No, you didn't."

"Yep, and it wasn't the money Grampa gave me or Aunt Vickie or Stacie. I made sure I kept your crisp fifty bucks set aside so you could buy it for me." I don't know why I'm such a prick. I've never been wronged by my family. Subconsciously I believe I was making some bold statement about how preventing me from playing video games for all those years led, rather than prevented, me to drugs and strippers and violence—all simulated on an amazingly sharp LCD screen, of course.

During that winter break from school, Stacie was attending her second residency for her MFA in Vermont. I had plans to read several books, snowboard, and *occasionally* play a few video games. Ten days later as I brushed my teeth to pick Stacie up from the airport, I realized I hadn't shaven or bathed in three days and my right eye had an unnatural red glaze. I'd successfully wasted the entire break zealously playing *GTA*. The game was as immoral and "wrong" as I'd imagined. I realized how bad it had gotten when I failed one of my missions as an up-and-coming mafia lord so I began randomly popping pedestrians on the street to relieve some stress. I stabbed grandmothers, leaving their purses on the sidewalk for the taking, shot a businesswoman at point-blank range in the head, and chased down a prostitute just to beat her to oblivion on the sidewalk, blood trickling from her mouth, all in hopes that the police department would send out the SWAT team with a tank. If they sent the tank, I could jack that ride, to begin inflicting some serious damage.

The first time my battery ran out after an all-day marathon, I rushed to plug in the AC cord so I could continue to drive the shiny, black mock-Cadillac I just stole through the streets of Liberty City. As I plugged into the outlet by the front window, a police car turned down our street. I literally snapped my body to the ground, spreading my weight flat against the carpet of my suburban home. My heart raced. I began to perspire, my armpits becoming damp. As I lay on the ground I realized what I'd just done, shut off the game, letting the unit charge for the remainder of the afternoon. In an effort to get some fresh air, I attempted to drive to the bookstore to get some coffee, but realized that the driving simulation in the video game, which encourages crashing your car into people, other cars, and buildings, was so accurate and life-like, I was unable to operate my car like a responsible human being. When I first backed out of my driveway, I floored the accelerator, a trick I picked up from *GTA*, spinning out the wheels, launching pebbles of gravel from our apron into the street. I took corners at thirty-miles per hour and punched the brakes at stop signs. But, to my credit, I successfully managed to circle the block without shooting anyone through my passenger window. As I was congratulating myself for this accomplishment, I decided I'd better pull the car back in the garage and find something else to do.

But I couldn't. I played again and again. The game made me nauseous. At first. Then I became immune to the gunshots and screams. Like a scene from *Clockwork Orange*, I was desensitizing myself to the simulated violence. The more I played, the more I couldn't stop. The game was liberating. It was a free pass to do all of the things that the real world prohibits. I could not-so-nimbly take a corner at sixty-miles-per-hour in Liberty City. Fuck that cop that was tailing my ass. Fuck him, you hear? I leapt from the car, pulled out my gat and popped a few caps into his dumb ass. Fuck that bitch.

My family was slightly concerned. When Stacie returned home she quietly said, more than once, "Don't you think you should put that down for a little while?" I couldn't. And I didn't. It was well into February when I finished the game. So, was it worth it? Did wasting almost two months of my life to plastic and wires and more plastic offer the reward that I craved? Oh hellyeah it did, because after completing the game, I was given a brilliant gift. Absolutely fucking brilliant. After 748 wasted people (twenty-two direct headshots), seventy-nine exploded cars, twenty-nine destroyed boats, five downed helicopters, sixty-four popped tires, five hospital visits, forty-three kilograms of explosives, and 7,962 bullets fired (only 3,826 made contact), yes, it really offers all of these morbid statistics when the game is complete, I won the grand-poobah of all prizes: an Elvis outfit. My mafia-tough character could don a white, gold-trimmed Elvis outfit to continue wreaking havoc and chaos on the streets of Liberty City. Brilliant.

It was actually Trevor, a senior in my third-period English class, who recommended *SOCOM* as the next game I should purchase. He said gameplay was "eerily realistic and accurate to real war scenarios." He would know, because not only is he an avid video game enthusiast, but he enlisted in the armed forces. He'd already completed fifty hours of boot camp training in order to be hurried through the process after graduation, with the hope of "seeing some action" before the end of the summer. He'd considered entering the Navy Seals program, which would require more extensive training, but his sponsor advised him to wait until graduation to make that decision.

Trevor was the best student I'd had that year. He was extremely well read, deciphering most of *Othello* on his own, explaining key scenes to his peers and even performing a portion of the play, complete with blocking, for the class. I told him the military was lucky to have such an intelligent man serving for them because he had a keen understanding and sensitivity of the world around him. After reading *First They Killed My Father,* a memoir based on the genocide in Cambodia, he made an appeal the day before Christmas break to his fellow classmates to be thankful for the things they had and to consider the fact that there were terrible atrocities taking place in the world around them. He stressed that we shouldn't become isolated Americans who live in a bubble of illusions and fairy dust. Someone in the back of class snickered when he sat down. A few students rolled their eyes, trying to covertly check their cell phones for new text messages.

This year I've already wished good luck and congratulations to two other students who enrolled in the National Guard. Jesse and Joe are both students who need the structure of the military. That's what I told their case manager at the school, because that's what you say to troubled kids who risk their lives so I can read books and take lazy naps in the summer sun. It made my stomach clench to say congratulations, but I didn't have any other options for them either. Joe told his case manager if he didn't sign up, he'd end up with a factory job that he despised, a wife that supported him, and would drink himself to sleep every night to try and forget what his life had become.

Jesse already possessed certain skills that the military craved. I discovered one morning that he already knew how to fire a gun, as he explained the gash on his skull: "Two niggers tried to jack my shit outside my apartment this weekend. I was trying to lock down the front speaker when the fuckers hit me from behind with a pipe. Fucking bitches scattered when I pulled my shit out of the glove box and fired one off at the sky as a warning." It was my job to write him a detention for use of the words "niggers," "shit," "fuckers," "fucking" and "bitches," but it somehow seemed inconsequential and irrelevant at that moment.

The day Jesse told me he enlisted, he stood at my door like a six-year-old asking his mom to let him play video games at the neighbor's house. He rocked on his heels in the doorway of my classroom. He looked at the ceiling, refusing to make eye contact, as he told me how well he scored on his entrance exam.

"You'll need to take correspondence courses for the comp class you got kicked out of, you know that, right?" I warned.

"Yeah, I know." It was the quietest and most meek I'd ever seen him. It was also the first conversation we'd ever had in which he didn't use one word of profanity.

"When do you start boot camp?"

"June eighteenth."

"They don't give you much time, do they?"

"It's probably best. I get into too much trouble when I have time."

I put down the book I was taking notes from, extending my hand to him. He accepted it and then stepped away from my desk again.

"Are you excited?"

He hesitated for a brief moment, "Yeah."

"Scared?"

"Yeah." I let the silence consume us. "But I don't have any other choices, you know that."

He was right. His dad never existed, it was rumored his mom was a meth addict, and his aunt, who he lived with periodically, was not fit to control him. Most days he slept in my class because he worked nights to buy groceries and pay rent on his apartment. But like Trevor and so many of the students that pass through my classroom in "regular" English class, he had an ardent eye for literature, understood Iago's evil in a way that my other students couldn't. During one class, he engaged in a heated debate with the class president, adamantly attempting to prove that Iago was an extraordinarily real character and not just an archetype of evil. He never completed his final thesis on the topic, but I passed him anyway.

A few weeks after Jesse's semester with me ended, I had a dream in which he coerced me to steal a van for him from my parents' neighbor's house (a result of too much chocolate and *GTA* before bed). In the dream I told him I couldn't possibly steal a car because I was a teacher so I had a reputation to uphold. He told me not to worry about it because everything was going to be fine, and if it wasn't, he'd take care of it. Unfortunately, in the dream I spotted the car, but got sidetracked with the prospect of snacks at my mom's house. By the time I headed out for the car someone else had already stolen it. In the dream Jesse was upset with me, but laughed when I offered him a portion of my granola bar.

Jesse just shook his head the next day as I retold the dream to him. He concluded that I had the dream about him because he was the "worst kid" I knew. I shook my head and said, "No, it's probably because you're the only kid I would believe when you said everything was going to be okay."

Personal catastrophes in my classes weren't limited to seniors being forced to decide what to do with the rest of their lives. Amber, one of the sophomores in my seventh period class, let her bag slide off her shoulder as she entered my classroom, announcing, "Hemery, I'll be in the bathroom." With the exception of her mascara, which was blacker than most days, she appeared normal: shoulders dropped underneath her black hoodie, which limply draped on her body—the typical teenager stance and wardrobe. Over twenty minutes had passed while the remainder of the class filled in a, c, c, d, d, a on Scantron exams, so I popped my head out the door to see Amber slumped against the brick wall, limbs and legs sprawling in all directions near the bathroom entrance. She was in tears. A friend sheltered her from the lunchtime traffic that sauntered by her, talking about how excited they were it was Nacho Thursday and gasping in disbelief that their boyfriends could be such assholes. The wall held her up while life moved on around her—the assumption she was just another victim of high school drama, possibly a breakup or a poor score on her geology test.

"Is it home?" I said, crouching next to her. She nodded, her thick-rimmed glasses now positioned onto her head so she could properly mop up her tears with the flopping sleeves of her hoodie. She winced when she rubbed her eyes. "I know, it's really hard to be dumped into a new school in the middle of the year, and I know you have *stuff* at home, right?" More whimpers and nods. "Amber, I need you to take that test in there, but I'll give you some time to recover, okay?" One last nod.

I walked past her, feeling guilty for leaving my classroom unattended, expecting to see my students spraying graffiti on the walls, "Fuck Hemery and his short story test right to hell!" But all was quiet. They hadn't even noticed I left. After another five minutes I stuck my head out the door again, nodding to Amber. She raised her hand and mouthed "two minutes."

Two minutes later her friend, who was serving as her shroud, opened my door, proclaiming that Amber needed me. Without hesitation I was kneeling next to her again, afraid to put my hand on her shoulder to console her, because I'd been trained never, under any circumstances, to touch a student. Her friend looked at Amber and said, "You told me to get him so you could tell him."

Amber mumbled what sounded like, "Cheese."

I smiled at her and said, "You brought me out of my classroom to show me cheese?"

She giggled like a fifteen-year-old should, and said, "No, *these*."

She carefully brought up the sleeve of her sweatshirt to reveal a gauze bandage wrapped several times from her wrist to her armpit. She undid the metal binding clips. With each rotation the blood from the gash burned a more vibrant shade of red. Again. And again she unraveled, until she exposed a deep cut that oozed with still-fresh blood and white puss. The incision was so deep that I wondered what she did with all of the flesh she carved out. Scarred wounds up her arm led to this fresh carving, a painful stairway that mapped out so much of her young life. The cut was long, wide, and most disturbingly, deep. She'd had to cut for hours to get that much flesh removed.

"What were you trying to do?" I asked.

"I know how to kill myself. I would have cut lower if that's what I was trying," she said—eyes drier now, but panicked.

"I really wish you had some strange addiction where you crammed cheese in your armpit and that's what you wanted to show me." Both she and her friend giggled again. "So now what?"

"I don't want my grandma and grandpa to find out; my grandpa will get mad again." *Again.*

"Well, here's how I see it. I care about you and that cut right there indicates there is something wrong we need to work at to make better. I only see one option, and the first step is getting you out of this hallway and getting some medical attention to that cut. Because if that gets infected, they're going to have to cut off your arm, and then where will you hide all your stinky cheese?"

Her nose was running much drier as she sniffled and smiled again.

"The next thing we have to do is get you to talk to a counselor. These are good people, I swear. I wouldn't give you to anyone who would hurt you, okay?" She nodded and began to stand up. I tapped her on the shoe, because I figured that contact was acceptable. I said I'd be right back. I found a teacher to cover my class, picked up her bag from my room, which I found to be surprisingly heavy, and walked with her and her friend to the counseling offices.

After explaining the situation to the counselor I trusted with her situation, I stood in his office until she was settled. She looked up at me and said, "You promise?" nodding her head toward the counselor.

"I promise," I said. "He's on the very short list of people I don't hate."

Many of my students embody everything my mother feared I'd become if I stared at the television monitor too long. And I wish she were right and the decline could be simplified to something that base. I wish that by simply unplugging the AC cord, these kids would have the opportunity to go to college, meet someone special, or find something that really satisfied them that didn't damage their thin, brittle flesh. It would be a hell of a lot easier to blame sixty-four-bits and a few hot processors, instead of Trevor's mom, who I had to call when he started missing an excessive amount of homework. I wish it were RockStar Games and not her, "How many goddamn times can I have this conversation with a teacher?" The realistic way my pixilated character could pull a glock out of his pants to fire upon the LCPD and not the way she said, "I just don't give a fuck anymore. He's eighteen; what the hell am I supposed to do?" Online warfare instead of, "I really can't talk anymore right now because I'm in the middle of something important." The theme to *All My Children* clearly blaring in the background. If only a government mandate eradicating all realistic, simulated video game violence could eliminate Amber's raw slashes induced from her father's decree that she must perform for him—a history of sexual abuse I feared no one could *select all* and *delete*.

Or maybe I hoped that Trevor was wrong about the "realistic accuracy" of *SOCOM*. He was mistaken about the way the mortars left a film of white powder on the screen or the rat-tat-tat sound of semiautomatic weapons. I hoped video games were more terrifying than reality. Maybe war really wasn't that awful.

Recently, while researching the next disc to purchase for my PSP, I came upon an advertisement in *Wired* magazine for a game that touted the slogan, "So real it renders fear." Reflecting upon *GTA*, I cannot recall any incidents where I was really petrified. When a rival gang member ambushed me from behind a dumpster and stabbed my character, I was surprised perhaps, but not terrified, because I'd saved my game only minutes before, so I could start again where I left off. The irresponsibility of game manufacturers is not creating violent scenarios, but claiming their special blend of violence was more forbidding than reality. Simulated horror couldn't compare to the emotions that bled through Amber as doctors sewed stitches into her arm. It wasn't fear of the needle; she'd grown immune to that pain. But perhaps she shuddered at the realization that their thread was useless to the cuts that would reappear in the upcoming months. Or the panic that Trevor or Joe or Jesse would smell as they writhed on their bellies in the dirt, listening to the rush of a waterfall, begging for someone to revive them. My only hope was that they saved often and could restart their games without losing too much.

Ruptures

Michael Hemery

Reconstruction

I've already begun to forget.

In my pocket I carry a miniature notebook in case a particular perfume or echo evokes some memory. When those transitory moments of enlightenment occur, I feverishly transcribe the details. Once exposed to the air of the present, they begin to crumble into ash. If I have an epiphany at a restaurant and don't write down at least a word of remembrance, or some rough sketch of the thought, the memory is lost by the time I return home. I've left an irretrievable part of myself entwined on that table with empty water glasses and heaps of napkins.

Even after my best conservation efforts to preserve memory and restore it to its original state, I find, after increased exposure to the *now*, the past begins to morph at will. The particulars of my youth—exactly what the sticker looked like that I gave Brianna Pendelton in second grade to demonstrate my love for her curly brown hair and asymmetrical smile. Was it the unicorn with the mirrored background or the embossed rainbow with the daisy at the base? Did she smile, blush, or slip the memento in her purse so the other boy she liked wouldn't notice my advances? I'm pained by these questions because without the particulars my existence is void of substance. What did summer taste like when I was nine? Aside from contracting poison ivy on my fingers, face, and legs, what else did I do when I was eleven? Was that the year my grandmother died, or was that much later? Even if you manage to hold on to one of those sweeping memories, the finite particulars are hazy.

I approach the past with caution. I cannot control its slippery nature, surfacing like a dormant oil slick on the freeway at the first flash of rain. That's the moment my driving instructor said traveling is the most perilous—not after it's been raining for hours, when all the grease and grime that's slipped from the undersides of cars has safely dissipated across the path—when our stories take shape into complete narratives that are manageable and easy to navigate. No, the real threat occurs the instant the first bead of thought pelts the road, awakening the concentrated patch of oil, memories assuming any glossy form they choose.

When I must engage in these intimate searches for the past, I've always visualized myself in some sort of blue submarine equipped with mechanical arms with gears. At the end of each arm is a two-pronged claw that lifts the folds of my brain to search the crevices for any trace of thought, as if I'm pulling cushions off the couch searching for house keys. This is how I've remembered, ever since my parents took me to see the *20,000 Leagues Under the Sea* ride at Disney World when I was two. The reason I'm able to summon the name of the ride is that I looked it up—otherwise it's only swatches of a blue-green background framing the porthole of a metal submarine. After minutes or even days of piecing together glimpses of stuffed toys, french-fries and Florida sun, the memories are replaced with more relevant concerns, such as whether it's cold enough outside for me to start wearing my sweaters to work. The past dissolves back into the dark murkiness of my head.

Sometimes the misfires of memory are temporary. I stood before my class this week discussing the persuasive writing techniques Eric Schlosser utilizes in his book *Fast Food Nation*. As I began to write "persuasive" on the board I stopped writing after "p-e-r-s-u." A fleck of chalk drifted to the floor as I tapped my chalk against the board. With my back to the class, I pressed my finger under each letter to sound out the word, forgetting if the next letter was an *a* or an *s*. I laughed and stood back from the board. One of the students in the front row rattled off, "p-e-r-s-u-a-s-i-v-e," but he said it too hastily so I couldn't remember what he said came after the *u*. I used the palm of my hand to wipe away the word and inscribed "Convince" on the board instead. "Okay, never mind how Schlosser persuades us," I said. "Let's discuss how he convinces us." I laughed. They laughed. But as soon as class ended I ripped off a scrap of paper from my lecture notes to write out "persuasive," repeating the process seven more times until I convinced myself that it wasn't lost.

I confuse spring with fall—I pause every time I mention those two seasons in order to visualize the orange leaves of autumn. Somewhere in my mind the word "fall" lies fallow underneath an orange leaf; only after I visualize the leaf with its imperfections and brittle wings can I salvage the name of the season. "Spring" has no direct association—I must first establish fall in order to identify it by default. Many memories must be unwillingly extracted by force. September through November have lost their individual identities, so I must mentally run through all of the months to remember what follows August. I cannot add eight plus six without using my fingers. After winter break, I labor over my classes' seating charts to re-familiarize myself with the names of the children that I've just seen two weeks before.

Although these lapses in memory are not new, I've just recently begun to pay more attention to them. At one point I considered recording everything in my notebook—not only appointments or childhood memories of piano lessons or eating M&Ms inside the canoe on stilts in my parents' backyard, but more of a comprehensive log of each hour of each day—what I ate, whom I spoke to, and where I sat down. Before committing to such an exhaustive endeavor, I overwhelmed myself with the prospect of so much information. Too many words would fill the tiny lined pages to wade through. I surely couldn't be strapped with the responsibility of choosing which memories were important and which should be discarded. I feared I might throw away something useful.

The regret of remembering and then losing the thought is far worse than not remembering in the first place. We've all had those memories that are on the "tips of our tongues," as we strive to recreate the exact moment in which we first conjured the memory, hoping to trick it back into existence. Failing to re-remember invokes an anxiety that I'm missing a scrap of myself. The acknowledged loss gnaws away, a ghost ship floating endlessly, unable ever to dock.

In addition to fretting over lost memories, I've also grown distrustful of collective memories. Their malleability. The tricks they play. I swear Nioki convinced me to throw rocks at the wasp's nest during recess, but my friend from elementary school swears it was Shane Barty. The last time I remember seeing my grandmother, at Halloween, in the large brown chair in her living room, a scarf covered her head to keep her now bald scalp warm. But my mom says we visited her much later, closer to Christmas. Though we both know the last viewing was in the casket, we've managed to forget what she looked like that day.

I fear I'll end up like my grandfather—wheeled about a nursing home from room to room, each day another series of lost actions.

"What did you have for dinner last night?" I ask him when I visit. The question isn't really fair. He doesn't always remember who I am. He stares at me without response. But I hope if I ask enough questions some memory will rattle, drift to the surface. As if enough questions will yield a response. I ask, "Was it a special meal like you get sometimes, one of the turkey or steak meals, or just a regular meal?" Nothing. "It doesn't matter anyhow, does it?" He nods.

Even those lines, quoted with the authority of truth, are only approximations. I said something very much like that to my grandfather one day and he responded with those actions, but perhaps I'm off a word or two, I can't remember. I wrote those exact lines in my notebook, but I jotted them down as I left the nursing home, maybe ten or fifteen minutes after I originally spoke them. It seems the best I can do is paint broad strokes of memory, estimations that seem accurate when I back away and look upon them from some distance.

The only shred of hope for my memory is that I'll live long enough to remember the distant memories, those that emerge from the past. Although Grandpa may not remember when I visited him last, he still recalls what he wore the day he began work at the Benedictine factory in Fécamp, at the age of twenty. He may now struggle to summon the English words to say, "I love you," but he can still reconstruct the tales of how he evaded Nazi soldiers in France during World War II. It takes some time, but he'll tell how he lay, belly down, in the wheat fields when surveillance planes flew overhead, weaving his body through threads of grain. Although the strokes have weakened his face, he still manages to smirk when he tells me how he threw a rock at a German soldier and shouted for him to get the hell out of France. I find solace in the thought that yesterday's dinner may be darkened forever, but I will be able to command the memories that define me into light.

My dad says the whole family is nothing but a bunch of liars. He says no story from his parents' past ever remained the same. Over his lifetime he was told that his grandmother died from complications of pneumonia, a gunshot wound during the war, suicide, and some other muddy memory that involved an affair. I asked him how you could die from an affair; he said he never bothered to ask. He says each story from his parents grows more convoluted with time, full of gaps and holes that make no logical sense. His mom used to tell him that the Hemery family had Viking roots. When my dad asked her what evidence she had that we were great warriors, she told him never to question what she said. He now believes we've always been poor fishermen who died at sea.

Other memories remain forever silenced. My dad believes his Aunt Simone may have been a prostitute—"She did what she had to in order for us to eat," Grandpa always told him. When my dad asked what she did, my grandfather would shake his head and say, "You don't need to know. No one needs to know."

The last time I saw Simone was at a dinner party in Cleveland when I was in elementary school. She was in her wheelchair eating caviar, bubbles of black eggs trailing down her chin. She waved me to her side and said, "I remember when you used to come over after school and play dominoes with me. Do you remember that?"

I'd only seen Simone a few times and always in the company of my dad. I was never allowed to be alone with her, because, as my dad said, she was "loony."

I didn't say a word but smiled at Simone.

"Do you remember, Michael?" she asked. "You'd sit on my lap and we'd play dominoes and drink wine. Do you remember?"

I looked around for my dad but found him on the other side of the room talking with one of his cousins.

"Michael," Simone snipped. "I asked you a question. Do you remember every day after school for two years we'd play dominoes and drink wine together? Do you? Do you remember?"

I chewed on the inside of my mouth, then nodded my head.

As a child my dad would walk with his mother up the hill each week to an unmarked grave, say a prayer for the dead, and march back to their tiny upstairs apartment. One week he asked his mother whose grave it was; she said *a friend*. The next month it was a niece, while the following year a neighbor. When he asked what the dead person's name was, Grandma answered, *she never had a name.* When he asked why not, she said *she didn't live long enough to get one.* When he asked why his dad never came with them she said *he doesn't know about her.*

Every memory lies. As each moment passes, it's gone, never to occupy space with the living again. Some might suggest that a picture or video of a birthday party captures the moment forever, but no snapshot or piece of film successfully recreates, say, the disappointment that panged through my chest when I opened a box containing a drum pedal and not keys to a new moped on my fourteenth birthday.

I remember how my head fit perfectly into my father's armpit when we lay on the front lawn calling out the images we saw in the clouds. Sometimes we even shouted out the same thing. I remember in fifth grade at my public elementary school when Mrs. Fowler stopped class early to tell us all about The Book of Revelations from the Bible. I remember the way she nodded when I asked her if we were really all going to die that way. I remember the torn armrest in the first limo I ever rode in, chunks of blue vinyl missing to reveal the white plastic underneath. I'd ordered it for Stacie's birthday the first year we were dating. I remember how she'd said she thought it was "perfect." I remember how I told my cousin I wanted to eat his pet snails because they looked spongy. The thunder bouncing off the mountains in Vermont. Squirrels dropping nuts from the oak tree onto the top of my stainless steel grill. Lake Erie. Sand. Mud. Waves.

Memories have no connective tissue, the sinew stripped clean from the thoughts that spill. I wish I could sew the moments together, double-knotting the ends and snipping out those that are irrelevant, and I fear if I don't say them now, here, they will be lost forever.

My memory will get worse, I know. At a Veteran's Day dinner at my parent's house, I watched my maternal grandfather agonize to recall the name of his friend who took a mortar shell to the face during WWII. He said his platoon of Marines, stationed in the Pacific, was crouched down behind a hill for hours, waiting for the enemy's fire to stop. My grandfather instructed his men to hold their positions and not to advance or stand up until they were ordered to do so. He explained to us that he and his friend both joined the Marines at the same time—both lying about their ages to enlist. He said this guy had freckles and red hair. He said he told the men over and over to stay down, but after three hours of silence, his friend stood up.

"Maybe he forgot what I'd told him," my grandfather said. "You forget stuff when you're out there. They train you to forget most things."

My grandfather said he tried to grab for the kid when he saw him raise his head above the crest of hill, but he was too late. As he pulled on the kid's pack, the shot took his friend's head clean off, so my grandfather only dragged a headless corpse back down.

"Goddammit," my grandfather shouted at the table, his open palm rubbing back and forth on his scalp. His eyes were shut, his head pointed to the floor. After several seconds he looked up, opened his eyes, and said, "Why can't I remember his name?"

This darkness grants a necessary respite. Favorable recollections form an inseparable bond with unpleasant memories, twisting into one another until they are unified. Recalling a summer afternoon of finger-painting with Mom on the patio inevitably conjures up the evening when I screamed, "I wish you were dead," when Mom denied my request to stay awake past my bedtime. A mind capable of recalling every scratch on the arm or creak in the wall would collapse onto itself. As would the mind of an eighty-five-year-old man envisioning the precise arrangement of freckles on his best friend's face before a mortar stripped it clean.

Un/doings

of origins

When the bell rang to end the first day of school, Scott Cameron snatched his book bag and ran for the open window on the far side of the classroom. He dove through it, tumbled outside, and sprinted home. The teacher shrieked. We third graders cheered. Leaving our new rulers and blank notebooks on our desks, we rushed to the window. Scott pumped his fist and disappeared.

When I got home, I told my mom I wanted to be Scott. "He didn't even *think* about what he was doing," I said. "And everybody loved it." Mom said I should be happy being me.

I'd always been a planner. I mapped out courses of action. I thought ahead. In kindergarten, I worried about the impact a coloring assignment would have on my college application. When the neighborhood kids decided to collectively lie to their parents, swearing they didn't have homework so they could play basketball all night, I did my homework. I didn't feel much remorse the next day when everyone said it'd been the best game of the season. Even when they explained how the older boys asked them to play a game, I still knew finishing my math homework was more important than a pickup game with sixth graders. But a room of third graders never applauded me for doing homework. When Scott received such grand attention for soaring through the window, I wanted to be something more. Everyone knew Scott's name.

The next day the principal told Scott to stand in the doorway. The principal's face didn't wince when the paddle hit, but his whole body shook. The pouch of skin underneath his chin quaked. The teacher stopped watching. But we couldn't look away.

Scott never cried.

This was what happened when you didn't do your homework or leave the classroom properly. Every decision had consequences.

When the paddling finished, Scott couldn't sit, so he stood in the back of the room for the rest of the day. I never turned around, but heard faint whimpers all afternoon.

of life

"He has a heartbeat," Mom said, shaking me awake in the lobby of the ER.

"They already did the ultrasound?" I asked.

My mom nodded.

"I should have been there," I said.

Mom led me to my wife Stacie's room. Her vomiting forced doctors to administer an IV and a catheter to complete an ultrasound. I'd been with Stacie the entire evening until the nurse drew blood. Blood and needles made me see millions of black dots.

I told Stacie I'd stand outside the curtain. The nurse said I'd better suck it up and get used to a little blood if I was going to be any help in the delivery room. I nodded. I willed myself to watch as she missed the vein the first time and went in again. The room was warm. I removed my jacket. There wasn't enough air. I stepped outside the curtain, put my back to the wall, and bent down, head between my legs. I had to do this, the nurse said. When I finally recovered, I walked back into the room where my mother was holding Stacie's hand. Mom asked if I was okay. I nodded.

After a few minutes the nurse said it was time for the catheter. The nurse explained under doctor's orders only one person could be in the room with the patient. Stacie asked for my mom. I thanked her, returning to the lobby where my dad sat. We talked about cell phones and music.

Now, as we walked back to the room, Mom said I wouldn't have made it. She said the catheter was rough.

"What did he look like? What did my kid look like?"

"He's the size of a grain of rice, with a tiny little heartbeat. It fluttered, like wings."

<u>of taking it</u>

"I swear to God, if you hit the glass one more time, I'll drag your ass in this house and beat it raw." Mr. Griffin slammed his back door. Kevin, my neighbor, and I had been kicking a red rubber ball back and forth on his patio, but neither of us had much control. We kept kicking the ball into the floor-to-ceiling windows that lined the back of his house. Kevin's dad was a loose cannon, shouting at kids who walked on his grass, threatening them with his shaking fist.

"Be more careful," Kevin whispered.

He kicked me the ball.

I kicked it back.

Kick.

Kick.

Miss.

The ball ricocheted off the side of my foot. It shot towards the window. Kevin dove to stop it, but couldn't stretch his arm far enough. Blood ran from his scraped knee.

The back door opened. The fist came out.

His dad yanked him inside by the shirt collar. I watched through the open window as Kevin's old man beat him. He never ratted me out, never told that I was the culprit.

I listened for a while, crying into my shirtsleeve, before running home with that ball tucked under my arm.

of disappointment

Mr. Saunders, my seventh-grade geography teacher, had just pulled down the U.S. map at the front of the room when voices stormed down the hallway. "If you want change, come with us. We'll be quiet, no more!" Fists pounded on doors, windows, and lockers. We gaped at the door, waiting for the voices to liberate us from something—from anything.

Earlier in the year Mr. Saunders had duct taped a map of Ohio over the door's window so no one could see in or out. Someone suggested we remove the map, so we could see who was in the hall. Mr. Saunders told us not to move. He explained the voices belonged to high school students protesting the third failed levy in the school district. He said Ms. Eugene, the junior high principal, warned the staff there might be a walk out. He said the students planned to leave high school in the middle of third period, convene at the center of town, and stage a sit in. He figured someone must have suggested rallying us junior high students to increase the numbers for the news crews.

"If you want change, come with us," the voices yelled.

"What do we do?" Mark, a preppy kid whose parents owned a local restaurant, asked.

Mr. Saunders drew a breath. "My official stance must be to stay put and wait for this to pass. I have to say that." He sat down on the stool in front of the class and removed his glasses. "But do you want the truth?"

We nodded.

"Decide what's right for you and deal with the consequences."

Two boys who sat in the back of the classroom and often skipped school to smoke behind the gas station bolted for the door, throwing it open. A flood of bodies rushed past shouting for us to join them. They moved so fast they became streaks of color and sound.

"We'll be quiet, no more!"

A tremor ran through my legs and up my spine. I yearned to be in that hallway raising hell. But students were supposed to obey the rules. If one of us broke free, he was quickly restrained by detentions or calls home. But I realized the school, the city, the cops were all powerless against a force. Not only did I want to march with the rest of the kids, but I wanted to lead the mass. I wanted a red flag.

A few more students began to stand. They shoved their books into their bags, swung the sacks over their shoulders, and marched out the door. Five, six, seven students left. I stared at Mr. Saunders to gauge a reaction. But he offered no emotion, only nodding when another student rose. Both of my parents worked for the school district, in the "lowest" of positions—janitor and media aide. When the district began its cuts, my folks would be the first to go. I believed in this protest more than anyone in the room.

Yet, I was terrified. In elementary school when I acted out, I was subjected to the blue chair—a cushy corduroy chair in our living room that was designated as punishment, a time out. I didn't frequent the chair, because I tried to be the model son. I was given five-minute timeouts for not eating my spinach or refusing to go to bed on time. My longest stay in the chair occurred when I called my grandfather a "fart face" after he beat me at Scrabble. Fifteen minutes in the chair. I cried into the fabric. I ran my wet face over the soft ribbed back.

I whispered to my friend, Adam, "What are you going to do?"

"I don't know," he said. Adam's mom worked for the district, too, as an aide. She'd be laid off with my folks.

"What will they do to us if we leave?" I asked Mr. Saunders. Four more students left the room.

He shrugged. "According to school policy they could suspend you." The noise in the hallway made it difficult to hear. "But that's an awfully large number of kids they'd have to kick out." The fists grew more violent on the windows and lockers. I was sure something would break.

I closed my book and placed it into my bag. Adam said he was going for it, launching from his seat before I convinced him otherwise. There were only eight or nine of us left in the room.

"What are we going to do if we stay—is there anything for points?" I asked. I'd never received anything less than an A on a report card. I'd be the first member of my family to attend college if I could earn enough scholarship money. I had an obligation to ask.

"Yes," Mr. Saunders answered. "But that's not what this is about, Mike. If you believe in this, go. March. But rebellion comes with sacrifices. If it wasn't dangerous, it wouldn't be worthwhile."

Five more students left. There were only four of us remaining, the "A" students. We ignored the door. The noise. Instead, we watched each other. We waited for someone to flinch. The slightest movement might have sent us out the door. But no one moved.

Almost immediately the hallways silenced, bodies draining into the streets.

"Open your books to page 46," Mr. Saunders said, his voice quiet now.

I stared out the door.

I retrieved the book from my bag. I opened it to page 46.

of static

"Come get me. I need beer," Daniel said on the phone, slur-ring his words.

"For the love of God, Daniel, it's Christmas Eve," I said.

My folks and I had just returned from dinner at my grand-mother's house. The phone rang while I was still taking off my jacket.

"But I drank all of Rich's beer. I got my fake ID, but I don't have a car, and I'm sure not walking to the store with this snow shit coming down."

I explained to my parents that Daniel was alone on Christ-mas Eve, so I was going to hang out at his mom's house for a while. Mom reminded me I was still only seventeen, so I had to be home by midnight, even if it was a holiday. I kissed her on the cheek, telling her not to worry, I'd be back before Christmas.

Daniel smoked on his mom's porch, only shorts and a hoodie protecting him from Cleveland's arctic winter.

"Well it's about goddamn time, Hemery, I'm freezing my nuts off out here."

"Why didn't you just wait inside?"

"I'm watching for Santa," Daniel said. He tried to stand. Losing his balance, he grabbed the porch railing to keep from falling.

"Where's your mom and Rich?" I asked.

"Some fucking party."

"So you're at home drinking by yourself?"

"I'm drinking for Jesus." Daniel reeked of beer and ciga-rettes. I helped him into my truck. He tried to wave me off sev-eral times, but I held onto him so he didn't slip. Pulling out of the driveway, Daniel reached for the CB my dad installed in case there was an emergency. He turned it on and clicked the microphone.

"Breaker, breaker 1-9," he said in a lousy country accent. "Anyone out there tonight?"

Static.

Daniel settled into the vinyl seat of the truck, resting his foot on the dash. "Breaker, breaker 1-9, I hope there's somebody out there tonight, because this is Broken Heart and I'm driving down the lonely roads of the Ohio turnpike right now thinking about my old lady and kid back at home in Tennessee. I got to say I'm missing them something fierce right now." Daniel went on to spin an elaborate tale about needing to drive his rig on Christmas Eve in order pay for his wife's surgery. He waved his arms as the story grew. At one point he used the sleeve of his sweatshirt to wipe his eye, drunk enough to believe his own story.

He released the microphone, letting it fall to the floor.

Static.

Then the speaker broke into silence. I never found the static of CBs to be lonely. At least the noise filled the empty spaces. What I found most disconcerting was the silence of a microphone clicked on, when you know someone's there, but not speaking.

Finally a voice began, "I hear you Broken Heart, this is Black Bear and I'm running that same stretch right now, trying to get home before Christmas."

Daniel grinned. He snatched the microphone from the floor to tell Black Bear the importance of family. Daniel said there'd be nothing better than being with the ones they loved. Daniel wished Black Bear a Merry Christmas. Black Bear returned the sentiment, telling Daniel to be careful so he could make it home safely to his family.

I parked outside the 7-11. Daniel slid out of the truck, returning a few minutes later with a case of Bud Light. When we returned home Daniel said I could leave, but I told him I'd stick around for a while. His friend, Zack, who lived across the street, stopped by to help with the beer. They stuck a lit candle in an empty wine bottle to watch the wax drip down the glass. They flipped through the phone book, searching for "Paul McCartneys" and "George Harrisons." They dialed the numbers telling the voices at the other end in spotty British accents that they wanted to get the band back together. People told them to go fuck themselves. Daniel ended every call by wishing the strangers a Merry Christmas.

Headlights filled the front window.

I cleared the empties into the garbage and told Zack we should probably take off. Daniel's stepdad didn't permit people in his house when he was gone. I shook Daniel's elbow; he drifted in and out of consciousness.

Zack and I bolted. Passing Rich and Daniel's mom in the driveway, I wished them a Merry Christmas. They were both drunk. Rich asked why the fuck I was at his house. He lit a cigarette and went inside. Daniel's mom asked about my family. I said they were doing well. She hugged me. I hugged her back. Daniel stumbled out of the house and said, "Well, what the hell is this, you're making a move on my mom?" She laughed. I wished them all a Merry Christmas and returned to my truck. Zack paused by my door to make sure I was able to drive. I told him I wasn't the one drinking.

Rich threw open the front door, cigarette burning in his lips. He grabbed Daniel by the sweatshirt, tugged it over his head just far enough to pin his arms. Rich punched him, fist to the face. Daniel fell down, freeing himself from the sweatshirt. His legs and arms were bare.

Rich pulled him back to his feet and said, "Where did all my beer go, you piece of shit?" He punched him again, in the stomach this time. Daniel giggled. They both breathed hard, clouds of frozen anger billowing from their mouths.

Daniel never made a fist, but instead opened his arms to form a crucifix. "Merry Christmas," he shouted.

Rich tackled him, beating Daniel into the bank of snow mounded near the driveway. Daniel's mom screamed.

I told Zack to get into the truck. I popped the clutch and squealed the tires into reverse, backing into Zack's driveway across the street. As we ran into Zack's house, I could hear Daniel's mom screaming to stop it. Then she yelled, "Hit him. Teach him a lesson!" Zack told me to follow quietly so we didn't wake anybody. He said we could watch from his bedroom window.

In the living room his mother lay on the brown, stained carpet, her breasts hanging dead to the sides of her body. She held an unlit cigarette. Their tiny white dog was licking a substance pooled near her hand. Her boyfriend slept on the couch, wearing a shirt, but no pants. A large glass bong, an open baggie of pot, and a syringe lay on the coffee table.

In his room Zack tried to apologize for his mom, but I shook my head and pointed out his window. Rich lifted Daniel from the ground, then punched him in the gut, dropping his stepson to his knees. Daniel's mom now joined in, kicking Daniel with her red, high-heeled shoe.

"What do we do?" Zack asked.

"I have no idea," I said. It never occurred to me to call the cops. In high school, I didn't think you could call the police on parents. They were the ones who called the cops on us.

Daniel stood up, stretched out his arms again, and took a slap from his mom. Rich brought him back down with a punch. Daniel vomited.

It was snowing now, light crystallized flakes—the kind in snow globes. Blood painted Daniel's face. The snow where he collapsed was tinted pink and brown.

Downstairs, someone tinkered with the bong in the living room.

Six years later, Zack would call Daniel to tell him he'd moved to New Jersey with his boyfriend. A year after that he'd be arrested in his car for giving some guy head for crack. In one more he'd be convicted for beating a girl. Once out, he'd rape another woman, leaving her for dead on the side of the road. But that night, Zack was just a kid asking me what we should do to help his best friend. He said he was terrified they'd kill him. He said there had to be something we could do.

I told him we'd wait until it got really bad.

Michael Hemery

After the Dash

I doubted the minister's sincerity. "None of us will ever forget Carol," he said at my great aunt Dottie's funeral. He'd been saying the wrong name for the entire memorial service held next to Dottie's open grave.

"If he says Carol one more time, I'm going to scream," Mom whispered to my dad. But she didn't. None of us did. My great aunt had no friends that we knew of, so the few immediate family members in attendance twittered among ourselves. My aunt shook her head. My grandfather sighed. Dottie's fifty-year-old son, Jim, kept rising from his seat to snap a picture with a plastic disposable camera. He took pictures of the minister, the wreath of flowers, and several different angles of the casket itself. He'd wind the camera, grinding the gear to advance the film, then return to his seat. The rest of us remained in our folding chairs while the man that none us had ever met before reminded us of the importance of remembering Carol. He said Carol was a loving mother and aunt. He said she had a fantastic sense of humor. He said she was a valuable member of the spiritual community.

Carol sounded like one hell of a lady.

Dottie was an eccentric who lived a few houses from my grandparents. She didn't drive but rode her bike with the large metal basket to the grocery store, sometimes making several trips a day, bringing home only what the basket could hold. Her plump face pushed her cheekbones up to her eyes, giving the impression they were permanently shut, until she blinked, which she did incessantly.

Aunt Dottie's house smelled of cat piss. None of the litter boxes were ever changed, so her half-dozen cats urinated on the carpet. She adored cats, referring to them as her babies. But despite her affection, she refused to let them on the furniture. To prevent this, her couch, kitchen table, television, rocking chair, and coffee table were all placed in discarded refrigerator and washing machine boxes, cut unevenly six inches to a foot from the floor. Despite these cardboard moats, the cats slept on the kitchen table and pissed on the couch pillows.

I don't remember many conversations with Dottie, save for the time I was ten and she asked my cousin Mat and me to clean out her garage. When we balked, Aunt Dottie said she'd find something in her purse to make it worth our while. Inside the garage was a large 1950s-era aqua-blue car that Mom said Dottie stored for a man she dated after her husband divorced her. The car remained there for twenty-five years. She hadn't spoken to the man since their breakup, but swore he stopped by every few years to check on his car. She'd hear the garage open, the engine turn over. She'd peek out her kitchen window to watch the man run the car up and down the driveway, then quietly disappear.

I pushed a broom in the garage, while Mat slid damp boxes filled with papers and books across the floor. Each time he moved a box, making room for me to sweep, dozens of mice scurried from one location to the next, their feet scrabbling over mounds of old newspapers and magazines. "No matter how much she's going to pay us, this isn't worth it," Mat said. We speculated how much we'd make for the afternoon of work. I thought we'd make at least five bucks each, while Mat claimed we'd end up with nothing.

Mat stacked boxes on top of other boxes, while I moved dirt from one side of the concrete slab to the other. We worked this way for a half an hour, sweeping around the dozens of dead, desiccated mice.

When Mat found an old *Playboy* magazine in a pile of garbage, we slipped behind the garage.

The corners of the magazine had been chewed away. When Mat turned the pages, tiny black mouse pellets slipped from between the pages. "These women are probably all old now," Mat said. "Can you picture them naked—their skin all wrinkly? Or maybe they're dead."

I told Mat he was sick for thinking about naked dead women. I said we should get back to work before we were caught. Mat said he was done working, said Aunt Dottie would never know the difference if we cleaned or not, said we might as well collect our money. When we knocked on the screen door after ditching the magazine, Aunt Dottie was listening to the Indians baseball game on her transistor radio. She rocked in her chair, the runners mashing the cardboard of its box lid with each movement. The game was so loud we had to knock twice.

Wordlessly, Dottie opened the door, twisting open the clasp of her change purse. She gestured for us to hold out our hands. In mine she placed a red plastic button. She pressed it hard into the palm of my hand, closing my fingers over the gift. Mat closed his eyes and shook his head. I said *thank you* before my face gave way to disappointment. Mat retracted his hand. He told Aunt Dottie that she didn't have to pay him, that he'd done the work for free. But she insisted. She said she wouldn't let us leave until all of her debts were settled. She fished around in her change purse. Fabric brushed against plastic, a zip of corduroy.

Mat grudgingly held out his hand again. Dottie placed a small feather in his palm, then twisted the clasp of her purse closed. The feather looked like one of the down feathers that sometimes blew out of the tiny hole in my blue winter jacket. Then she took the objects back and wove the feather through three of the button's four holes, tying it off at either end. She handed the feather-button back to me, blinked several times, then returned to her rocker, stepping over the lip of the box.

"I told you she was crazy and we wouldn't get paid," Mat said as we walked back to my grandma's house. I pulled the feather-button from my pocket. It was dull and worn. "Let me have that," Mat said, taking the object from my hand. Then he flicked the feather-button into the road. It skipped across the asphalt until it spun to a stop at the curb.

"We should go get that," I said. "What if she sees it when she's out riding her bike?"

"The crazy old bat can't see anything," Mat insisted. "And even if she does, so what? It's just garbage anyhow."

I began to go back for the feather-button, but Mat pulled my sleeve. "Leave it," he said. "If she does find it, maybe it'll teach her not to be so crazy and cheap."

The family accepted her quirks. For the annual Fourth of July picnics, Aunt Dottie would ride her bike down for hotdogs and potato salad. She'd straddle the bar of her bike, resting the paper plate of food on the handle bars. As soon as she finished eating, she'd peddle back to her house without saying goodbye.

After she died, Mom and Jim were in charge of Dottie's house. While emptying the kitchen Mom screamed when she opened one of the cupboards. On the second shelf was a stuffed muskrat. They named it "Musky." Before Jim returned home to San Francisco, he sold or threw away all of his mom's belongings—chairs, couches, ceramic knick-knacks. The only things worth salvaging were a suitcase full of pictures and the muskrat, which he packed in his carry-on bag.

That's all I know.

Mom says I'm wrong. There were only three cats and one box lid—for the rocker, a gift when she retired from the local college. I didn't know she ever worked. I still believe there were more box lids, but there's no one to arbitrate. When Dottie died, her existence was offered up for interpretation. Slipped memories. Miscounts. Wrong names at the cemetery.

The worst funeral was for Grandpa's brother, Johnny. Grandpa said his brother lost his mind years ago. He believed the FBI had a tap on his phone, so he tore the jack from the wall. Grandpa never visited Johnny. A nurse would stop by his house once a day to clean and feed him. He died during the summer of my sophomore year of college. Mom said I should go to the funeral. She said it would be nice if I came so the living outnumbered the dead.

There were six of us, but my mom and grandfather were the only two who knew Johnny. The minister began the service with a prayer and a call for us to say something personal about the departed. Grandpa said, "He was my brother."

"Is there anything more you'd like to say?" the priest asked.

Grandpa shook his head. The rest of us were quiet.

"Well, as I'm sure you know, Johnny liked good whiskey and to spend his money on dogs at the track," the priest said. "Hopefully God will look past these faults and see the man you knew."

Between the service and the burial, Grandpa invited us to lunch at Olive Garden, his treat. He thanked us for coming, because he said it would have been mighty sad if no one had showed.

"Why the hell did the minister say that about Johnny?" Mom asked.

"Say what?" Grandpa asked.

"The gambling and drinking bit."

"Well, that's what I told him about Johnny," Grandpa said. "I left out the part about how he'd shoot at the neighbor's dogs when they'd go through his garbage or how he'd hang his underwear on the mailbox." The waitress brought the round of drinks Grandpa ordered for us.

"You could have told him about when you two were kids on the farm."

Grandpa swirled his whiskey and ginger ale. "I can't really remember much anymore," he said. "What does it matter? All this talking is for the living, not the dead." He ordered another round before we even finished the first.

After Johnny's burial, Grandpa said most of his family was buried together in this cemetery, in the same block. He said he'd bought a spot for himself next to them, his stone already carved with his name and date of birth. The number after the dash was all that was missing. He said he wanted to find the graves before we left. He wanted to see his second wife, see what he'd look like next to her.

We followed him around the graves as he drove up hills and back down. He leaned out his window, shouting it had to be around here somewhere. Finally, he parked his car to search on foot. We all helped. The six of us kicked the dirt from toppled headstones, reading the names of people we didn't know. *Loving mother. Caring uncle.*

The pack of us ambled around the cemetery, the alcohol from lunch warming us in the cool summer breeze. After an hour, my grandfather threw up his arms in disgust. He rubbed his right knee. He said it ached, so he was done.

"What's the point, anyhow?" he asked. "When I go, it'll be someone else's problem to find the grave."

"But don't you want to see your family? To pay your respects?" Mom asked.

Grandpa thought for a moment. "Maybe you're right," he said. Finally, we found them.

I've searched for Dottie's feather-button in drawers and boxes in the attic, but I'm sure we left it on the street that afternoon. I thought maybe I went back for it. I would have given it to my son when he was older. I'd press the button into his hand, just like Dottie did to me. I'd tell him this was Aunt Dottie. I'd tell him what I know. We'd make up the rest between us.

The End

I

Tucked between a chic outdoor wine bar and an overpriced women's clothing store, my wife Stacie and I discovered an art gallery in Sarasota that sold bugs. Hundreds of butterflies, mounted in frozen patterns of motion inside airtight, acrylic boxes, hung from an enormous, yellow wall. Although the blues, greens, and reds of the butterfly wings were enchanting, a sinister, long-bodied critter hanging at the end of the wall, away from all of the other displays, caught my attention. The bug resembled a distended grasshopper, its six-inch green and tan exoskeleton framed by two sets of translucent pink and green wings, like those papery umbrellas gracing tropical drinks. Attached to its armored underside were two sets of short arms drawn into the body, while two more legs, lined with spiked black barbs, dangled from the creature's bottom. Despite the striking hues of color at the base of its wings, the bug was fierce, surely the inspiration for horror films and campfire tales, a sultry vampire with fangs. Removing the case from the wall and turning it over, I noticed the bug's shell seemed nearly impenetrable, all soft spots covered by rigid plates, evolution ensuring this one would last. Traces of glue clung to the bug's abdomen, securing it to a plastic stake. Two minuscule, tentacle-like arms were drawn around the mouth, wide and sharp enough to nip off the tip of my pinky.

"So, you're a bug man?" asked the white-bearded owner, a chatty middle-aged man wearing cargo shorts, a red Hawaiian shirt, sandals and a Panama hat.

"Not necessarily," I said. "This is just a fascinating insect."

"We don't carry many bugs anymore," he said. "The women want the pretty butterflies—they usually get freaked out when they see weird specimens. In fact, this is the last one of these I'm going to carry. I told the artist I can't sell these to the rich women. They run out of the shop. No good for business."

"I think it's beautiful," I said.

"This one was a rare find in this perfect condition."

"What is it, exactly?" I asked.

"A Madagascar locust," the owner said. "Can you imagine thousands of those sweeping onto your crops, darkening the sky? And the sound they must make, it's no wonder they thought the end was near."

"Who?" I asked, hanging the box back on the wall. "Who thought the end was near?"

"The people in the Bible," the man said. "Oh, I forgot to mention, that's the exact locust that historians believe was referred to in the Bible—the plagues and all."

Without asking for a price, I hastily dug in my back pocket to retrieve my wallet.

I had to own this locust because I still longed to solve mysteries I unearthed as a child. In elementary school when I tired of hearing Mom read The Hardy Boys and the *Adventures of Narnia*, I asked if she'd read to me from the Bible. She'd suggest the story of Noah or one of the Christmas tales, but I'd insist on the book of Revelation. Sprawling out on the hardwood floors and tightly closing my eyes, I'd listen as Mom read about each seal that was broken open, revealing a new layer of terror for the destruction of man—seas turned to blood, horses with lion heads spewing sulfur, and the plagues of locusts. I loved the part with the locusts—lion's teeth, faces of men, the hair of women, all topped with a gold crown—ravaging humans under the leadership of Apollyon, an angel king known as "The Destroyer."

When I first questioned her about the book, which was introduced to me accidentally by my fifth-grade public school teacher, Mom explained that Christians were being persecuted at this time, so many historians believed John wrote the passages as a message of hope in a secret code only understood by Christians. I had no interest in the Christians' redemption at the end of the book; I'd often ask Mom to stop before we reached that part. Instead, I quaked with excitement as I thought of the mystery—man's demise wrapped up in a tale of Hollywood blockbuster proportions, with its gore, drama, and most importantly for me, secrecy. I thought if I heard the story enough times I'd crack the code and understand the message of the author, like the clues to some hidden treasure. But as Mom concluded each reading, I'd open my eyes and shrug. "I still don't get it," I said.

Mom would laugh and say, "You're not the only one."

I worried the bug would get tossed around in the cargo hold of our return flight from Tampa to Cleveland, damaging its tissue-paper wings, so I packed the bubble-wrapped locust in my carry-on luggage with my laptop and magazines. As we approached the security checkpoint, I thought the screeners might question the cargo, assuming it served some devious purpose, like nail clippers or deodorant, but they didn't search my bag. Slipping my shoes back on after walking through the metal detector, I said to Stacie, "They're worried about shampoo bottles, but they just let the plague that will destroy all of mankind slip right through."

The locust now hangs just to the left of my computer monitor. At first, I studied the creature each time I sat down to write, check emails, or pay bills. It had been seven years since I last opened a Bible, for an undergraduate Genesis class, and even more years since I'd given up on religion. But I again found myself reading the book of Revelation, hoping the marks on the legs or tears on the wings would provide some insight into the mystery. The story was still captivating, but I wished I were terrified of the locust, the tangible form of my childhood story, an ominous warning. The locust didn't frighten me, so much as it filled me with wonder. Closing my eyes, I imagined thousands of locusts descending upon the earth, their pink wings chariots of sound, for one final battle.

After a few weeks, the locust became more of a decoration, coming down from the wall less frequently. Maybe once a week, I noted how content it seemed in its acrylic case, angelic, even, its bent left leg giving the impression of holy ascension. The top of the case is now covered with a dusty film, yet inside remains the mystery, staked to my wall in silent martyrdom.

II

"Uncle Larry's bees are gone," Mom said one morning when Stacie and I joined my parents for breakfast at a local bagel shop.

"What do you mean 'gone'?" I asked, spreading cream cheese on my bagel. "Weren't his hives full just a few weeks ago?" My uncle owns an organic produce farm just south of Cleveland, and since he purchased the land nearly thirty years ago he's had beehives at the back of his property to provide fresh honey and pollinate his crops. This was the first time the hives had ever been abandoned.

"He went back there a few days ago to get some honey and there were piles of wax and other debris from the hive heaped outside the stacks. When he opened the hives up, they were empty—not even a dead bee. After they emptied the hive, not leaving a single piece of dirt, they all abandoned it."

Before I was born, my dad also tended to the beehives in the back of his suburban yard. He'd explain the complexity of the bee's social network. He told me, "I loved just watching them interact and carry on—like a miniature and more perfect version of us."

Now, at breakfast my dad began explaining how he'd seen a program on PBS that investigated a massive disappearance of bees across the world. Apparently, some seventy-percent of bees are gone on the West Coast, and no one has any idea what's happening to them. "There are tons of theories," my father said. "Some say it's cell phones or pesticides, but no one knows for sure what's happening."

I didn't want to think about the bees, because really, their fate is not a mystery at all—the specifics may be murky, whether it's the chemicals or the communication towers, but their disappearance shouldn't come as a great surprise. The real shocker for man is how our end won't result in a bloody battle of good versus evil, swarms of insects the size of our open hands annihilating us. Instead, we could easily perish from abandonment. Our gods, who owe their very existence to us, have abandoned us, cleaned house like the bees and returned to their homes. They're calling home their creations one by one, the bees, the polar bears, the chestnut trees. Soon, all that will remain of the planet are humans with all of our intelligence. If the enemy was clearly defined, humans would surely rally to victory, attacking the locusts with nukes or heat-seeking lasers. But you can't defeat departure.

We sat for the rest of the morning in relative silence, aside from the occasional exchange about work or our relatives, while I periodically stirred the honey that had settled at the bottom of my mug.

Michael Hemery

Infinity

Leopards

The fingers of both my hands were woven and locked together, palms facing upward. Only my two middle fingers were separate from the masses, sticking straight up, undulating back and forth like the tides dictated their movement, rather than the muscles in my hands.

"Like this?" I asked, straining to keep my palms upright as I offered my masterpiece to my Sunday school teacher, Mrs. Johnson, who was talking with another child across the room. I clapped the tips of my middle fingers together to gain her attention, not understanding that I was flipping her and the other five-year-olds in the room the bird, twice. The room was located on the second floor of the church, above an annex jutting from the sanctuary like a tumor. The walls were painted a mute yellow, like a fading daffodil, with little decoration aside from a few bent tacks and a creased poster featuring a faded rainbow with a Bible quote. A cork bulletin board housed our art projects from the prior week—renditions of baby Jesus, his body torn from the cardboard of shoebox lids, with mismatched colored beads glued on the face to represent eyes.

Each Sunday, after twenty minutes of songs, prayers and communion, the minister called the children to the front of the church for "children's time," three or four minutes of Bible parables that involved visual aids like balls of yarn and duct tape. We children were more enthralled with the props than Jesus's devotion so would raise our hands to find out the essentials: "Can we keep the yarn?" After at least one kid screamed that he missed his mother and was escorted back to the pew with his mom, we were ushered out the back door next to the organ, traveling through a series of poorly lit, dusty tunnels until we reached a stairwell that led to the second floor. We were divided by age and given a church-related activity to complete. This week we sat in a circle on metal folding chairs learning the "Here is the church, here is the steeple, open the doors and see all the people" hand gesture, which concludes by opening your hands to a mock-sanctuary full of wiggling fingers. But for the third time I erroneously linked my "church" together, fingers twisting in places they didn't belong, revealing the two lonely, vulgar members of my congregation.

Mrs. Johnson's daughter Tammy sat next to me giggling when she glanced down at my fingers. She proudly showed me her hands—all sorts of celebration and revelry amongst the six fingers waving about on her lap. Mrs. Johnson quickly stood up from her chair across the room, straightened her long, red, flowery dress, and squatted next to me to shroud my middle fingers with her open hands.

"Listen up, everyone," she said loudly. "Your hand church is just like a real church, it needs a foundation of faith to fill its pews. You need to take time to make sure each finger is in place before you open your doors."

I stared at her hands veiling my church and whispered, "Am I not going to heaven because my church isn't right?"

Mrs. Johnson shook her head and helped me unwrap my tangled fingers from one another. "No," she said more quietly than before, "all you need to do is pray."

"For what?" I asked, wanting to ensure I offered God the appropriate request to avoid eternal damnation.

"Pray for God to help you with what you struggle with the most, and right now that is your hand church."

"That seems like a waste of a prayer," I said. Even at age six I remember thinking it ridiculous to ask God to fix a silly hand game.

"There are no frivolous prayers, Michael," Mrs. Johnson said. My hands were now separated, but Mrs. Johnson still sat crouched next to me. "God listens to those sorts of prayers, helping out all of His children with whatever it is they need."

"I thought He only wanted to hear about curing people and helping out leopards and stuff."

"Lepers," Mrs. Johnson said. "God cares for sick people, not animals. And no, God listens to each prayer, no matter how big or small. Pray for help, okay? Do you have any other questions?"

I looked up from my hands and was about to ask her again why people would pray about a hand game when there were starving people in Africa, but instead I asked, "Can you explain infinity to me?" Earlier that month my mom introduced the concept of infinity to me when she exclaimed that she loved me "infinity plus one." When I asked her what infinity meant she told me to ask my dad. He said infinity was a philosophical concept that had no beginning and no end, going on forever. I told him that's what Mrs. Johnson said about God and he said the mathematicians came up with it first. I became infatuated with the concept of infinity—it made my head tingle when I thought about it. My dad eventually agreed to replace my bedtime story with the retelling of the theory of infinity. I still didn't understand it, but I enjoyed the way it made my head feel tight, like it was using my entire brain.

"It's not logical," he said one night before bed. "I guess that's the problem. It's not something we're supposed to understand. But that doesn't mean you should stop trying."

I hoped Mrs. Johnson had a better explanation. Instead she said, "You, mister," poking my stomach with her finger, "have bigger things to worry about than infinity. You need to fix your hand church by next week. Understand?"

I nodded.

"Now promise you'll go home and pray for your hands."

"I promise." I held up my fingers to show that they weren't crossed, the only tangible evidence that a child is lying.

"This is what faith is all about," Mrs. Johnson said. "If you have faith that God will help you, then He will help you."

I hypothesized that faith and infinity were somehow linked, which diminished some of the thrill of the number puzzle for me. One night before bed my dad said you just had to have faith in infinity. I liked trying to figure out the idea of a number that went on forever in either direction. When I stopped trying to figure it out and just accepted it on faith, the concept of infinity lost some luster.

When I was five, I'd developed a somewhat obsessive habit of reminding God each night in my prayers who He had to protect. I'd list the names of each family member and those friends I was speaking to at the time, asking God to allow them to make it through the night without dying. After my great uncle Bob showed up drunk at my grandparent's Fourth of July party, I intentionally omitted Bob from the list. The night after the finger debacle in Sunday school, I closed my eyes after my dad finished his infinity explanation and began to run through the extensive list of names of people I determined should be saved: *Mom, Pa, Mat, Kathleen, Aunt Vicki, Uncle Larry, Grandma, Grandpa, Grammie, Grampie, Mary Joe, Aunt Bettie, Uncle Dick, Rich, Chris, Marty, John,* and *Steve.* I also made a special request for God to keep watching over the leopards, even if Mrs. Johnson said He didn't care about them. I told Him after seeing a special on PBS how hunters killed them for their fur, I thought they'd needed more help than the lepers. At the conclusion of my prayers I said (in my head, of course): *Well, that's about it. And if you ever want to explain infinity to me, I'd be more than willing to listen. Nothing more, I guess. Well, there is one more thing—this whole hand church thing, but only if you have nothing else going on. It's probably not an important prayer. Focus mostly on keeping my family alive tonight. Oh, and the leopards. Don't forget about them. Amen. Over and out.* I always ended with "over and out," a phrase I'd heard my dad say dozens of times into the microphone of the CB in his truck. I tacked the hand church appeal onto the end of every prayer for a week, never making it a greater priority. I would have hated to sacrifice one of my family members for my hand church.

The following week when I returned to Sunday school, Mrs. Johnson asked all the first graders to run through their "here is the church" routine. She said, "I know that you've all been practicing." I realized it never dawned on me to practice. I figured it was enough to pray and, like Mrs. Johnson said, God would take care of everything. My hands began to sweat as each child performed the routine before me with ease. After Tammy wiggled her six fingers around proudly and everyone clapped, Mrs. Johnson said it was my turn. She asked if I'd been praying. I nodded, looking down at my hands. I concentrated on putting my fingers together in my lap, trying to remember how she'd showed us the previous week. My hands were slippery with sweat and the fingers easily glided into each other, forming the damp "foundation" of my church. I looked up to notice the entire room of children and Mrs. Johnson leaning forward in their chairs, staring not at my face, but at my hands. Mrs. Johnson had both of her hands on her knees. Nodding her head, she said, "Go on, it'll be fine."

I stared back down to my hands. "Here is the church," I said, showing my hands to the still room. Tammy nodded approvingly. "Here is the steeple." I connected my two pointer fingers together and turned in my chair so everyone could see my now outstretched hands. This felt right. Everything was meshing precisely how it should. I tried to peek inside my hand church, but Mrs. Johnson said, "Mike, don't cheat. Have faith." Mrs. Johnson suggested my hand church had something to do with faith, and I supposed that meant everything would work out, like the concept of infinity, even if I didn't understand why.

I took a breath and said, "Open the doors and see all the people." I closed my eyes, said a shotgun prayer, *Please, please, please,* and flung open the doors of my church. Based on the prevailing silence in the room, I didn't even have to open my eyes to know what was in my hand. When I did open my right eye slightly, I saw only my two middle fingers wiggling uncontrollably, flicking off the Sunday school class again.

That night I stopped praying for assistance with my hands.

Three years later when my grandmother died of cancer, I stopped listing my loved one's names. I only asked God to worry about the leopards.

The Nod

"I understand that it's tradition, but I'm trying to tell you he doesn't want to go, and I told him he didn't have to," Mom shouted into the phone in the kitchen. I sat on a wooden chair while the curly phone cord connected to the wall whapped me in the head as Mom paced back and forth. The summer before sixth grade, our church required that all Sunday school students attend a three-day camp in order to obtain confirmation into the church (we were also guaranteed free Bibles). All of the kids in Sunday school attended the same *real* school and knew each other intimately. I was the only one from another school. When the Sunday school teachers left the room to get art supplies or snacks, the boys would launch from their seats to flick my ears and sock me in the arm. Luckily, the girls ignored me, instead discussing which boys they'd made out with, while Meghan, the tall girl with braces, announced that she'd let Tommy somebodyoranother feel her up after gym class that week. I figured church camp would consist of three days of private beatings and rampant sexcapades. I thought perhaps I could better find spiritual enlightenment in the bruise-free comfort of my own house. Mom was infuriated at the Sunday school teachers when I explained my reasoning and wanted to know why I hadn't told her the problems earlier. I made her promise not to say anything about the harassment when she called the church to get me out of the confirmation requirement.

"I understand that's how it's done, but I'm asking you to change how it's done," Mom said.

"No, I don't see how spending three intense days together in the woods is going to build up Michael's faith any more. He's met all of the other requirements for confirmation and he's gone to Sunday school every week for six years. Please be flexible with this."

"I don't really care what message this sends to others, all I know is Michael would rather not spend the week away, and I will be very disappointed if he does not get confirmed with the rest of the students."

The minister finally agreed to Mom's request, under the strict condition that I read the Bible for the three days in which all of the other fifth-graders would be at camp. Mom said she'd be sure of it, but when those days eventually came about, she told me to go ahead and play outside and not worry about what she told the minister.

On the day of my confirmation, I kneeled on a red-carpeted step in the front of the sanctuary with the other fourteen students. Evan, the boy who tortured me the most, kneeled next to me. While the minister spoke of the integrity of this confirmation process, Evan whispered to me, "We missed you at camp. We had a great ass-kicking in store for you."

"Each of you is expected to remain an active member of this community of faith," the minister said.

"But you'll still get what's coming to you," Evan whispered.

"Would everyone please stand and welcome these new members of the United Methodist Church," the minister pronounced. I heard the congregation standing behind us, but no one clapped. No one ever clapped in church. After the organist played a fervent hymn, the people would nod and turn back to their leaflets. I'd always detested that silence right after the performer hit the last note of the song. Aside from a polite nod, she was never recognized for her accomplishments. I thought there should be more whistling and hooting and hollering in church. But all we got that Sunday morning was a silent nod, just like everyone else who stood up before the church.

I was handed my free Bible and the congregation was encouraged to stay for a reception after the service to greet us new members of the church. I told my parents I'd rather skip the formalities, and head home to play in the yard—hoping to evade an "ass kicking" for at least a week.

Evan never had the opportunity to give me that beating. I was no longer required to attend Sunday school courses and we always attended the 9:00 a.m. service. Evan came at 11:00 a.m. Then, one Sunday, two years later, the minister announced, "Evan was found dead in his shower last Saturday morning. The coroner has yet to determine if it was an overdose as the police are indicating based on evidence found at the scene. I'm asking each of you to pray for Evan's family members in their time of need." The congregation silently nodded and turned the page of their leaflet to prepare for the next hymn.

Not for Him

"Godisgreat. Godisgood. Thankyouforthisgoodfoodwehave. Amen." I could say grace in less than two seconds, depending on the length of the pause between the three lines. My mom once timed me and said, "I wonder if God even understood what you said." I assured her He got the message. But when the whole family gathered for Easter and Thanksgiving, I'd add some impromptu lines like, "Thank you for bringing us all together" or "Please continue to bless us all." I'd also slow the prayer down slightly. Not for Him, but for the grandparents who may not understand.

Signs

"Could you please stop rubbing Jesus's forehead," said Reverend Mitchell, the minister of our church who began only the year before, my first year of college. He held his hand over the receiver of the phone. I'd told him I could wait in the hallway outside of his office until he finished with his phone call, but he waved me into the dimly lit room, pulling out the wooden chair in front of his desk. The windowless room was lit by a green banker's lamp, which illuminated only three or four feet in any direction. I could see the titles on only a few of the books, such as *The Beginning of Desire* and *A Testament of Hope*, which were neatly stacked on the dark cherry bookshelves that lined the room. Reverend Mitchell remained on the phone for more than five minutes and after properly inspecting all visible corners of the room, I'd absent-mindedly begun rubbing the face of a ceramic baby Jesus nativity figurine placed near the front of the desk. Jesus had no markings of eyes or a mouth—only a glossy surface, begging for a rubdown. I winced and mouthed, *Sorry*, promptly removing my finger from Jesus's cranium. "Sorry Ron," Reverend Mitchell continued on the phone. "What was that?"

Reverend Mitchell was a rotund African-American minister who preached to our predominantly elderly, white congregation. Before he began his first sermon, he proclaimed that he intended to "reawaken our souls with some soul," and broke into an African-American spiritual, holding the low notes and stretching out his hand as if to grasp the invisible air before him. Mrs. Elbertson, the eighty-something-year-old woman who blew her nose incessantly during services, held her hands to her ears until he'd finished. A few other couples whispered to one another and shook their heads. Eventually, the old folks grew more comfortable with Reverend Mitchell, appreciating his inclination toward dramatic flair, how he'd toss his weight across the staging area, reaching deep into the pockets of his black robe to retrieve a handkerchief to wipe the sweat off his bald head. He'd sing every week, but even when he wasn't singing, he sang. Since his bass voice boomed throughout the church, Mr. Robinson, the older man who volunteered to set up the sound system, decided that Reverend Mitchell didn't need a microphone. Reverend Mitchell's voice was brawny and loud enough to keep even my dad awake for an entire hour of church—no small feat. Before Reverend Mitchell, I'd poke my mom in the leg when my dad began to bob his head and close his eyes. She'd pull the hair on his arm, causing him to cringe and massage his skin, looking hurtfully at Mom.

But my dad isn't entirely to blame. None of us were too enthralled with church. I'd protest each Sunday as I buttoned my dress shirt and Mom announced how much she loathed ironing her ruffled skirt. But we'd all pile into the truck and sulk off, for me, at least, because I feared being damned to hell. The guilt of not going to church was slightly more gut wrenching than the nauseous twinge that formed on the drive to church. Spending an hour there seemed like a waste of a perfectly carefree morning. I never understood what any of the adults were talking about anyway, so would doodle on the offering envelopes while the minister droned on about salvation and eternal happiness. I'd sketch stick figure renditions of myself slaying dragons or create complicated mazes for my dad to try and escape from during the sermon. The best part of church was when it was over. Then, Pa would stop by Spudnuts for a dozen donuts and let me pick out which four I wanted for breakfast. I'd labor over which to choose—jelly or cream filled, French crullers, or those dense chocolate donuts my dad called "sinkers" because they'd sink to the bottom of your stomach, lingering there for the remainder of the day. When we returned home we'd tear off our constricting dress clothes and charge to the kitchen table, where Mom made coffee and mixed Ovaltine into a glass of chilled milk for me. I'd peruse the comics in the paper while my parents read the real news. We loved Sundays. Well, after church.

"Thank you, Ron, and may God be with you this week," Reverend Mitchell said, returning the phone to its cradle. He reached across his desk with his gigantic hand, picking up a pen and a small yellow pad of paper, before settling into his high-backed, plush leather chair. He twirled the pen in and out of his fingers. "Now, Brother Hemery, what is it I can do for you today?" Reverend Mitchell addressed all of the men in his parish as "brothers." The salutation made me feel like part of an underground society, privy to the clandestine knowledge Reverend Mitchell possessed. Despite my fascination with Mitchell's delivery, I still had no idea what that knowledge was. Instead of understanding the content of his sermons, I'd lose myself in the hypnotic musical tone of his voice, sure he was declaring something of value.

"Well," I said. "I actually had a question for you. I've been thinking about what I'm going to do after college, and I was wondering how you knew you wanted to become a minister."

"Ah." He rocked back in his chair, setting the pen on the desk and folding his hands together. "You, brother, are inquiring about the calling."

"The what?" I asked.

"The calling—when God reaches out to those blessed few who are chosen to lead his flock toward salvation." He pulled the handkerchief from his pocket and dabbed the sweat forming on his head. "Do you believe He is calling you?"

"Well, I'm not sure," I said. "He may have the wrong number."

Reverend Mitchell put his hand on his chest, chuckling, which transformed into a roaring chortle that echoed off the walls hidden in the office shadows. "Tell me, my son, what makes you think he's tried talking to you."

I didn't necessarily believe God had spoken to me, but as a sophomore in college, I'd begun to run out of career options. I'd dropped out of the communications program my first year because I found radio work to be redundant and unfulfilling. After declaring an English major, I scheduled a meeting with one of my favorite literature professors to discuss possible vocations. He presented me with a brochure the department published in 1978, the year after I was born. The leaflet entitled "Career Paths for English Majors" featured black and white photos of men with beards working with ditto machines. After struggling to come up with any valid options, he suggested I look into teaching or writing something or another for someone that needed something written. Still lacking direction, I figured the next step must be to declare a double major to broaden my career possibilities. I chose the next least practical major: theology.

There were very few religion majors, and those who made the commitment often took their studies very seriously. One such student was Bill Meyers, a fellow sophomore I met in a Milton course. I'd been writing my name in big block letters on the outside of my notebook before class began when I noticed Bill writing odd characters in his notebook. I introduced myself and inquired what he was writing so intently.

Michael Hemery

"I'm teaching myself Hebrew," he said rather casually. "In two years I'm going to the seminary and figured I'd better brush up on necessary languages." I turned my notebook over to conceal the oversized "Mike" with poorly sketched flames flaring from the letters. Over the course of the year Bill and I spoke at length about his religious devotion. He was a devout Catholic. We'd often engaged in fiery debates over religion in the student lounge. He believed the Bible was the Word of God, whereas I had a much looser interpretation of the text—mostly because I'd never really read it. But I did know enough to be adamantly against Catholicism and their lack of acceptance and understanding towards women and homosexuals. Bill and I both wrote for the school newspaper and composed a series of editorials debating religion—I proposed it should become much more liberal while Bill conjectured that religion had strayed too far to the left and needed a resurgence to the right.

Despite our differences, Bill and I remained close acquaintances. One day in the lounge I asked him how he knew he wanted to be a priest. He said, "I guess I've just always known. I can't imagine doing anything else. Some say they receive a sign, but for me it's just part of who I am. It's more my destiny. My life has been a sign."

Having absolutely no post-college direction, I began toying with the idea of seminary school. I thought I could revolutionize the church from within—continue the discussion Bill and I had been having on a more global level in an attempt to urge congregations to be more accepting towards others. I was enamored with Bill's sense of awe towards spirituality and hoped that the seminary would teach me to love religion and crush the emptiness I felt every time I thought of church. When I spoke with Bill, I felt as if I was missing something. Religion seemed to be a cross-cultural phenomenon—Native Americans, Asians, Europeans, and Africans were all deeply moved by the sacred. I, too, desperately wanted to obtain that fervor for the divine.

For the past twenty years I'd been going through the motions at church, but God never "spoke" to me. If I entered the ministry I might gain the opportunity to share in the sense of wonder others experienced, something I'd been unable to unearth at church or anywhere in my life. Church was entirely unmoving. Each time the minister talked about the sense of "wonder" Jesus Christ gave him, I "wondered" what the hell he was talking about. Church made me sleepy. I wanted to know what caused people to fall to the floor and shake in ecstasy. I wanted to know why wars were started over faith. I wanted to share in that connection with a God that the majority of Americans claim to have. I hoped seminary could train me to feel. At the very least, I figured by entering the ministry, I might finally read that Bible.

I focused on the faceless Jesus figure on Mitchell's desk. "See, that's the thing. I don't really know if I've been called, as you say. I didn't realize that was a requirement for the ministry. I suppose that's why I'm here. I want to know how you came to decide to become a minister. How do you know if you're being 'called?'"

"The calling is different for each person," he explained.

"But what was it like for you?"

"Subtle."

"How subtle?"

"Nearly silent."

"So, did He say something to you? Like could you actually hear the voice of God?"

"That depends," Reverend Mitchell said.

I was growing tired of this enigmatic conversation and inadvertently began rubbing Jesus's forehead again. Reverend

Mitchell reached for the statue, moving it to the other side of his desk.

"It depends," he said, "on each person's own, individualized need. God caters the message for each special person. God knows exactly what that person needs in order to be awakened to his or her purpose in life. It's different for each person."

"So, what did He say to you?"

"Quiet, quiet things."

"Such as?"

"It's difficult to say in words."

"So, he didn't *say* words?"

"No."

"What did he say?"

"Feelings."

"He *said* feelings?" I leaned back in my chair and sighed deeply.

"Michael, we humans don't always need to use words to say something. That sigh you released just said volumes about your frustration and confusion as you embark on your own spiritual journey. You didn't use words, yet I understood what you were feeling."

The room went silent and seemed even darker than when I entered. "Okay, I guess I should just go, because I think maybe I shouldn't be here." I began to stand up.

"Brother, please sit back down and tell me why you're *really* here." Reverend Mitchell clasped his hands together again. I was amazed that his massive hands could even mesh into one another. I slowly lowered myself back into my seat.

"I told you—I just wanted to talk about being a minister and see how you knew that's what you wanted to do."

"Stop worrying about everyone else and start worrying about what God is trying to tell you. What is God saying, brother?"

"I don't know." I wiped the sweat off my lip with the back of my hand. "It's just I don't know. I've been taking a lot of religion classes at school and I'm thinking it would be good to help people out and I was thinking being a minister might be a good job. And..."

Reverend Mitchell stopped me short. "That's your first mistake. It's never a job—the ministry is a lifestyle. If God asks you to speak his Word, you bring your work home with you, you take it to the grocery store, you take it to the movies. You embody the ministry."

"Right. Lifestyle. So, I'm thinking it would be a good *lifestyle*, but I don't know, I mean when I was a kid I wanted to be a carpenter and then a park ranger and a marine biologist. And just five months ago I thought I'd be a DJ and spin records, so maybe this is just one of those phases."

"Did God tell you this was just one of those phases?"

"Like, what? Did Jesus appear on a slice of toast and tell me to think about being a minister? No."

Reverend Mitchell didn't laugh. "It's not that obvious. God speaks to us in the quiet voices we hear when we stop and really begin to listen."

"That's another question I have for you—what is all this talking God is doing? Because the only voice I ever hear is when I talk to myself in my head. Is that what you mean, like talking to yourself?"

"Like talking to God."

"Does His voice sound different than your own voice in your head?"

"Sometimes."

"And how do you know?"

"He speaks to your heart and not your ears."

"And one last time, so I'm totally clear on this, how did you know you wanted to be a minister?"

"The silence." He held out the last "s" sound.

"No words?"

"Not ones I could hear."

"And did he speak these non-words in a sudden revelation, like an awakening, or was it something you figured out over time?"

"Yes," Reverend Mitchell said, smiling in his chair.

I sat there for a moment and asked, "Like, does a construction worker get a calling or an airplane pilot?"

"Possibly, but I don't know. God never asked me to fly a plane or build a house. He just wanted me to build a community of faith. It's ultimately all about faith. Faith in what you can't explain or understand. Faith is all about believing what's in your heart and not what's in your mind. Faith reminds you that what you believe is more important than what you know."

Although I did believe Reverend Mitchell was being as honest as he could be about his own awakening, I felt as if I'd just had a twenty-minute discussion with a bag of fortune cookies filled with clichéd riddles and generic advice. I thanked the minister for his time and he said he'd be in touch if he happened upon any religious retreats that may offer further guidance. He said he often received notifications of seminars that might provide me with a sign. "Always keep your heart open," he said as I left, "and listen for signs from God." I promised I'd keep my ears open and walked into the bright fluorescent lights of the hallway.

The next week I received a letter from Reverend Mitchell that my church was going to sponsor and pay for me to fly to Houston, Texas, to attend the "Calling Conference," a three-day symposium designed to present answers and direction to teens who were interested in becoming the future leaders of the church. I notified my college professors I'd be missing class on

Friday, packed a bag, and boarded a plane for the first time in my life, anticipating some sort of sign.

The sign read: "God's children, register here." I figured I was in the right place, so I joined a winding line with dozens of kids that led to a small table in the lobby of the Dallas Holiday Inn. The line seemed not to budge because there was only one woman with large, teased hair working the registration table. Each teenager handed the woman his confirmation card, filled out a nametag that sported a large cross drawn in red magic marker on the right side, and was given keys to his room. I stared forward, hoping the process would soon expedite itself, when I noticed her.

Standing a few feet from the table was an adorable petite girl with sandy blonde hair and dimples that seemed ever present, even when she wasn't smiling. She wore a tight shirt with swirls of red and blue and jeans that clung to her legs. In the monotony of the line, I fixated on the way her hair brushed her shoulders when she turned her head back and forth, laughing with the other girls who stood next to her. I probably should have been paying more attention to her eyes, as I hadn't noticed that she'd been returning my stare, assumedly for some time. When I happened to notice her fixed gaze, I looked back at the stack of registration papers in my hand.

"Who loves you?" a voice bellowed from near the back of the line like someone shouting cheers at a baseball game. Everyone in the line as well as the guests in the lobby turned to see who'd just disrupted the quiet solitude of the place. Near the back of the line a boy with shaggy brown hair that just covered his eyes shouted again, "I said, who loves you?" He wore a white "Got Jesus?" shirt. A large wooden cross dangled from a thick silver chain around his neck. "Jesus loves you!" he said, responding to his own question. I wondered why the religious fanatics always wound up in my line. At amusement parks or on sub-ways, it seemed as if I was always the target for fundamentalists sharing their rhetoric. I'd nod, wave my hands about like I didn't understand their language, and swiftly move in the opposite direction.

He shouted again, "Who loves you?" In unison the line erupted with: "Jesus loves you!" And again. And again. I was mortified. The guests in the lobby stopped sipping their coffees and lifting their bags off the porter's cart to stare at this line of extremists declaring their love for Jesus. The guests' conversation about plans for the afternoon hushed into whispers, pointing fingers, and shaking heads.

"Who loves you?"

"Jesus, Jesus, Jesus!"

It was at that juncture that I understood precisely what I was standing in line for. This guy was not some isolated nut job on the sidewalk in front of a coffee shop testifying for Jesus. This was a line of nut jobs who were considering a career, no a *lifestyle*, of being nut jobs. None of the kids seemed the least bit uncomfortable with the commotion they were raising. Hands clapped. Two girls hugged one another in the frenzy. I wasn't upset because they were fanatic about religion specifically—anyone who openly exhibits that sort of exuberant public emotion is added to my nut job list. There are people who worship a certain breed of dog and plaster the back windows of their cars with "I'd rather be walking my schnauzer" stickers. Or baseball fans who don't own a piece of clothing that isn't embroidered with some sort of MLB logo. I don't need to know that you'd rather be golfing. And I especially don't need your public declaration of utter devotion to Christ.

I was accustomed to a sleepier style of Christianity back home, and not just because I slept through most of the services. It was a quiet church. If you weren't paying attention, you may miss the religion all together and think it was just punch and cookies on the patio. Even despite Reverend Mitchell's zeal, my church never exhibited signs of showiness about religion. They abided more to a "figure it out and leave us alone" philosophy. Religion was never forced upon anyone. I liked that. The minister before Mitchell once said during a sermon: "There is a thin line between Christianity and atheism, and I walk that line every day." I don't know what the context was for that line, because I hadn't been paying attention to the beginning of the sermon. But after that statement, he spoke about the struggle of religion and how, in the end, it didn't matter what you chose—to be Christian, Buddhist, or atheist. What mattered was how you lived your life. He then offered a quote from Gandhi: "I like your Christ, I do not like your Christians. Your Christians are so unlike your Christ." The minister said actions are the basis of life, qualifying them as Christian actions or Buddhist actions or Jewish actions are inconsequential. Words mean nothing, he said.

"Who loves you?"

"Jesus!"

Someone was ringing a bell. I turned my back to the stares of the hotel guests who now laughed outright and ceased to whisper. But even more dreadful was that several of the guests joined in on the chant. Even one of the hotel workers who checked in guests was chiming in with a few *Jesuses*. I closed my eyes and pressed slightly on them with my fingers, imagining when I opened them this nightmare would be over. But instead, when I opened my eyes I saw the girl with the sandy-blonde hair, her face now flushed. She'd stepped out of line to separate herself from the girls around her who were shrieking, "Jesus, Jesus, Jesus." The girl looked at me, shook her head, and mouthed, "Fucking idiots."

A boy walked away from the registration table with his room key. The line surged forward, working its way closer to the sign.

A prayer gathering in the hotel's auditorium after dinner was the only required activity for that evening. I skipped dinner and devoured a granola bar, which I'd packed in my carry-on bag, alone in my room, attempting to wrap my mind around the disaster I'd witnessed in the lobby. As I sat on the bed, three teens, my roommates for the next two nights, opened the door. They wore tight-black shirts with embroidered emblems of crosses, doves and a chalk-like sketch of Jesus on the back. Their biceps were enormous, bulging from the sleeves of their shirts. After introducing ourselves, the largest of the boys explained the ground rules for the next three days. He said they were all friends from Georgia and they went to bed by 9:00 p.m. sharp so they could wake up at 4:30 a.m. to pray together, "When the world is still silent from distractions. We don't tolerate distractions." They advised me to be in the room and asleep by 9:00 or don't bother returning, because it'd be locked. He said I was welcome to join them in the mornings for prayers, as long as I wasn't a distraction.

The three of them began setting up a sanctuary in our room—turning the TV around and placing crosses on the bathroom counter. I gathered my bag and headed down to the auditorium, hoping to see the girl from the line. I situated myself in the last row of the large, stifling hall that seethed with heat and lacked any airflow. Near the front of the auditorium hung several banners with doves and crosses and rainbows. The room was already full and soon the service began. Speakers who looked more like men's fashion models than ministers spoke to the audience, which flailed and whimpered when the men mentioned Christ's love. I sat in my seat, fraying the end of a strap on my bag, searching the room for the girl. Near the conclusion of the service, one of the models made a call for anyone wishing to openly embrace God's Word to "come on up and receive Him." Dozens of kids scampered to the front of the hall, pushing each other out of the way to be first. They formed a line next to the stage and one of the models stood behind each kid as the other placed his palm on his and her head saying, "You have been blessed with the spirit of Jesus Christ." One after another, each teenager would fall over in a fit of ecstasy. After being caught, another man would lead him or her off stage. I was embarrassed for everyone in attendance. I thought this display lacked sincerity or truth. It was more smoke and mirrors than genuine conversation about the pursuit of the divine. I stood up and slung my bag over my shoulder, planning to head back to my room and sleep off this outlandish scene. As I scooted my way out of the row of weeping, ecstatic, future ministers, I took one final look to the front of the room to witness the girl from the morning toppling over after just being whacked in the forehead by the model. She writhed in the arms of the other man, while several other pretty girls and boys ran up to her to embrace her for a "group hug."

I returned to my room, now completely transformed into a shrine (complete with incense and framed sketches of Mary and Jesus), well before it went into lockdown. I called my mom, begging to return home now, but she said it would be too expensive to switch flights. I should try to make the best of things. My three roommates also informed me they would be sleeping in the two double beds, and if I was a loud sleeper, it'd probably be best if I found another spot in the room to sleep. I curled up on the floor in the corner, used my bag for a pillow, and didn't wake until the next morning when one of the boys began invoking God's spirit with a flute.

After breakfast we were steered into small meeting rooms for breakout sessions with names like, "The voice within" and "Je-

Michael Hemery

sus, his light, and you." These sessions were surely designed to encourage and support us in our struggles for self-enlightenment, but they ended up being showcases for the kids who actually knew their Bible verses. The session leaders began with questions like, "What Bible verses speak to you and inspire you?" Kids were furiously waving their hands in the air, naming all sorts of verses, quoting them verbatim. I knew that Jesus was born in a stable with some donkeys and the first half of the Bible didn't mention him much. Whenever it was my turn to speak I made up some babble about how the Bible spoke to me as a whole, rather than in individually segmented verses.

"But what is your verse, Mike?" the group leader asked, carefully reading my nametag. He was perfectly coiffed like the rest of the adults who led the conference. "What is the one that speaks directly to you?"

I shifted in my seat. I couldn't answer.

He moved on to the boy who'd memorized the Gospel of Matthew.

None of the sessions discussed the ministry or practical matters like schooling. After the day of workshops wrapped up, we were herded into the auditorium for a final prayer session to conclude the event. The next morning, after breakfast, we would gather one last time and then be left to our own devices to recognize the mysteries of God. That evening, a model led the group through song after song that everyone, but me, knew the words to. More songs were sung, hands were heaved into the air, and a few people passed out—no doubt overwhelmed by all of God's love.

As the model gave us his final blessing, a boy with curly brown hair tapped my shoulder and informed me that a bunch of them were assembling on the roof of the hotel after the service to sing songs, play guitars and pray. They decided the roof was the ideal place to conduct the after show, even closer to God at

277

that elevation. I politely thanked him for the invitation and told him I'd think about it. I turned to leave but felt someone clutch my hand. The girl from the line intertwined her fingers with mine and led me out of the auditorium.

"Try to keep up," she said as she tugged on my arm. She had a thick, twangy southern accent, perky and full of rich sound. She smelled of smoke and perfume and wore a long, loose multi-colored skirt and a tight black top. She clenched a tiny white purse. I could still hear hundreds of off-pitch voices behind us singing the closing song, "This little light of mine…I'm going to let it shine."

"Can I ask where we're going?"

"Just shut the fuck up and follow me," she said. As we strode across the green-carpeted halls of the hotel, she turned abruptly at the "Emergency Exit Only" door and flung it open with her shoulder, still dragging me. Emergency alarms screamed until the girl pushed the door shut when we were safely outside. I realized this was the first time I'd smelled real air in days. The sun was just setting beyond a small artificial hill the hotel had built to set the property off from the large airport looming in the background. The sudden rush of light and fresh air was almost painful, as I'd grown used to the dull fluorescent lights and stale recycled air.

The girl's hand was warm and the silver rings she wore on all of her fingers dented my flesh. We walked in silence for awhile, climbing the small hill twenty yards from the hotel. She released my hand and flopped down on the grass, her locks fanning into a halo around her head. She slipped off her shoes. Her bare feet caressed the soft grass.

"You gonna stand up there all night or are you gonna come down here and keep me company?" she said.

As I lay down next to her, I thought of my mother and tried to concoct an excuse for the eminent grass stains that would appear on the back of my shorts.

"So," she said, "is God calling you?"

"Better yet," I asked, "is God calling *you*? I saw you yesterday up front, crying and falling over."

She laughed, sat up, and opened her purse to pull out a pack of cigarettes. She held the pack out to me and I shook my head. She shrugged, located her lighter, and flicked it several times. She placed her cigarette in her mouth and held her hand over the end as she flicked the lighter, sheltering it from the breeze blowing from the airport. "It's all bullshit," she said. "I haven't seen this much bullshit in years."

"I'm Mike, by the way," I said.

"I see that," she said, pulling my nametag off my chest. She wore no nametag. "Nice to meet you, Mike." She took a drag from the cigarette and exhaled, the smoke curling into the darkening sky.

There was a thirty-something-year-old man with a scraggly brown beard and an off-white robe a few yards down the hill from us. He was meditating in yoga positions and mumbling in a sing-song tone, his words running together and rising in pitch, "Jesussaveusallfromtheeviloftheworld." He broke out of his trance when we began talking behind him, shook his head, and went back to his low mumble.

"And you are?" I asked.

"A seventeen-year-old girl from Louisiana who would rather be anywhere but this bullshit conference."

"What's your name?" I asked.

"Sarah," she said. She placed the cigarette in her mouth and held out her hand as a formal introduction.

"So why are you here?" I asked. "I mean if it's all bullshit, why did you come?"

"Because my mom wants me to take the 'divine road to life.'" She laughed. "After she and my dad broke up, she thought I should come to Christ Camp to be more like her and less like my dad." Sarah lay back down and I propped myself up on one shoulder to watch her speak. "So she brought me here and is one of the chaperones. If I fall over and make her believe I've been consumed by God, like I did last night, she'll get off my shit. Plus, she may buy me a new outfit if she thinks I'm going to be a minister." She took another hit, the cherry of the cigarette now the only light on the darkened hill. A mass of voices was gathering volume on the hotel's roof. Someone strummed a guitar and another cheered, "Who loves you?"

"Jesus!"

"God, I wish they would all fall off the roof," Sarah said.

"So why did you pick me?" I pulled out a blade of grass and poked it into my calf. I gestured toward the roof. "It seems like there are plenty of other good-looking guys you could have smoked a cigarette with on the hill."

She rolled over to face me and flicked her still-lit cigarette into the grass. "Because I could tell you don't buy into any of the shit, either."

"I'm still thinking it may be a possibility. I mean, not like these guys with the jumping and singing and stuff, but I could still maybe look into becoming a minister. I haven't totally ruled it out."

"I'm sorry," she said. "I didn't realize you were taking any of this seriously. You looked just as annoyed as I did by all of that crap."

"Well, it all seems fake and showy. I guess if I were to go into the ministry, I'd want to change the way the church is run." I told her about a sermon I'd heard at a friend's church where the minister referred to homosexuals as "Satan's minions" and suggested that these minions were sent to earth to destroy the righteous. I told her my plan was to start a new church where things like sexuality and race and even religion itself didn't matter.

"And how would you do that?" she asked. Her accent was intoxicating. When she grinned, her dimples were even more prominent.

I explained how I'd get rid of Bible verses and sermons about old stories. Instead, I planned on talking about acceptance and just being a good person.

"So let me get this straight," Sarah said, lighting another cigarette. "To make your church better, you'd get rid of the Bible, the sermons, the hatred, and pretty much anything that resembled religion?"

I played with the blade of grass. "Yeah, I guess so."

She laughed and lay back down, running her bare feet across the grass. "It sounds like this," Sarah gestured toward the kids on the roof, "isn't you. And I'm sorry and may be overstepping my bounds, but it doesn't sound like you have too much religion in that heart of yours." She reached over and touched my chest. Sarah took another drag of her cigarette. "If nothing else, I bet you could fill that church because you're cute." She grinned and shifted closer to me. I could feel her arm against mine.

"I never would have expected this was how this weekend would come about. I thought I'd have this grand religious awakening."

"With a beautiful girl," she added.

I laughed, "Yes, with a beautiful girl."

On the roof kids sang some song about Jesus being bread.

"Here's the question," Sarah said. "Where would you rather be? Up there or down here with me? No hard feelings if you want to be up there. But whatever your answer is—that should tell you a lot about this struggle you're having."

"I can't imagine being anywhere near those kids right now," I said.

Sarah smiled and took another hit of her cigarette. The man in the robe packed up his mat and walked back into the hotel, leaving us alone on the dark hill.

"Well, I should probably think about getting back to my room, because my roommates are going to lock me out soon," I said.

I explained their policy and she said, "So, don't go back to your room."

"Well, if I don't go to my room tonight, then where will I sleep?"

As I sat on the grass, staring at Sarah, I tried to figure out where I was going to sleep. I really didn't know where she thought I could go. It was about the time that I could taste the lingering cigarette smoke on her tongue that I understood what she was suggesting. We proceeded to make out on the hill for about a half hour, the songs of Jesus being sung in the distance.

When the cool rain began to fall, I couldn't help but think my life was turning into some romance novel: "Our wet bodies surged together as her shirt clung to her breasts." We ran inside the hotel, continuing to kiss in the elevator. She pressed the button for floor eight. Her wet hair hung in her face until she violently ran her fingers through her locks to tease them back to life. She skipped out of the elevator, holding my hand as we walked toward her room. She slipped the key into her hotel room but motioned for me to wait a moment as she stepped inside. She emerged a few seconds later. "My fucking roommates are all in there sleeping. It's only like ten o'clock. Goddamn, now what?" I loved her accent. I even started to pick up on the slight drawl in my own words.

We made out all over the hotel. We went to the top floor and made out on the dining tables, in the kitchen, and up and down the elevator. When other kids from the conference would walk by, I'd struggle to pull myself away, but Sarah sustained her kiss for them to see.

"I feel like I've known you for a long time," I said as we took a break in the dining hall on the top floor of the hotel. We watched the flickering lights of the runway through the tinted glass windows.

"That's because I let you kiss me."

At 2:00 a.m. she said she needed to return to her room to try to get a little sleep before her trip home the next day. I walked her to her room and kissed her at her doorway, wiping the mascara that was working its way down her face. We made plans for breakfast in the morning. I went for a walk in the hotel lobby, sure that my roommates had barricaded the door hours ago. Three in the morning seemed like an appropriate time to call my friend Daniel back in Cleveland.

"You're seriously calling me at this hour?" he asked as he cleared the sleep from his throat.

"But she's awesome, I mean, she's everything I'm looking for."

I had a tendency to fall in and out of love pretty easily. With the right mood music and the proper lighting, I could fall in love with a parking meter.

"Dude, you're out of your fucking mind."

"No, ya'all just don't get it."

"Did you just say, 'ya'all?'"

As I explained how we connected, Daniel expressed his disappointment that we'd only kissed and not gone any further.

"But I think it was something more than that," I said. "Maybe it was the sign I've been looking for from God—He was telling me to change the world." The phone went quiet. "Daniel, you still there?"

"Yeah," he said. His voice was muffled, like he was covering the phone with his hand, but I could still hear him laughing. In the background his Zippo lighter clicked open. "I just want to make sure I get this right because it's 3:00 a.m. and I may still be drunk—God had you make out with some girl at church camp to tell you to become a minister?"

"That makes it sound so shallow, but yeah."

"Shit, if that's how God works, then I may be Jesus-fucking-Christ himself with all the ass I've hit in the past year."

I spent the rest of the night composing rhyming poetry for Sarah and filched a plastic rose out of a display in the hotel lobby. I left both outside of her door. I crashed in a chair in the hotel lobby, trying to figure out if this was the sign Reverend Mitchell told me to watch for. In the morning she held my hand at breakfast and rested her head on my shoulder during the last church service. We exchanged phone numbers and made plans to see each other as soon as I could save enough money for a flight to Louisiana.

The following morning I dialed the number Sarah had given me, but the man who answered explained that she wasn't in. When I asked if I could leave a message he tersely replied *no* and hung up. I looked up her address in the conference directory and forced Daniel to join me at the florist shop so I could mail a dozen roses to her mom's house. The note read, "The past forty-eight hours with you have been amazing. I think we were brought together for a reason." Daniel told me it was too much, but I informed him he didn't understand the connection we had.

Sarah never called to let me know she received the roses. I wrote three more times, asking her if I had the right address or if my other letters were delivered. Still nothing. Gradually, after nearly a half-dozen letters and another dozen roses, I ceased to write. I returned my attention to my classes and failed a few geology tests.

After two months, I'd almost forgotten Sarah until I received a letter when I came home from school. Sarah thanked me for the flowers, but told me that I'd misunderstood her intentions. She said I was a sweet boy, but she lied about her age—she was only fourteen. She also explained that she'd been dating a thirty-eight-year-old recovered drug addict and made out with me to see if she still wanted to be with him. "Because you were such a gentleman," she wrote, "I saw it as some kind of sign that I needed to be with him. I know that doesn't make a lot of sense, but thank you. If it weren't for you, I'd probably still be stuck with my parents and forced to go to school. I'll never forget you. Love, Sarah."

Formal Defense

"Well, Mike, this is the part I'm sure you've been looking forward to—it's time for you to defend yourself," said Dr. Badinski, the head of my college's religion department. I sat at the head of a long, glossy wooden table in a tiny room on the third floor of the humanities building. To my left and right sat all the members of the religion department. Seated at the other end of the table was Dr. Heptner, a soft-soften priest who taught several religion classes at the school. He consistently taught courses in the afternoon after lunch, and his feathery voice would lull me nearly to sleep. My advisor, Dr. Ulrich, sat to my right, with the college chaplain, Dr. Mattus, beside him. Dr. Badinski was to my immediate left and Dr. Remington, the world religion professor next to him. The men all wore suits; Dr. Heptner never wore his traditional priest collar in an academic setting.

Dr. Badinski told me that the entire department had read my paper on *The Brothers Karamazov,* so the panel of professors was prepared to ask me questions—the formal defense for my senior religion thesis. I fidgeted in my suit at the end of the table. I'd been working on the paper with my randomly assigned supervisor, Dr. Ulrich, turning in proposals, outlines, and rough drafts. I'd chosen to focus on Dostoevsky's *The Brothers Karamazov*, with a particular focus on man's struggle to obtain religious enlightenment. I conjectured that the search for spiritual truth is not easy to obtain, as some would have us believe. I surmised that born-again encounters were manifestations of man's desire to be led and contained little religious worth. I concluded that much of religion was gibberish devised by man so he may feel at ease with the uncontrollable and unknown. I acknowledged that some may sincerely find true spiritual illumination and conversion, but only after dedicating a lifetime to gaining this understanding.

My choice of topics was inspired by several events. After receiving the last letter from Sarah, I wrote her several more brief letters in which I informed her she was incorrect about our "relationship" being a sign, about her feelings for this older man. In the last letter I even told her she may have been incorrect about her own age. Even though she clearly explained all of these points to me, I refused to believe her and had faith she was secretly pining away for me somewhere in Louisiana. It wasn't that I needed her, but rather I needed a sign. I was sure she was it. After several more weeks of obsessively checking the mailbox each day after school, I became even more disillusioned with religion and the notion of "signs." This retreat would have been the perfect opportunity for God to speak up, but I heard nothing. Sarah was the only optimistic moment of my time in Texas and even that had crumbled into ash. I used my experience with Sarah as a sign against the church and finally decided to be honest with my own feelings. I stopped attending church altogether. After twenty years of reciting rote monologues without any emotion, I slept in on Sundays, eventually climbing out of bed to flip through the ads in the Sunday paper. My parents also stopped going to church. We also stopped getting donuts.

Reverend Mitchell called me once a week for several months after the trip to Texas to schedule a post-conference discussion. I ignored his phone calls, and he eventually ceased to make them. I came to understand that signs are another human construct to make the chaos of life fit into a nice, neat, prefabricated existence. The challenge, I found, is to begin living life in spite of the chaos, in spite of the "evil" that exists. Yet, I was still fascinated with religion, especially man's compulsion towards the spiritual, but I began to think that organized religion preyed upon that innate desire for faith to control people.

At the same time I was having this religious unawakening, I was becoming particularly infatuated with a college class on the historical Jesus—the "truth" behind the real man who was a political revolutionary, turning over money changers' tables, eating dinner with society's outcasts, and elevating women to the same social status as men. Dr. Badinski taught the course, and throughout the semester we read work by Dominic Crossan, who presented a rather bleak view of Christianity, stripping away all of the religious rhetoric (Mary wasn't a virgin, Jesus never performed any magic tricks or miracles, and his body never rose from the grave, but was probably torn apart by wild dogs).

Dr. Badinski's class grew smaller each week, as students would stand up in the middle of lectures and proclaim that Dr. Badinski was a "heathen" before storming out of the room and encouraging others to join them. Ironically, Dr. Badinski was a devout Protestant who openly admitted he followed the church not *in spite* of the knowledge that Christ might only be a man, but *because* he was a man and not some magician who could perform parlor tricks. Dr. Badinski encouraged those students who disagreed with these theories to remain in the class to make their own faith stronger. He said a solid foundation is key to enlightenment. By the end of the semester the class shrunk from thirty students to twelve. I was delighted with the small class, because I felt like the close group of us was obtaining some sort of privileged, secret information that, most of all, made sense. My struggle ended in that class—as I accepted Jesus for the first time but not "into my heart," like some sort of religious conversion. I accepted him as a guy who simply was trying to make the world a better place by accepting the weak, the poor, and the outcasts.

I realized this message had nothing to do with signs. After understanding the truth behind the real Jesus, I swore myself off of organized religion entirely, vowing never to return, as I had faith enough in Christ, the man, not to need some sort of reincarnating magician who could walk on water or miraculously feed the hungry with a couple chunks of bread. I rejected religion to find solace in man, despite his obvious flaws and weaknesses.

It was this struggle in *The Brothers Karamazov* that became the concentration of my senior religion thesis. I focused on mankind's battle to reach religious enlightenment when he factors in reason and rational thought, underscoring the importance of the Grand Inquisitor scene. I believed Dostoevsky rejected "easy" religion and instead respected the man who struggles each and every day to understand existence and his connection to it. In my thesis proposal I wrote, "I believe it is necessary to embrace Ivan's ideas as we struggle through our own religious faith. I don't believe people can have any kind of faith until they address Ivan's doubt. No one can call himself a true, religious being if he hasn't questioned a God that created a world where young children are raped and tortured. But in quite the same light, an atheist cannot truly dismiss the notion of God without recognizing that small voice of doubt in his own mind—the voice of Alyosha and Zossima. One has to recognize both of these issues that the characters raise before he can make any legitimate stand on his own religious feelings."

After I explained all of this to the room of religion professors, several of the men lobbed light questions at me regarding the paper and my own spiritual struggle. My advisor, Dr. Ulrich, was silent for the beginning of the questioning process. A half-hour into the discussion he finally cleared his throat and said, "As most of you know, Michael and I have had a long year together." Dr. Ulrich disagreed with my thesis entirely—he believed Dostoevsky was not drawing attention to the struggle of faith, nor was he saying that true faith comes through effort. He also disagreed with my newly accepted heathenism and believed I was attempting to undercut religious faith by writing the paper.

He continued, "Despite being a technically well-written paper, I find Michael's thesis offensive toward those who truly have had a religious conversion overnight. I believe he is using Dostoevsky's words to serve his own ends and I am in complete and utter disagreement with his ideas. I believe it is assuming to speak for people who are born again and suddenly see the Truth as a result of some sort of religious awakening."

I raised my hand to speak, but Dr. Mattus cut me off. "Just to clarify for Michael and group, Don, you are saying that someone who is born again has just as much faith as one who struggles a lifetime to understand religion, right?" Dr. Ulrich nodded.

I began to speak but Dr. Remington started up, "I agree with Dr. Ulrich. Although it appears that Michael has fully supported his argument based on the text, and I don't necessarily disagree with his interpretation of Dostoevsky as Dr. Ulrich does, I do disagree with Michael's ideology. Religious awakening is entirely possible and deserves just as much weight as those who fight a lifetime for their religion. Who is to say how God speaks to us?"

Dr. Mattus said, "But does it deserve just as much credit? The conversations I have with parish members who truly think about religion are much different than those who blindly accept my sermons. There is no conversation, just acceptance. And is that really a foundation of faith?"

For the next twenty minutes the men engaged in a discussion of the struggle for religion. They pounded fists on tables and cut one another off mid sentence. I attempted several more times to interject my thoughts, but the professors ignored me and argued the acquisition of religion amongst themselves. Dr. Badinski entered the fray. I remained silent, calmly watching the men grow more agitated. Dr. Heptner was also silent at the other end of the table. Several times he closed his eyes tightly and shook his head.

After a half-hour of discussion Dr. Ulrich finally said, "What I am trying to say is that Michael is expressing a voice of young naiveté—he is too young to understand faith and that is demonstrated in this paper." He picked up my tome and tossed it onto the table—it slid and hit my arm.

"Dammit, Don," Dr. Heptner shouted. The room went silent and turned to the gray-haired priest at the end of the table. He used the edge of the table to hoist himself upright and said, "Just shut up, Don. Shut the hell up." Both of his hands gripped the edge of the table and his brow was furrowed. "As you all know I'm retiring this year and I've been waiting twenty-five years to tell you this, Don: You're absolutely fucking wrong and full of shit."

Dr. Badinski gagged a bit on the coffee he was sipping.

"There, I said it and I don't care. I'm retiring and it makes no difference at all. What this young man is presenting is the heart of all great religious debates and you know damn well that people don't give a shit about God, all they want is a quick fix to their problems without any real struggle. I see it every day—we all do." Dr. Mattus nodded his head. "There are only a handful of people who have found any sort of true enlightenment. And some days I'm not so sure I'm even one of them. But I can't waver on that pulpit. Not once, Don, not once. Because you know goddamn well what happens if we don't keep up that act—the church will be empty and I'll be preaching to myself. But those who are truly enlightened, those who I *want* to have discussions with, those are the doubters who question every word I say. Religion doesn't come overnight. It doesn't. So what I'm saying is you're fucking wrong."

He eased himself back into his seat, shuffling through the pages of my paper. The men all looked toward the department head, Dr. Badinski, who chuckled slightly. "Well, Michael, I have to say this has been one of the more heated thesis discussions we've ever had." Dr. Ulrich did not look up from the table. "I'd first like to mention that it is my recommendation that you pass your senior thesis with an A, because not only was this a fine paper, but never before has a student's work so engaged this room nor has a student's paper ever inspired a retiring priest to say 'fuck.' Twice." He stood up and said, "I think that's a good way to end this."

I pray when our plane takes off. I pray before it lands. I prayed when they found a suspicious lump in my mom's breast. I make my wife toss salt over her shoulder when she spills it on the table. I knock on wood when I mention how happy I am.

I lost the gold cross that my mom gave me for my sixteenth birthday in a mosh pit when I was twenty-one. I found it scratched nearly to shreds under a man's shoe. I asked him to lift his foot in the middle of the concert. I don't know how I knew it was there.

I told my wife I hope there is an afterlife so we can be together. I agreed with her that reincarnation would be fine too, as long as we're together. I meant it.

I tell my wife I love her infinity plus one.

I join my wife, mom, and dad for breakfast each Sunday morning, not after church, but instead of church. I eat bagels instead of donuts. I heard they're healthier.

I think religion is a creation of man. I blame religion for most of the world's problems. I don't blame God.

I don't trust religion. I don't trust man. I trust infinity.

I believe things happen for a reason. I believe I can say this because I don't suffer much.

I think best when I'm in the shower or mowing the lawn. I'm pretty sure it's just my own voice talking to itself.

I still pray for the leopards, which are now near extinction. I still pray for man to become kinder and more accepting and more intelligent and more aware. I'm pretty sure it's just my own voice talking to itself.

I think that's a better way to end.

Michael Hemery

Acknowledgments

I would like to sincerely thank the following people for offering so much of themselves, never asking for anything in return. You have made it all worthwhile. Sue Silverman, Laurie Alberts, the Vermont College of Fine Arts MFA program, Kathy Hemery (your strength and own books have always inspired me), Dan Hemery (you taught me how to be a man, even though I never mastered the chainsaw), anyone that's ever been struck by my water balloons on the Fourth of July, the physical laborers who work their bodies each day—what you do will always be more important, Michael Dolzani, the eighth-grade Power of the Pen advisors who kicked me out of the club for writing an essay entitled "Dangerous Curves"—that made me want this all the more, Michael Alfaro, Eric Anderson, Kathryne Starzec, Drew Hood, Ryan Vana, my son (you are way better than any superhero), and my wife, Stacie Leatherman, my love, best friend, and first read, who insisted I revisit my talents and write. If it weren't for you, these essays would never have happened and I'd be a much higher rank in *Gears of War*.